AN INTRODUCTION TO
COUNSELING
A HANDBOOK

George D. Demos, PhD, ABPP
Richard "Buck" Marrs, EdD

AN INTRODUCTION TO COUNSELING
A HANDBOOK

iUniverse books may be ordered through booksellers or by contacting:

iUniverse
1663 Liberty Drive
Bloomington, IN 47403
www.iuniverse.com
1-800-Authors (1-800-288-4677)

ISBN: 978-1-5320-0614-2 (sc)
ISBN: 978-1-5320-0615-9 (e)

Print information available on the last page.

iUniverse rev. date: 11/11/2016

Dr. Richard (Buck) Marrs has been a full time professor in the Department of Teacher Education at California State University, Long Beach since 1968, and has supervised over four hundred student teachers in grades K–12. Also, he has been a practicing psychotherapist since 1972 specializing in treating families and their dysfunctional children and adolescents.

Dr. George Demos is a licensed clinical psychologist and Professor Emeritus of Counseling Psychology at California State University Long Beach. He received his PhD in psychology from the University of Southern California.

Dr. Demos has over 200 publications, including author or co-author of 14 books, several psychological tests and many articles in Professional Journals.

An Introduction
to Counseling:
A Handbook

George D. Demos, Ph.D, ABPP
California State University, Long Beach
and
Richard "Buck" Marrs, Ed.D.
California State University, Long Beach

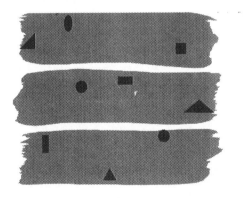

CONTENTS

PART IV
THE SCIENCE OF COUNSELING

PART V
THE PREPARATION OF THE COUNSELOR

PREFACE

This book is intended to serve as an introductory learning tool for the counselor-in-training. Furthermore, the authors believe that the practicing counselor, even an individual with many years of experience, can benefit from having the text in his office as a source of reference, a handbook, and as a refresher on points that too often become obscured by time.

It should be helpful to list the typical occupational titles of people in public schools, colleges and universities, public agencies, in private practice, and in business and industry who do counseling. These people need to prepare for acquiring competency as counselors and to maintain and sharpen this competency once it is acquired.

Titles in the public schools include: guidance counselors, school psychologists, school social workers, child welfare and attendance workers, and deans.

In colleges and universities: counselors, counseling psychologists, clinical psychologists, physicians, psychiatrists, career counselors, housing officers, placement counselors, advisement personnel, and student activities officers.

In private practice: marriage and family counselors, career counselors, counseling psychologists, clinical psychologists, educational psychologists, and clinical social workers.

In business: personnel specialists, industrial psychologists, human resource specialists, rehabilitation counselors, and staff development officers.

From the foregoing, it should not be assumed that the authors expect this book to be "all things to all people"; they do not even idealize it as being "all things to all counselors." However, it is their hope that it will offer some knowledge, some methodology, and some skills to each reader, qualities that can enhance his/her competency when he/she participates in the counseling process.

For too many years, arguments in the field of education have persisted over which is the more important: for a teacher to know how to teach, or to know what (that is, the subject matter) he/she is teaching. This controversy of methodology versus content has raged on and on, seemingly "ad infinitum" and certainly "ad nauseam."

It would seem a reasonable premise that a teacher can only function as a teacher when he/she knows both what he/she is teaching and how he/she should teach it. Any deviation from this is simply a delimiting of their professional competence. Quite obviously, this applies in the same way to the counselor.

It is a major thesis of this textbook that counseling is both an art and a science; in other words, there must be both a 'how' and a 'what'. In fact, as the saying goes, you can't have one without the other.

> Art … means a high level of skill (outstanding skill).
> Skill is doing something well. (2, p. 41)

The extent of the smoothness, the poise, and the charm with which the counselor executes techniques – the elements of methodology – will determine to a significant extent the degree of success with clients.

> Science … means a high level of knowledge (the product of understanding), which is both extensive and intensive. (2, p. 27)

Informing/advising is one of the techniques used by the counselor. If data is presented with considerable skill, one is an artist. But unless he/she possesses the knowledge he/she elects to give, there cannot be an "art of informing." The counselor must know something before he/she can inform anyone.

Just as certainly, no matter how profound the depth of one's knowledge, if the counselor is unable to communicate this data to the counselee, then the process of informing cannot be carried out.

Part I is concerned with the bases of counseling. The philosophy of counseling, including meaning, objectives, and principles, is presented. The reader should remember that this philosophy (and the contents in all of the other chapters of the book) is discussed within the frame of reference of the guidance counselor who works in public schools, colleges, or universities. The members of allied professions, such as marriage counselors, physicians, or social workers, can easily make a transfer of learning of some, or even much, of the data discussed. The authors have no doubts about the intellectual capacities of these professionals and know them to be able to quickly recognize information of value to them and to transcribe it into a meaningful concept for application into their own practices.

Counseling and group guidance are differentiated, and clear, definitive guides that will help the counselor determine when he/she should use counseling or when he/she should use group guidance are offered.

The important distinction between counseling and psychotherapy is made, with considerable reference to the judgments of several authorities on this question.

Ethics of counseling are discussed. This is a vital area for counseling, because unless an occupation determines ethical standards which are honored by its practitioners, it cannot justify the claim that it is a profession. To avoid being unethical the practitioner must first become aware of what constitutes ethical practices. It is like manners – some people omit saying "Thank you" out of ignorance, not an intent to be discourteous.

The need for research that might provide data on the effectiveness of counseling is emphasized, along with an elaboration of the many diverse variables which often can impinge on an evaluation, making it less valid in many instances. Instruments for evaluating counseling are recommended. Their use may not overcome some of the difficulties in achieving a scientific measurement of the value of counseling, but these devices do provide a concrete means for making improvements in counseling. Improvement can be achieved by discovering weaknesses and then carrying out plans for eliminating or lessening these weaknesses.

Part II discusses the functions of counseling. The key function – in fact, the essence – is the counseling act, in which the one-to-one, face-to-face relationship between two individuals occurs. Whatever else the counselor does, most of his/her time should be devoted to this one-to-one relationship, or as it is sometimes labeled, interviewing. His/her other functions should emerge from or contribute to this private relationship with his/her client, student, patient, counselee, or whatever term the professional wishes to attach to the individual he/she is seeking to help.

The words "counseling" and "interviewing" are often used synonymously. Some authorities frown upon the use of the word "interview," claiming it does not accurately depict what occurs in the professional relationship. In this text, whenever either term is used, the meaning intended is the " ...one-to-one, face-to-face relationship between an individual who seeks help and another person who is professionally educated to give this help." (1, p. 219) The only variation from this interpretation comes in referring to certain other functions of the counselor that go beyond his actual relationships with the people he is serving.

The counseling record is examined. Here, whether the professional be a physician, who has long been castigated for his indecipherable handwriting and hurried record scribbling, or a guidance counselor, whose scrawl often challenges his own eyesight and ingenuity as he tries to transcribe his notes, there is a need for guidelines that will enable the professional to save his valuable time by reducing his writing to a minimum. An Interview Record form is included that uses a system of checking appropriate items, so that only a little writing should be necessary. Each professional can adapt this to his/her own practice or use it as a model in constructing a form applicable to his/her own needs.

Referrals are an important part of a practitioner's functions. When, how, to whom, and why to refer are factors considered. A Referral Form is suggested, and a hypothetical Referral List is presented to illustrate to the counselor the value of having ready access to the names, addresses, and telephone numbers of those professionals to whom he can refer his clients (or patients, etc.) when necessary.

To assist the counselor in those situations when group guidance should be used, some of the group procedures are described.

The concept of the counselor – a practitioner – becoming involved in creativity and research is examined. In a young profession there are many frontiers of knowledge to be explored, and many potential innovations to be put into service; the challenge is worthy of our best minds.

The counselor's role in professional and community organizations and services is explored. Certainly the counselor can only do so much in each twenty-four-hour day. As one of the author's venerated counselor-educators once said, "I can't find time to do many things I should, mainly because I dare not shirk my responsibilities to my students." The counselor must not abdicate his/her prime justification for existence, which is counseling. He/she should enrich his/her contributions to his/her clients through a continuous program of professional and personal growth, which certainly goes hand in hand with creativity and research and/or participation in professional and community organizations and services.

Part III presents seventeen techniques of counseling: informing, interpreting, clarifying, evaluating, reviewing, inquiring, questioning, discussing, motivating, suggesting, referring, nonverbal responses, brief replies, reflecting, empathizing, supporting, and reassuring.

Each of these techniques is discussed, designated in terms of when it should be used, and illustrated with a sample of counselor-client dialogue.

In Part IV, the knowledge needed by the counselor to carry out the seventeen techniques of counseling is considered as the scientific basis for the counselor being able to acquire and practice the art of counseling.

Part V deals with the education required for counseling. The authors refer to their recommendations for undergraduate and graduate counselor education proposed in "College and University Counseling." (1, pp. 234–236) In addition, they elaborate on this proposal with additional innovations and a detailing of specifics.

The necessity for a counselor to acquire work experience outside the helping professions is emphasized. However, the restricted "ivory tower" world of the teacher is not a very practical training ground for counseling. Far better that the counselor-to-be serve in a variety of jobs, ranging, for example, from manual labor to office work in different industries, such as manufacturing, finance, merchandising, etc.

In Part VI, the kind of personality best suited to counseling is examined – what his/her interests should be; the aptitudes he/she ought to possess; the severity and extent of his/her needs and which ones can be best set in counseling; his/her personality traits and their compatibility with the characteristics needed for effective counseling; his/her value system and how it blends with the values most reasonably expected in one who is to counsel; whether his/her values may clash with or be distorted by those of his/her clients; his/her goals and whether counseling integrates nicely with noncareer goals; and finally, his/her health and whether he/she is mentally and physically qualified to function as a counselor – these are the elements out of which we can draw a portrait of the "counselor-to-be."

The authors are indebted to many people for the extremely valuable contributions that these individuals have made to their professional development. They would like to enumerate the names of these persons and regret that a partial listing must inevitably omit several whose help they have esteemed. To all of these people the authors express their profound appreciation. To those outstanding educators that space permits including herein, acknowledgment is offered with gratitude and fond memories: Dr. Earl F. Carnes and Dr. John C. Gowan.

Finally, the authors are grateful to each other for the enriched professional life each has bestowed upon the other and for the opportunity to collaborate on so many publications.

George D. Demos, Ph.D.

Part I
BASES OF COUNSELING

Chapter 1

PHILOSOPHY OF COUNSELING

S ince this book is concerned with presenting the knowledge and skills that counselors should possess, it is important to explore early the reasons for the necessity of counseling. A rationale for counseling can be arrived at through a discussion of the meaning, principles, and objectives of counseling. Each of these serves to indicate the "why" of counseling.

Why counsel? Unless there are satisfactory answers to this query, what thinking student can justify the choice of the counseling profession for his career? Indeed, how can a practicing counselor maintain his self-esteem unless his rationale for counseling leads to the conclusion that counseling is an indispensable professional service?

☞ *The Meaning of Counseling*

"...counseling is a one-to-one, face-to-face relationship between an individual who seeks help and another person who is professionally educated to give this help." (4, p. 219) It is immediately apparent that an individual does not have to possess the title "counselor" in order to be qualified to counsel. But he/she must be a professional, and he/she must limit his/her counseling to within the scope of his/her professional competency.

Counseling is one of the most intimate of all professional relationships in which two people interact and communicate with each other. It is certainly characteristic of the finest in our Western traditions, providing an environment in which the emphasis is on the individual and his personal fulfillment.

The nature of the help being provided by the counselor is "assisting the individual in making wise choices and adjustments." (3, p. 4) These choices involve a wide range of activities: for example, determining a major, choosing an appropriate subject, selecting an occupation, evolving a career, choosing a husband or wife, deciding on a hobby, or adopting a budget. The adjustments that confront individuals are equally diverse: adapting to new environments, dealing with fears and hostilities, resolving dilemmas, changing self-concepts, altering level of aspirations, getting along with others, maintaining self-esteem, and enhancement of self. Choices and adjustments may be classified into three areas: educational, career (or vocational), and personal-social.

> When guidance is concerned with curriculum, cocurricular activities, studying, learning, and preparation for a vocation, it is classified as educational guidance. (9, p. 7)

> Guidance which includes vocational interests and aptitudes, surveying vocations, selecting vocations, and getting a job is classified as vocational guidance. (9, p. 8)

Personal-social guidance involves problems in such categories as mental, emotional, ethical, social, marital, financial, health, etc.

It is important at this time to reflect upon the definitions of counseling as expressed by different authorities:

> Counseling has been described as the face-to-face meeting of the counselor and counselee. Within the guidance services, counseling may be thought of as the core of the helping process, essential for the proper administration of assistance to students as they attempt to solve their problems. (15, p. 12)

> Counseling is a service of verbal assistance by one person who wishes to help another person in a puzzled or troubled state by influencing his behavior so as to relieve the puzzled or troubled state. (2, p. 61)

> Guidance is the assistance given to individuals in making intelligent choices and adjustments in their lives. (12, p. 25)

… we may define counseling as a learning process, warm and permissive in nature, by which one human being, properly trained, helps another to come to a closer realization of his total personality. (23, pp. 103–104)

> Counseling is a personal face-to-face relationship between two people, in which the counselor, by means of the relationship and his special competencies provides a learning situation in which the counselee, a normal sort of person, is helped to know himself and his present and possible future situations so that he can use his characteristics and potentialities in a way that is both satisfying to himself and beneficial to society, and further, can learn how to solve future problems and meet future needs. (22, p. 3)

Throughout the literature on counseling, there is considerable confusion, disagreement and fuzziness in the use of the words "counseling" and "guidance." Some authorities use them synonymously. Others consider "guidance" a broader term that encompasses services other than "counseling." To further confuse the issue, the term "pupil personnel" has been inserted into the literature, sometimes to replace "guidance" and in other instances to represent more of a variety of services than is usually associated with "guidance."

The attachment of the word "guidance" to "counselor" is a redundancy in some instances, though perhaps because of the divergence in the use of the terms, even educators occasionally may become confused.

Whenever the word "guidance" is used in this text, it refers to a professional service designed to help individuals in making wise choices and adjustments. A guidance worker is any professional who is so engaged, and this includes people other than counselors, such as teachers, supervisors, and administrators.

Whenever the word "counselor" is used in this text it means "professional counselor," and it means "guidance counselor." A professional guidance counselor is defined as a qualified individual who helps another person to make wise educational, career (or vocational) and personal-social choices and adjustments.

Some colleges, universities, and agencies are referring to their counselors as "counseling psychologists." In the public schools the titles of "counselor" and "school psychologist" are used, representing two different occupations and requiring different educational preparation. It is believed that "guidance counselor" – dropping the word "guidance" whenever the usage of the word "counselor" alone does not confuse the users – is the best identifying label for current usage.

In regard to the use of titles, it is important to consider the following:

> Above all, the school has a right to expect that the
> counselor will be proud to be known as an educator, that
> he will make no pretenses, either publicly or privately,
> of being something better than "just an educator." (11)

The only time the word "counseling" will not refer to the definition given in this chapter is in *Part II: Functions of the Counselor*. In that section of the text, the occupational activities of the counselor, other than the actual act of counseling as we have just defined it, are described. As implied by the term, the functions of the counselor point out that there are other responsibilities incumbent upon the performance of counseling. What these activities are and their relationship to the one-to-one relationship are the subject matter of Part II, which in no way should confuse the reader in holding fast to the meaning of counseling as defined in this chapter.

☞ *Principles of Counseling*

Each of the following principles is applicable to the concept of counseling. Counseling is a young profession, and the subject matter forming the bases of the science of counseling is still in the process of evolving into a framework of comparative stability. Consequently, there are few principles to which all counseling authorities subscribe. If the reader or his instructor disagree with a principle, the application of the third principle discussed further on makes possible this disagreement.

It is important for the reader to be alert in recognizing how the principles integrate with each other, and how the acceptance of a given principle contributes to the utilization of others.

Individualization. The adult and the child sitting on the log have long symbolized the ideal learning situation. From this emphasis on the individual, public education has unavoidably moved a long way into larger and larger groups as American society has attempted to cope with its belief in education for all.

In some texts, "guidance" becomes "guidance services," and in most usages, "pupil personnel" becomes "pupil personnel services." At the college level, "student personnel services" is used in most instances, rather than "guidance services" or "pupil personnel services," the term employed for California School Guidance Counseling Services.

Guidance Services include:
Individual Inventory Services
Counseling Services
Career Planning and Placement Services
Research and Evaluation Services
Career Counseling Services
Coordination/Consultation Services
Advisement/Program Placement Services

Pupil Personnel Services include:
Guidance Services
School Psychology Services
School Social Work Services (including Child Welfare and Attendance Services)
School Health Services

Student Personnel Services (4, p. 231) include:
   Counseling Center
   Testing Service
   Career Planning and Placement Service
   Admissions Office
   Housing Service
   Financial Aid Office
   Health Service
   Records Office
   Foreign Students Office
   Student Affairs Office
   Career Counseling Services
   Handicapped Students Services
   Advisement Services
   Veterans Services
   Adult Reentry Service

As we stated in the Preface, this chapter and all other chapters of the book are presented primarily within the frame of reference of the counselor who works in public schools, colleges, or universities. For these people, counseling is the service – the educative process – which counteracts the impersonalization that often comes with the group situation. Counseling focuses on the individual – one person, not the group (two or more people).

The importance of this principle in a democratic society cannot be overstressed. If many of the following principles are to be maintained, if each American is to have equal opportunities for self-enhancement, certainly there must be provision for expert assistance at those times when each person seeks specific personal attention in resolving his problems, meeting his needs, enriching his understanding of self, relating his self to his present or possible future environment, in maturing, etc. There should be little doubt why Frank W. Miller refers to counseling as "the most important service offered to pupils." (14, p. 56) This may be extended beyond the milieu of the school, substituting the word "people" for "pupils." Individualized help for a person – lawyer to client, dentist to patient, etc. – is something unique in interpersonal relationships. It is needed by each of us, it is one of the privileged heritages of being an American.

Emphasis upon the individual can, of course, occur in groups whenever the group is devoting its attention to aiding one of the members of the group or each member of the group. This matter of when and why the group should be utilized is covered in *Chapter 2. Counseling and Group Guidance.* As emphasized in Chapter 2, however, the utilization of the group situation should be carefully controlled to prevent any usurpation or infringement of the counseling process (the one-to-one situation).

In a discussion of existentialism in counseling, Landsman (13) points out that regardless of the positions taken by existentialists, all such theorists place "emphasis upon the self." The existentialists are not the only philosophers who adhere to the importance of individualism, but their thinking is cited here as an example of one of several possible philosophical bases for our focusing on the individual.

Learning Process. As it is used here as our second principle, learning means "the acquiring of understanding or skills." (9, p. 25) Regardless of the diverse viewpoints as to the most appropriate counseling methodology, there is little justification for any thesis which proposes that counseling is not a learning activity.

It is, of course, possible that learning will not occur, for the counselee may refuse to learn, may not want to learn, may not be able to learn, or may terminate the relationship before learning can be achieved. But none of these difficulties nullifies the principle that counseling is a learning process, which it certainly is when it is successful. When the counselor fails, and there is no learning, it does not destroy the "learning process" principle so long as the intent of the relationship is learning. If an automobile salesman and his customer are together in a "selling relationship," this is what their interaction may be called regardless of whether or not the customer buys a car. It is the rationale involved in the inception of the relationship which determines its identity.

Human Freedom. From the spirit of '76 to the immediate moment, Americans have agreed on and have fought for the concept of freedom.

To exclude this principle from counseling would be unthinkable; counseling provides an environment in which the client is free to make his own choices and adjustments.

Not only is the client free to choose and to adjust in terms of his self-concept, level of aspiration, needs, personality traits, etc., he is free to delay decision making and adjusting. If he is not interfering with the rights of others, injuring others, or performing illegal acts, he should not be coerced, sold, persuaded, or led into actions: "...the foundation of freedom – the right of the individual to the pursuit of happiness as he chooses to pursue it" underlies the counseling relationship from beginning to end. (10, p. 145)

One of the prime reasons why a counselee often approaches a counseling appointment with resentment is that he was told he "should" see a counselor or worse, that he "must" see a counselor. The freshman who receives a form letter directing him to report to the Counseling Center or the transfer student who must meet with a counselor are examples of possible causes of a counselee's resistance to counseling before he is ever exposed to it. The hoary adage, "You can lead a horse to water, but ..." still applies.

In such situations, it is fitting to invite freshmen and transfer students (plus all other students) to avail themselves of the counseling service whenever they wish. Detailed explanations of the services offered by counselors should be called to the attention of the students at frequent, strategic intervals. But there should be no infringement of the individual's freedom; he should be permitted to stay away from the Counseling Center if he so chooses.

Helping. The core, the foundation, and the structure of counseling are tied into the principle of helping, for the very essence of counseling is helping.

The naive, the immature, the unknowing, the unskilled, the prejudiced, et al. – in varying degrees of deficiency – come to the counselor seeking assistance. It is not that the counselor "plays God" or pretends to be a fountain from which all manner of wisdom flows. Rather, within the scope of his education and experience, and in terms of his specialization or generalization, he strives to aid the individual, to provide the kind of assistance the person desires.

The techniques used in providing this help are discussed in Part III, the section dealing with the art of counseling.

With the ever-increasing complexity of living, everyone needs help from many professional sources: from the physician, dentist, lawyer, counselor, etc. It is the personalized assistance that makes the counseling relationship unique in human relationships.

Influencing Behavior. What the counselor and counselee do in the counseling relationship should have an effect on the counselee's future behavior. This is inevitable if the counselee learns anything in counseling. Accordingly, counseling influences behavior.

> The counselor is attempting to influence the behavior
> of the client – this is obvious; otherwise he wouldn't be
> engaged in counseling. (17)

Caution should be exercised in delimiting the meaning of "influence." Having an effect on behavior means that the counselor serves only as a catalyst, contributing to the client's acquiring understanding or skills which then facilitate the making of wise choices and adjustments himself.

Thus, this principle does not mean that the counselor should try to manipulate, maneuver, cajole, or persuade the client to make certain choices or to adjust in a prescribed pattern. Instead, it should pertain to counseling methodology, which is selected only to aid the client. The "influence" is exerted through techniques chosen by the counselor which are intended to show the counselee the facts needed, the alternatives to consider, etc., so that the counselee has "techniques of action" that can move him in the direction of the resolution of his difficulties.

Self-understanding. With the previous emphasis on the importance of the individual, it follows logically that we can add: counseling enables the counselee to achieve more self-understanding.

The human being is perhaps the most complicated entity in existence. A lifetime is not nearly long enough for anyone to attain as much self-understanding as he could use for the enhancement of his living. Self-understanding may range from a casual insight, occurring in one interview, to a scientific program involving the in-depth acquisition of knowledge concerning personality traits, psychological needs, interests, aptitudes, values, and goals.

In most instances the client will be seeking more self-understanding in order to make a choice of an adjustment, which also requires other data such as understanding of self in relation to the world of work in order to make a wise career plan. However, it is possible for a client to seek greater self-understanding simply in order to get more enjoyment out of living, to acquire peace of mind, to change his self-concept, or to modify his level of aspiration.

Environmental Understanding. As important as the realization of self-understanding is for a counselee, it is equally vital that he continuously enriches his knowledge of his present and probable future environment.

This is one principle that is violated too frequently by too many counselors, particularly in career counseling. Unfortunately, some counselors are naive about the world of work, so they shy away from it and concentrate on aiding their clients in self-understanding. It is for this reason that the word "should" must be inserted in the wording of the principle: Counseling "should" enable the counselee to achieve more environmental understanding.

Adding to knowledge of his/her present environment is essential if the individual is to make wise choices and adjustments. This environment could include school, home, church, clubs, etc. It is apparent that each person lives within a variety of environments, which in turn means a diversity of choices and adjustments. And, while the understanding of self and environment are separated into two sections for presentation, in actual operation they are in most instances related to each other and not separated.

A continuous alertness to probable future environments, coupled with increasing understanding of what may be involved in these possibilities, are needed in career planning, marriage planning, educational preparation, and leisure-time activities.

Adjusting. This principle and the following one are the expressions of what the helping process is attempting to do. Counseling assists individuals in adjusting.

The word "adjusting" has many interpretations. It is used here to refer to an individual's " ...doing things that lead to his being satisfied or happy with his environment ... To be satisfied means that you are pleased with yourself, others, and things, and in general enjoy life. If you are happy, you are deeply satisfied." (9, p. 5)

Few people ever achieve adjustment and then sustain it for an indefinite period of significant duration. Most individuals find themselves dissatisfied with one thing or another on a daily basis, but spasmodically – just as the intervals of satisfaction come and go.

Even if it were possible for a person to achieve constancy in his/her satisfaction with himself/herself, with others, and with all aspects of his/her living, a strong case can be made against this seeming utopian happiness. Briefly, the person who is happy is hardly motivated to improve. If he/she has no motivation to be other than he/she is, why would he/she willingly embark on any activity which would require exertion, time, or money, or any combination of these?

Some dissatisfaction or some tension usually is necessary if a person is to learn, to change, or to improve. Consequently, while the counselor is involved in helping his/her client to adjust, it is important for the counselee to attain a functional degree of satisfaction without achieving (even if it were possible) a state of bliss or contentment which would take the edge from any motivation for improvement or progress.

Making Choices. Choosing a vocation, planning a career, determining a college, deciding on a major, selecting a husband or wife, finding a hobby, and discriminating among alternatives for solutions to problems are examples of the massive importance involved in making choices. A poor choice can lead to maladjustment in varying degrees, or it can have a devastating effect upon the course and pattern of a person's life. Counseling helps individuals to make choices.

It should be kept firmly in mind that regardless of what methodology a particular counselor may prefer, that counselor should never make choices for his/her clients. Instead, he/she should help them do what is necessary to reach the point at which they can make their own choices.

Presentation of alternative solutions to a problem is permissible, so long as the counselor refrains from indicating even a subtle preference for a particular alternative. The essential goal is that the client sharpen his/her problem-solving methodology so he/she will be better able to attack his/her next problem after the resolution of the current one. There will be other problems as long as he/she lives.

Maturing. Many difficulties that people encounter are the product of immaturity. For example: "Of all the many obstacles on the road to marital success the critical inhibitor is immaturity – mental, emotional, social, and/or moral immaturity." (5, p. 19)

The brat, the irresponsible youth, the (so-called) adult who has tantrums, the compulsive job-hopper – these are but a few of the seemingly limitless assortment of instances of immaturity. Counseling provides a situation in which the individual is aided in approaching mental, emotional, social, and moral maturity.

If the learning process is to become a reality in the counselor's office, or in the classroom, the home, the church, in business, etc., the individual must continue to make significant progress towards attaining true adulthood. Retarded progress towards maturity usually inhibits learning, may impede it altogether, and certainly does not facilitate it.

Many counseling techniques serve to stimulate the individual's maturing through a helping process, one that involves the client, always freely, to accept or reject, to verbalize or remain silent, to respond or defer response, and to think or feel or both.

Methodology. For too many years counselor educators have allowed themselves to become involved in defending or refuting a particular school of counseling methodology or theory. The directive versus the nondirective (or client-centered therapy) battle has been fought on too many battlefields.

It is time to turn to a principle that offers freedom of choice to the counselor. This principle will no doubt elicit sharp disagreement from some authorities and from those who wish to campaign zealously against any viewpoint that is in variance with their own. The counseling methodology should include any particular technique which will best meet the counseling needs of each counselee. This, of course, postulates the eclectic viewpoint.

Eclecticism has its weaknesses as well as its strengths. Some possible disadvantages are the "jack of all trades, master of none," limitation; superficiality in application of a particular technique; the absence of those skills usually available with the specialist's repeated usage – again and again – of certain techniques within one methodology; and the distortion of a technique due to a lack of depth in understanding it.

In spite of these possible liabilities, it is believed that each counselor should be free to choose his/her way of performing. The adequately educated, highly professional and ethical counselor will endeavor to master those techniques which he/she must use in doing the type of counseling for which his/her education has prepared him.

Just as certainly, the ethical counselor will refrain from attempting to use every technique (all of which are theoretically available to the person who is eclectic in his methodology), and will confine himself/herself to utilizing only those techniques which he/she is professionally competent to use.

If a particular technique in which a counselor is unskilled should be used with a certain counselee, it is the responsibility of that counselor to refer that counselee to a counselor who is known to be skilled in the technique. This permits any counselor to adhere to the principle that when he/she is qualified to act, he/she does so; when he/she is not qualified to proceed, he/she refers to another counselor.

Problem Solving. As previously mentioned, it is more important for the client to sharpen his problem-solving skill than it is to resolve a particular difficulty. This is not to belittle the significance of problems, many of which are monumental in their importance. But problems are unending. Each time a person is able – with help – to resolve a difficulty, using scientific or logical procedures, he moves closer to being able to handle subsequent problems independently, providing the counselor is careful to avoid fostering a dependency relationship.

"The chief objective of the guidance worker should be to work himself right out of a job." (20, p. 222) It might be added: "This is true of the physician, dentist, social worker, and others who dedicate themselves to the welfare of people." (8, p. 14) Attempting to get persons to the point at which they can solve their problems without professional help is an ethical goal which should not be construed as being economically threatening: " ...none of these professional people need concern themselves, in terms of loss of livelihood or even a diminishing income, for there will always be an ample supply of persons who need help." (8, p. 14)

Whatever technique he/she may be using, the counselor should remain alert to this principle: Each counselee should be aided in moving toward more independence in problem solving.

Value System. It has never ceased to be a source of amazement to the authors in their counseling practice that most clients have never evolved a value system – an organized pattern of what an individual considers worthwhile (e.g., honesty, courtesy, etc.).

It is difficult for an individual to make certain decisions, resolve particular difficulties, or effect special adjustments if he/she does not know what traits, activities, things, etc., he/she considers worthwhile or eminently important to him. Counseling helps the individual to determine his/her value system.

What a person considers worthwhile has a tremendous impact on his decision making. The authors, recognizing the importance of values in career planning, have created the *Rating Scale of Vocational Values* (18). For example, if in career counseling a client discovers that one of his vocational interests is accounting, and that he possesses sufficient aptitudes to succeed in this occupation, one of the additional factors he/she should also know is whether or not he/she values this type of work. To be highly interested in accounting and to be able to do it are not enough if the person does not value it. If he/she is ashamed of himself/herself for being an accountant, if he/she does not respect accounting, if this work seems insignificant to him/her, if it ranks low on his/her own personally evolved hierarchy of worthwhile occupations, then – in any of the foregoing examples – the prognosis for his being successful or satisfied as an accountant is poor. Just as we tend to dislike what we do not understand, we are inclined to reject or leave what we regard as unworthwhile.

When a person determines his/her values and organizes them into what he/she considers a meaningful pattern, he/she is then much better prepared to face a diversity of problems. Accordingly, when a client acquires a value system, this should be helpful in aiding him/her to make progress in problem solving.

Goals. A common fallacy of many people is to focus their attention on "the means to an unknown end." This is illustrated by the college student who concerns himself with choosing a major without knowing what goal or goals his/her major is intended to help him/her achieve. Of course, a major may be a goal, and each particular subject within the major could be interpreted as a goal. It is important that the basic goal – which must be determined before making a decision about the subordinate goal or goals – should be considered first. Then in logical order, the other goals leading to it (and serving as means as well as ends) may be ascertained.

A surprising number of college students, as well as high school students, do not have a vocational goal (or even a nonvocational goal such as acquiring culture, becoming an educated individual, etc.). Even fewer people have an awareness of such major life goals as marriage, civic projects, recreational pursuits, etc. Counseling assists the individual in choosing his goals.

There are temporary goals which, when achieved, cease to exist: for example, getting married, getting the education needed to qualify as a nuclear physicist, learning how to play bridge, etc. There are permanent or continuous goals which may be lifelong. Notice how a slight change in the wording of the temporary goals makes them permanent goals: having a happy marriage, keeping abreast of the evolving content of nuclear physics, and playing bridge with more and more skill.

Evaluating. Just as the acquiring and continuous sharpening of the skill of problem solving is an important asset for anyone in living, so is the process of evaluating.

To evaluate means to determine the strengths and weaknesses of someone or something. Each counselee should be aided in moving toward more independence in evaluating.

These are necessary steps in the evaluation process: locating criteria which may be used to determine the strengths and weaknesses of whatever is to be evaluated; developing criteria (if no standards are available); and recognizing that some strengths and weaknesses carry more weight than others in arriving at a conclusion concerning the person or thing being evaluated.

In so many of the other principles it is necessary for the client to engage in evaluating if he/she is to make significant progress in adjusting, making choices, evolving a value system, etc.

It is essential for the client to gain an awareness of the need for obtaining facts and relating them to standards. They can then be used as means of finding the strengths and weaknesses in the choices being considered. Possible courses of action can then be contemplated, and necessary adjustments can be made.

Common weaknesses in clients (as in all of us) are evident in our natural inclination to look only for strengths while ignoring weaknesses, to distort facts to fit preconceived conclusions, or to interpret data according to prejudices or emotions. Evaluating is a scientific process which may enable the client to eliminate or alleviate these weaknesses by adhering to a factual and logical procedure.

☞ *Objectives of Counseling*

In the relationship between a person who seeks help and an individual who is professionally educated to give this help, there are several goals which the counselor should strive to achieve. While it is obvious that the most basic objectives in counseling should be the realization of each principle of counseling, there are a few other important goals that each counselor should attempt to attain. These goals will be briefly discussed in this section.

As in the case of the principles, authorities are not in complete agreement on all of the goals we discuss here. Certainly, however, each goal is worthy of consideration as a desirable outcome in a particular counseling situation.

Realism. The counselor often comes face to face with a dilemma. On the one hand he/she would like to achieve the objective of helping the individual acquire a realistic self-concept and level of aspiration. On the other hand the counselor wants very much to avoid any destruction of the client's self-esteem. The comments cited below serve to emphasize how crucial this dilemma is.

> No amount of education, no amount of inspiration, and no amount of vocational guidance will change the fact that the great bulk of human workers must always be employed on the lower levels." (10, p. 187)

… most of our students will remain in, or near, the jobs at which they begin … (10, p. 187)

> If we are going to be realistic and truthful and if we are not going to contribute to future frustration, we must abandon the inspirational ballyhoo that any boy can be president, and we must encourage our students to choose occupations in which they may hope to be reasonably contented if cherished promotions do not materialize. (10, p. 187)

> Personality disturbance is the result of threat to the self-concept. The self-concept becomes disturbed when the maintenance or enhancement of the self is frustrated or thwarted. (18, p. 147)

It was Thoreau who said that most people live lives of quiet desperation, and Eliot who pointed out that all life is an endless struggle to think well of oneself. And among the many important contributions of Snygg and Combs in their text *Individual Behavior: A New Frame of Reference for Psychology* (19) is their thesis that each individual's defense of himself is his most pressing and crucial need.

The counselor's dilemma, then, lies in helping the individual to think better of himself/herself while he/she is discovery those weaknesses that limit the scope of his/her aspirations, a discovery which may be shattering to his/her self-concept. The hope, of course, is that the counselee will be able to modify his/her self-concept and level of aspiration within a framework of reality that permits the inclusion of realistic goals, plans, and activities.

Responsible Independence. Responsibility and independence are each characteristic of maturity. In combining them here, the intent is to put forth the concept of an individual who is willing and able to answer for his actions, and who does not require control by others.

Patterson believes that "the goal of counseling is the development of a responsible independence." (18, p. 62) However, his interpretation is from the mental health point of view: "Responsible independence is perhaps an external definition of mental health." He further states that "self-actualization is perhaps the internal point of view of responsible independence. A more general and inclusive term is self-esteem." (18, p. 62)

The authors' explanation of responsible independence focuses attention on the counselor's need to refrain from fostering client dependency and to avoid exercising control over his behavior. "Counselors in particular must avoid the temptation 'to build a clientele' by encouraging client dependence." (8, p. 13)

The positive approach of the counselor in attempting to achieve this objective should be " ...to help the individual to help himself." (1, p. 12).

Detecting Talent and Ability. The counselor's mind should remain alert in order to observe any signs or clues that a client possesses a particular talent.

In this space age, with its demanding requirements for more and more scientists, professional workers, administrators, and executives, any counselor is certainly remiss in a key professional obligation if he/she is not alert to the discovery of gifted individuals. Helping the individual to ascertain what talent or talents he/she may possess is not only of prime importance to the client, but of significant value to society.

There is more to the discovery of talent than the identification of the scholastically gifted. There are other talents to be explored, such as administrative, artistic, athletic, clerical, commercial, computational, creative, dramatic, executive, literary, manual, mechanical, musical, organizing, scientific, service, and societal. (6) It is saddening to reflect upon the number of people who may possess one or more talents, but who go through life without ever being aware of their latent gifts.

Whenever possible, and when it is appropriate to the client's reasons for seeing a counselor, there should be a search for talent, if it is integrated with the following objective of actualizing talent.

Actualizing Talent and Ability. When an individual discovers he/she possesses a talent or talents, it is merely academic unless he/she proceeds to do something about it or them. Super and Crites (21, p. 619) stress the importance of detecting and using talent. Accordingly, it becomes necessary for the counselor to strive toward the objective of helping the individual to actualize his talent or talents.

Detection of talent simply as an academic exercise or to satisfy a client's curiosity is not worth the expenditures involved in using the tests, instruments, and other means of gathering data. It can be justified on the grounds that the client will move into a program of development designed to bring his/her talent to a level appropriate to its vocational, educational, cultural, or recreational application. It is most regrettable when talent remains undiscovered, but it is tragic when the talent is discovered but not developed and not utilized.

Improvement of Counselor. No system is better than the people who make it work. It follows that counseling can be improved only by enhancing the capabilities of the counselors.

> A great deal of what you communicate to your client is
> not what you say but what you are. (16)

Each counselor should actualize "responsible independence" for himself by sharpening his effectiveness as a counselor. *Part V: The Preparation of the Counselor,* offers suggestions for the student and the practitioner of counseling who are concerned with achieving this objective.

It is a fact that a person seldom remains static; he usually is either progressing or retrogressing – professionally and personally. If he/she desires to improve, the individual must engage in activities designed to facilitate progression rather than retrogression. Research, creativity, professional reading, self-analysis and environmental investigation are procedures which should contribute to the enhancement of the counselor personally as well as professionally.

Confidentiality. The counselor-client relationship is a sacred one, professionally speaking. What the client says and what he/she reveals to the counselor must be kept confidential to the extent permitted by law.

It is hoped that the laws will be extended to include all counselors within the boundaries of "privileged communication." Until such time, the counselor who is not now a privileged communicant should do whatever he/she can, professionally and legally, to achieve the objective of keeping the counseling relationship confidential.

A counselor should not discuss any of his/her clients with another person unless this individual is being utilized as a consultant or a referral source. If the client wants his/her counselor to give information resulting from the counselor-client relationship, authorization in writing should be secured by the counselor from the client. Every protection should be provided to safeguard the confidential nature of the counselor-client relationship, including keeping records in a room to which only authorized personnel have access.

Referring. Whenever a counselor knows that another counselor or another professional is better qualified to assist his/her client, a referral should be made. Referrals should be made whenever this will provide the best possible professional service for the client.

An important part of the counselor's education should involve knowledge of the scope and limitations of his professional service, together with an understanding of the nature of the service provided by other professionals who can serve his/her clients. Because of the ego factor involved, there could be a tendency for a counselor to continue working with a client beyond the point at which his/her professional judgment indicates a referral should be made.

Each counselor should remember that an essential ingredient in any profession is a code of ethics, and adherence to the code is necessary if he/she is to qualify as a professional. Referring certainly may be necessary in any profession under certain conditions and in particular circumstances. When it is necessary, it should be done.

Public Relations. Whenever the counselor, or any member of the counselor's staff (e.g., receptionist, secretary, etc.), has contact with a client or a potential client by letter, telephone, or "face-to-face," there is an impression of the counseling service which may range from strong feelings of pleasure and good will to resentment, irritation, or even hostility.

It is not necessary for the professional or his/her staff to respond to the public in terms of the old axiom of the merchandising industry: "The customer is always right." Anyone connected with counseling should pursue the objective of helping each potential client understand the nature of the counselor's services (including scope and limitations), the cost (if applicable), and in general to offer acceptance, warmth, and understanding, if only for the fleeting moment of contact during which the potential client is being referred.

For many years, the authors have stressed the significance of counseling centers having a high-quality receptionist, for this person often is the only contact a potential client has with the counseling service. The receptionist should function on a professional level, rather than a clerical one, and have the time, energy, education, and experience to equip her/him to greet, accept, and inform the public with such competency that people go away enthused about counseling, even though they may not have seen a counselor.

Each counseling center has an obligation to enhance the public image of counseling. Steps should be taken to correct any of the following distorted impressions: only sick people go to counselors; counseling is just for the maladjusted person; counselors are provided by schools to deal with problem students, dropouts, truants, failures, and deviates; there is not time enough to help the normal individual; etc.

The American public has the right to be informed concerning the nature of counseling. What a person does not understand, he often fears, distrusts or ignores. If the public is to accept counseling and to use this service, people must be informed on a continuing basis about counseling.

☞ References

[1] Arbuckle, Dugald S. *Guidance and Counseling in the Classroom.* Boston: Allyn and Bacon, Inc., 1957.

[2] Byrne, Richard Hill. *The School Counselor.* Boston: Houghton Mifflin Company, 1963.

[3] *Colorado Criteria for Evaluative Study of Programs of Guidance Services: Part I – Introduction and Purposes of the Survey.* Office of Director of Guidance Services, Colorado State Department of Education, June 1964.

[4] Demos, George D., and Bruce Grant. *College and University Counseling.* From *Guidelines for Guidance: Readings in the Philosophy of Guidance,* edited by Carlton E. Beck. Dubuque, Iowa: W. C. Brown and Company, 1966.

[5] –––––. *How to Have a Successful Marriage.* Columbia, Missouri: Lucas Brothers, 1966.

[6] –––––. *Rating Scales of Vocational Values, Interests, and Aptitudes: Manual.* San Diego, California: Educational and Industrial Testing Service, 1966.

[7] *Evaluative Criteria: Guidance Services.* National Study of Secondary School Evaluation, Washington, D.C. 1960.

[8] Grant, Bruce, and Richard Oldenburg. *A Philosophy of Guidance Services.* Columbia, Missouri: Lucas Brothers, 1964.

[9] Grant, Bruce, George D. Demos, and Willard Edwards. *Guidance for Youth.* Springfield, Illinois: Charles C. Thomas, 1965.

[10] Hoppock, Robert. *Occupational Information.* New York: McGraw-Hill Book Company, 1963.

[11] Hoyt, Kenneth B. "What the School Has a Right to Expect of Its Counselor." *Personnel and Guidance Journal,* October 1961, pp. 129–130.

[12] Jones, Arthur J. *Principles of Guidance.* New York: McGraw-Hill Book Company, 1963.

[13] Landsman, Ted. "Existentialism in Counseling: The Scientific View." *Personnel and Guidance Journal,* February 1965, pp. 568–573.

[14] Miller, Frank W. *Guidance: Principles and Services.* Columbus, Ohio: Charles E. Merrill, 1961.

[15] Moser, Leslie E., and Ruth Small Moser. *Counseling and Guidance: An Exploration.* Englewood Cliffs, New Jersey: Prentice-Hall, 1963.

[16] Murphy, Gardener. "The Cultural Context of Guidance." *Personnel and Guidance Journal,* 34, 1955, pp. 4–9.

[17] Patterson, C. H. "Control, Conditioning, and Counseling." *Personnel and Guidance Journal,* April 1963, pp. 680–685.

[18] –––––. *Counseling and Psychotherapy: Theory and Practice.* New York: Harper & Brothers, 1959.

[19] Snygg, D., and A. W. Combs. *Individual Behavior: A New Frame of Reference for Psychology.* New York: Harper & Brothers, 1949.

[20] Stoops, Emery, and Gunnar L. Wahlquist, *Principles and Practices in Guidance.* New York: McGraw-Hill Book Company, 1958.

[21] Super, Donald E., and John D. Crites. *Appraising Vocational Fitness.* New York: Harper & Brothers, 1962.

[22] Tolbert, E. L. *Introduction to Counseling.* New York: McGraw-Hill Book Company, 1959.

[23] Zeran, Franklin R., and Anthony C. Riccio. *Organization and Administration of Guidance Services.* Chicago: Rand McNally & Company, 1962.

[24] Hagermoser, Lisa & Kratochnill, T.R., *Treatment Integrity*, A.P.A., 2015.

☞ *Suggested Additional Readings*

Arbuckle, Dugald S. *Counseling: An Introduction.* Boston: Allyn and Bacon, 1961.

Beck, Carlton E. *Guidelines for Guidance: Readings in the Philosophy of Guidance.* Dubuque, Iowa: W. C. Brown and Company, 1966.

Creamer, Don G., ed. *Student Development in Higher Education.* Cincinnati: American College Personnel Association, 1980.

Gallagher, Phillip J., and George D. Demos. *The Counseling Center in Higher Education.* Springfield, Illinois: Charles C. Thomas, 1970.

Gowan, John C., and George D. Demos. *The Education and Guidance of the Ablest.* Springfield, Illinois: Charles C. Thomas, 1964.

-----. *The Guidance of Exceptional Children.* New York: David McKay Company, 1965.

Grant, Bruce, George D. Demos, and Richard Oldenburg. *Improving Counseling: An Evaluative Instrument for Improving Counseling Centers.* Columbia, Missouri: Lucas Brothers, 1964.

Gysbers, Norman C. "Career Guidance at the Crossroads." In New *Imperatives for Guidance,* edited by Garry R. Walz and Libby Benjamin, pp. 2–29. Ann Arbor, Mich.: ERIC Counseling and Personnel Services Clearinghouse, 1978.

Herr, Edwin L. *Guidance and Counseling in the Schools: The Past, Present, and Future.* Falls Church, Va.: American Personnel and Guidance Association, 1979.

Krumboltz, John D., and Carl E. Thoresen. *Behavioral Counseling.* New York: Holt, Rinehart and Winston, 1969.

Lewis, Judith A., and Michael D. Lewis. *Community Counseling: A Human Services Approach.* New York: John Wiley and Sons, 1977.

Miller, Frank W., James A. Freuhling, and Gloria J. Lewis. *Guidance Principles and Services.* 3rd ed. Columbus, Ohio: Charles E. Merrill, 1978.

Patterson, C. H. *Theories of Counseling and Psychotherapy.* New York: Harper & Row, 1966.

Pietrofesa, John J., Bianca Bernstain, J. Anne Minor, and Susan Stanford. *Guidance: An Introduction.* Chicago: Rand McNally, 1980.

Shertzer, Bruce, and Shelley C. Stone. *Fundamentals of Guidance.* 4th ed. Boston: Houghton Mifflin, 1981.

Warnath, Charles F., ed. *New Directions for College Counselors.* San Francisco: Jossey-Bass, 1973.

Wirtz, Willard. *The Boundless Resource.* Washington, D. C.: The New Republic Book Company, 1975.

Wrenn, C. Gilbert. "Personnel Perspectives Past and Present." In *New Imperatives for Guidance,* edited by Garry R. Walz and Libby Benjamin, pp. 456–491, Ann Arbor, Michigan: ERIC Counseling and Personnel Services Clearinghouse, 1978.

Chapter 2

COUNSELING AND GROUP GUIDANCE

In some instances, the use of the group may be the most effective approach to helping one member, or each member, of the group. For this reason alone, attention must be directed toward the utilization of the group whenever it is most appropriate. Bennett believes that "guidance is a learning process. Some aspects can best be carried on individual face-to-face situations ... others can best be carried on through some type of group situation." (1, p. 17)

A prime factor which warrants focusing attention on the group process is the need for clarification of what it means, when not to use it, and when to use it.

The group procedures reported in *Chapter 9, Group Activities,* further prescribe the extent to which the group may be utilized.

☞ *An Interpretation of Group Guidance*

One of the terms used in place of "Group guidance" is "group counseling." Since counseling has been defined as a one-to-one relationship between counselor and counselee, and group means two or more persons, the term "group counseling" cannot logically be used to represent a counselor's relationship with two or more persons. Another term, "multiple counseling" (2) is also erroneous for the same reason.

A definition of group guidance that avoids the pitfalls of the foregoing terms would be: group guidance occurs whenever a counselor (or other guidance worker) is assisting a group of individuals in making wise choices and adjustments.

There is one other instance in which the term "group guidance" may be stretched to include an unusual situation. This involves two or more counselors (or other guidance workers) assisting one individual or a group of individuals in making wise choices and adjustments. From the cost standpoint, and considering the number of professionals available, it is a rare occasion when two or more counselors or other guidance workers can simultaneously work with a group.

☞ *When Not to Utilize Group Guidance*

Before examining when to use group guidance, it is appropriate to direct attention towards when not to use it. There are many instances of the good which could accrue from group guidance being distorted by its misuse.

Not to Effect Economy. Of all the abuses in using group guidance, the most flagrant has been the submitting of the group situation for the one-to-one relationship to save money.

Admittedly, an administrator who is forced by money restrictions to limit his counseling staff to two counselors when he needs four or more is faced with a practical problem that does not yield to simply saying, "Do the best you can under the circumstances." A high school principal faced with this situation might also have only twenty-five teachers when he should have fifty or more. If he has 1600 students, each teacher has to have an average class load of 64 pupils, and each counselor has to have a client load of 800 pupils. This administrator might be able to reduce teacher load by using the auditorium to have lecture courses of 400, 600, 800, or more students per class period. He could have his counselors set up group guidance classes in the gymnasium, meeting with 100, 200, or 400 to 800 per session.

These are examples of efforts to effect economies, to attempt to operate in an impossible situation. It does not mean that the school will accomplish what society expects it to do. To subvert or distort the guidance service by expecting group guidance to replace counseling or expecting to do what it was never intended to do should not be attempted as the supposed solution to mass education in a poor community.

If the school or organization cannot afford counseling, it should not attempt to have it by utilizing untrained people; nor should it try to get by with an abuse of the group process in a miscalled guidance situation.

Instead of acquiescing to budgetary limitations, which on the surface seem to prohibit the employment of enough counselors, administrators should present to their community the need for counseling through a well-organized program of public relations designed to acquaint the public with why counselors must be employed, how many are needed and what they will be doing when hired.

Too many educators have failed to grasp the significance of the work performed by counselors. In *Guidance for Youth,* (3, p. 4) there are quoted statements by two of the great educators of all time. It would be prudent for each educator and citizen to reflect profoundly upon the meaning and implications of these thoughts.

> All of us who are working in the field of human relationship ... are engaged in the most crucial enterprise in today's world. *Carl R. Rogers*

> It would not be too much to say that on the success or failure of our guidance program hangs, in all probability, the success or failure of our system of public education. *James B. Conant*

> ... it is not upon the physical sciences that the future of this planet will depend. It is upon us who are trying to understand and deal with the interactions between human beings – who are trying to create helping relationships. *Carl R. Rogers*

On the other hand, a group of educational administrators meeting on the campus of the University of Illinois " ...placed major priority on group work and group therapy skills. Recognizing that they could not hire enough counselors to work with students individually, they wanted the counselors to work with groups of teachers." (4, p. 2)

At least these administrators were making a laudable attempt to bring guidance into their school districts through the teaching staff. However, this is not the way to provide professionalism in guidance services, any more than it would benefit the teaching profession to have teachers train well-meaning parents to function as teaching assistants.

Let there be enlightenment with the public supporting sufficient financing to get adequate instructional programs and guidance services.

Not to Replace Counseling. Even when there is enough financing to provide enough counselors, there can be instances in group-oriented institutions such as schools and churches where counselors are using groups instead of the one-to-one relationship.

There always is a temptation to use the group when several clients need similar information. If 8 or 10 students – or 50 or 100 students – choose the career of accountant, the counselor may easily decide to meet with all of them at once to help them (if they are in high school) choose an appropriate college, or (if they are in college) to select subjects that advantageously supplement an accounting major. So, if the counselor proceeds on this basis, the typical group meeting usually will consist of a lecture by the counselor or a question-answer session in which the aggressive students dominate the questioning.

Whenever two or more individuals have a common problem, the counselor may be inclined to get them together, even though the nature of the problem does not lend itself to the advantages to be gained from the group situation. When an individual wishes to approach the resolution of his problem in privacy, it doesn't matter how many other people have the same problem, he should not be placed in a group with them.

A top social studies teacher with many years of experience in working effectively with groups of varying sizes – but with no education or experience in counseling – should not be assigned to conduct a group-guidance class or function as a counselor with groups. Instead a counselor should be hired.

Principals should stop using their best teachers, who also possess warm, sensitive personalities, to work with groups until the teachers can go back to school to take counseling courses and return as counselors.

Counseling cannot be replaced if individuals are to receive adequate professional help in making wise choices and adjustments.

☞ *When to Use Group Guidance*

Some of the many eminent advocates of group guidance may vehemently disagree with the following proposition on when to use group guidance. Nevertheless, the authors strongly contend that, basically, there are only two fundamental situations in which the group might be more effective than the one-to-one relationship; these will be discussed in this section under the headings of orientation and group interaction.

All group guidance should be offered only when the emphasis is on helping one individual or all individuals in the group; the emphasis should not be on the welfare of the group.

Orientation. Whenever two or more people are entering a new environment helping them get acquainted and become familiar with their new surroundings, in this case as a member of a new group, should be considered.

Examples of this situation would be pupils leaving one educational level to enter another, say from elementary school to junior high school; individuals leaving civilian life to enter the army; or people leaving one company for another firm.

Sometimes there is a degree of security when several people are together when they are initiated into their new environment. Tom the freshman may feel more comfortable meeting with the counselor in his new school if he is surrounded by other freshmen. It doesn't always work this way, for another individual might prefer being alone when he meets his counselor.

Another example of the value of using the group for orientation is to inform people of the existence of a counseling service, its nature and functions, how to use it, when to use it, why to use it, and who should use it. It is almost unbelievable how many students tell a counselor, "I didn't even know this place has a counseling service," or, "Why didn't someone tell me that I could see a counselor when I needed help?"

The public is usually unaware of the counselors in private practice and in public agencies who are available to help them. Unfortunately, a code o ethics prohibits the counselor in private practice from advertising his/her services, so it is most difficult for him/her to inform the public of his/her availability and the services he performs. However, it is perfectly ethical for school administrators to inform students, parents, and the community about the school's counseling service. Too many principals seem to take it for granted that the citizens in their school district know what each member of the professional staff does. Even in this age, the following query is heard too often: "Counselor? What is a counselor?" Educational administrators then wonder why they don't get more public support for their guidance programs!

Bennett (1, pp. 135–143) discusses the following orientation services in schools as being applicable to the group approach: preadmission and postadmission activities and Freshman or Orientation Day or Week, each of which is designed to acquaint students with their school. The orientation course also is suggested as an aid to introducing students to the school and for helping them in a variety of ways. When a guidance course is offered by a school, it may be an administrative device for providing time to give students the opportunity for studying those things that they think are most important to them. (3, p. 11) This can be fine, provided the course is integrated with the counseling service.

Group Interaction. Whenever the counselor assembles two or more clients for help in the group situation, probably the chief benefit which may accrue from this relationship is the interaction of the clients with each other.

Interaction just for the sake of interaction is, of course, nonsense, but when it occurs as a means of achieving certain purposes, it may be worthwhile. Some of these goals are mentioned below.

In the group " ...members learn to help others while they are obtaining assistance from others." (5, p. 24) This can be most valuable for persons who need to relate more effectively with others – those who tend to be too shy, who are fearful of social contacts, who lack confidence in socializing, and who are seeking the acceptance of others.

Some people become uncomfortable when they leave a familiar group to join a group of strangers. "The individual needs to learn to function effectively in various group situations." (6, p. 24) It is, of course, important to assist such people in acquiring social poise, grace, and related abilities.

Today, when there are many complications involved in the evolution of the rights of minority groups in this country, it can be vital. " ...to direct efforts toward putting democratic ideas into social practice – toward helping members of different groups (socioeconomic, ethnic, religious, etc.) to cultivate mutual appreciation and to work out ways of cooperation." (6, p. 6) As in all group guidance, it is essential to keep firmly in mind that it is the welfare of each member of the group that justifies the existence of the group. If and when the group supersedes any individual or all individuals in the group, it should be abandoned.

Presenting one's problems to a group of peers and finding that the others have the same or similar problems; asking the members of the group to join in a mutual exploration of the nature of a difficulty and how to attack it; and examining together the possible alternative solutions are all examples of possibilities for group work. However, care must be taken to avoid creating peer dependency.

A discussion of an issue in which all participate certainly can contribute to the social and intellectual development of each member. One of the key criticisms of this approach (which has been used most effectively by many experts in the small-group method – see *Chapter 9, Group Guidance)* is that it sometimes becomes a pooling of ignorance. From the intellectual viewpoint this is lamentable; however, if there are residual social values for each individual (assuming the subject matter has not been distorted, perverted, or falsified to any harmful extent), the group has served its purpose well.

When accurate scientific data are needed by the members of the group, the interaction process should be replaced by another method that permits this purpose to be achieved.

☞ *Suggested Additional Readings*

Burton, Arthur. *Encounter.* San Francisco: Jossey-Bass, Inc., 1969.
Cartwright, Dorwin, and Alvin Sander, editors. *Group Dynamics: Research and Theory.* Evanston, Illinois: Row, Peterson & Company, 1953.

Cohn, Benjamin, Charles F. Combs, Edward J. Gibian, and A. Mead Sniffon. "Group Counseling an Orientation." *Personnel and Guidance Journal,* December 1963, pp. 355–356.

Froehlich, Clifford R. "Group Guidance Approaches in Educational Institutions." ??? 7-155.

??? Bacon, 1962.

???

Little, Steven, Bray, Melissa & Kehle, Thomas, *Behavioral Intervention in Schools,* A.P.A., 2009.

Chapter 3

COUNSELING AND PSYCHOTHERAPY

I n the preceding chapters, there has been reference to several terms such as "counseling and group counseling," which are included in the literature of guidance, often to the confusion of students and practitioners alike. Certainly, belonging in this family of confusing labels is the term "psychotherapy."

Some authorities treat "counseling" and "psychotherapy" as if they were synonymous. Others use these words in a context that indicates that the writers regard the labels as being different, but the nature of the difference may be allowed to persist as being uncertain, obscure or unexplained.

☞ *The Nomenclature of Therapy*

The use of the word "therapy" had its origin in the field of medicine. To the physician it means treatment, healing, remedy for disease, curative action or a prescription for improving a patient's health.

"Psychotherapy" also emerged from the medical profession as being descriptive of treatments for mental illnesses. But even though psychotherapy had its roots in the medical profession, this does not preclude its adoption for usage by other professions. However, when one makes such an adoption, he should assume the ethical responsibility of carefully defining the word as he uses it in his profession.

A related word, which also has its basis in medicine and has been included in the professional vocabulary of the education profession, is "diagnosis." The physician uses the word diagnosis to mean the recognition of disease from its symptoms. (A "symptom" is any perceptible change in the body or its functions, indicating disease, a condition in which health is impaired–sickness, illness or an ailment.)

In spite of the medical connotation, educators have long utilized the term diagnosis to mean "what is wrong," "a decision reached," or "scientific determination." So long as the educator confines his usage to situations such as the following, he/she is on solid ground.

Educator #1: What's your diagnosis concerning Max?

Educator #2: There is nothing wrong with his intellectual capacity. His learning difficulties stem from cultural deprivations and a language handicap resulting from his having parents who do not speak English. However when an educator makes the following kind of diagnoses, he is going beyond the ethics of his profession.

Educator #1: What's your diagnosis concerning Al?

Educator #2: He is a manic-depressive.

It should be obvious that the medical profession cannot restrain other professions from using a word that originated in medicine, as long as the word is not used to identify an act that is restricted legally and/ or ethically to the practice of medicine. When counselors use the term psychotherapy, they should know precisely what they are saying; when they practice psychotherapy, they should know exactly what they are doing and, of course, whether they are qualified. It should be a truism to add that their interpretation of psychotherapy – whatever meaning they adopt – should not be the medical one.

The concept of psychotherapy is examined in this chapter, with the authors reserving the right to propose their explanation of the term within the framework of guidance services. First, interpretations from different authorities should be offered, and it is incumbent upon the reader to exercise his freedom of choice in selecting the definition he regards as being the best for the term. Furthermore, there is an obligation to adhere to the meaning chosen, both philosophically and in practice.

☞ *Interpretations of Psychotherapy*

Release of Tensions. Recently, while swimming in a heated pool, a physician remarked, "This is good psychotherapy." What he meant presumably was that the swimming enabled one to release tensions and that the warm water was relaxing.

This definition seems to be stretching the word psychotherapy into a scope so broad that its all-inclusiveness would make it virtually useless. If swimming can be called psychotherapy, so can any sport, game, or recreational activity which is enjoyable and diverts the participant's attention away from his problems – just as sleep, eating, and drinking can. Even work can be psychotherapy if it enables an individual to gain release from frustrations accumulated in recreational and/or nonwork situations. In fact, occupational therapy has made just such a contribution, but note that it is referred to as "occupational" therapy, not psychotherapy.

This expansion of the word psychotherapy that would encompass various cure-alls, which emerge from multiple sources, simply places too large a scope on the word. It reminds us of a statement made by a psychiatrist: "Everyone is neurotic." If the word "neurosis" can be inflated to encompass all people, then it becomes the norm, and the concept "normal individual," as it is used within a mental health frame of reference, must either be abandoned or regarded as synonymous with "neurotic individual."

It is a reasonable assumption that the psychiatrist was exaggerating in order to emphasize a point: that each person has latent neurotic tendencies which theoretically could be actualized under certain conditions. This is similar to Levinsen (7) indicating that since each person has weaknesses, the incidence of mental illness is one out of one rather than the often-stated one out of twenty.

But to say that all people have neurotic tendencies is not as useful as it might appear at first glance. The same can be said about many other diseases – including physical ailments. Other words may be inserted in place of "neurotic," for example, "tubercular," "infectious," or "degenerative." Accordingly, what is to be gained by saying each person has latent neurotic tendencies, tubercular tendencies or infectious tendencies? It is simply another way of stating that each of us, under certain conditions, could become sick – mentally or physically. Since this is an obvious truism, it does not appear to serve any useful purpose.

Thus, to label psychotherapy as any activity which releases tension or relaxes is as much an abuse of the word as it would be to expand the helping element of counseling to mean "any word or act which assists the counselee." There should be more precision in the meaning of these words than the ambiguity in the foregoing definitions.

Synonymous. Some authorities contend that counseling and psychotherapy are synonymous in meaning. After digesting the preceding section, some of the comments below will, at the least, be confusing and, at the most, aggravating.

> ... whether he is a 'psychotherapist' or not, the counselor may often find himself required to deal with situations that should be met with psychotherapeutic skills. (1)

It should be obvious that every professional may find himself in a situation in which his client, student, or patient might benefit from the application of psychotherapeutic skills, but this should not be the only requirement for proceeding to practice psychotherapy. The counselor who is not a psychotherapist should refer to a psychotherapist those clients who need psychotherapy.

It has also been said that " ...the most intensive and successful counseling is indistinguishable from intensive and successful counseling psychotherapy." (2, p. 7)

The question that arises from this statement is, why are counseling and psychotherapy alike when each is intensive and successful, but as implied, dissimilar otherwise? Also, what is counseling, and what is psychotherapy?

Lifton (3) interprets psychotherapy as being that which is advocated by a group of theorists who do not differentiate between psychotherapy and counseling.

> Advocates of this point of view perceive as therapeutic any relationship which enables the individual more clearly to perceive his needs and to modify his behavior. Treatment is oriented toward enabling the client to clarify his self-concept and toward enabling him to practice new methods of adjustment in a protected setting. Any change in the client's attitude toward

> himself is considered to change the client's total personality. Rogers, Rank, Taft, and the Gestaltists fall within this frame of reference. (8, pp. 10–11)

Note that the word "treatment" is used in the foregoing. Also, observe the reference to "change" in relation to the explanation of psychotherapy, even though the proposition that counseling and psychotherapy are the same is being presented.

Albert has observed that "the more the 'experts' seek to define counseling and psychotherapy differentially, the more the two areas seem to blend and overlap." (1) It is precisely to counteract this semantical confusion that this chapter is included in the text, for the authors intend to propose a definitive explanation of psychotherapy for the consideration of students and practitioners.

The foregoing is not intended as a threat to counselors, social workers, and other professionals who may wish to incorporate "therapy," "diagnosis," "patient," and other medical terms into the jargon of their own profession. It should be evident that the adopting by any occupation of nomenclature commonly associated with another specific occupation may be unethical, unwise, unfair, or a combination of these – unless the occupation doing the adopting makes certain that the terms are adapted (defined and utilized within the scope of the occupation's functions) as well as adopted.

A Curative Process. After perusing the previous section, it may be startling to reflect upon the viewpoint expressed in this section, which by its heading obviously pertains to treatment.

"…psychotherapy deals with the pathological and seeks to cure." (17) While the proponents of this interpretation emphasize the involvement of medical treatment, they may also include the "change concept" as indicated below:

> … psychotherapy denotes a process usually implemented by interview techniques, which seeks to alter the client's receptor or response system to such a way that healthy behavior will occur in situations where

unhealthy behavior has been typical. It is, in short, a kind of relearning, or re-education. It should also be emphasized that the old behavior is seen as pathological, and the new behavior is seen as healthy. (17)

Even though the "change concept" is expressed in the idea of movement from "old behavior" to "new behavior," the emphasis remains on medical treatment as exemplified in the words "unhealthy behavior," "pathological," and "healthy."

Reaves and Reaves (12) differentiate between counseling and psychotherapy in terms of choices and illness and involve the words "client" and "patient" in their differentiation.

> Counseling differs from psychotherapy. The primary objective in counseling is that of stimulating the individual to evaluate, make, accept, and act upon his choices. In contrast, the objective of psychotherapy is the intensive treatment of emotional illness. The term "client" suggests someone in an adverse situation with or without exaggerated neurotic defenses. The "patient" implies someone who is pathologically sick and requires intensive evaluation and care.*

There seems to be a definite need for the counselor to stand on his own "professional" feet, looking the other professions squarely in the eyes, when he proclaims, "As a counselor I have services to perform that are professionally unique. It is enough that I strive to master my own art and science, without attempting any unwarranted infringement upon any of the functions of the other professions."

> Counseling, if it is to become a real profession, must have the dedicated, informed, and constant allegiance of a core of counselor educators and real counselors in

---

* It is interesting to note that at the time this quotation was written, one of the authors was a counselor and the other was a physician.

the field who aren't the least bit ashamed to be known as counselors. We must quit bowing so deferentially to the psychotherapy-oriented, who for some reason or another are willing to claim much of the glory, but who at the same time seem to be unwilling to do very much to help the counselor prepare for the types of tasks which he realistically faces on the firing line, in the school, in the college, or in the agency. (4)

A more ambiguous reference to psychotherapy as a curative process is presented in Patterson's (11) integration of such nomenclature as "psychological methods," "systematic knowledge of the human personality," and "the improvement of mental health." The focal point, however, is the "improvement of mental health."

Unless one wishes to concede that everyone is involved in contributing to the improvement of the mental health of all one's associates, coupled with the assumption that professional assistance (as rendered by the physician and psychiatrist) should not be separated from the layman's impact on others, there still remains the necessity of discriminating to terms of what the nonmedical professional should do, if anything, in dealing with the health of those he is attempting to help.

There is little question that a parent, friend, or any professional can make significant contributions to the mental health of others through offering support, encouragement, hope, comfort or reassurance, all involving the restoration of confidence. Any football coach worthy of the name uses "psychological methods" to get his team up for a game. An astute baseball manager recognizes that he cannot handle all of his players the same way if he is to get the most out of them. One ballplayer needs continuous pats on the back, while another requires pressure. One person responds best to suggestion while another must be commanded. Use of psychological methods to get employees to produce is a basic requisite of the most elementary form of management. When a supervisor chooses the wrong method for a particular employee, the by-product of this action may be a lessening of mental health. When the department manager selects the appropriate method for a certain employee, the byproduct can be a resulting improvement in mental health.

By no stretch of the imagination can it be conceived that the football coach, the baseball manager, the supervisor, or the department manager perform psychotherapy. If their administrative methods are to be designated "psychotherapy" as having a meaning applicable to the jargon of football, baseball, supervision or management along with other expressions such as: "red-dog," "squeeze," "control," and "delegate."

Unless psychotherapy is carefully defined by all who use it, the current confusion will continue and probably spread. Unfortunately, in its present usage by diverse occupational groups, the word has become unscientific and almost meaningless; it parallels the futile semantical theory that "everyone is neurotic."

Another statement on the meaning of psychotherapy has some interesting implications: "The term psychotherapy refers only to those processes directed by a skilled, professional individual toward improvement of a client who needs help to remedy a defined pathological condition." (8, p. 10)

Note the terms in the foregoing: "a skilled professional individual," "client," and "pathological condition." Questions which immediately arise are What professionals? Skilled in what? Why "client" instead of "patient" if the goal is to help the individual to remedy a defined pathological condition? Does "defined pathological condition" mean that a diagnosis of catatonic schizophrenia, compulsive-obsessive personality, sociopathic individual, has been made? If so, what professional, other than a physician or psychiatrist, can justify – legally and/or ethically – making such a diagnosis? If the diagnosis is not made in terminology that identifies the pathological condition, how can it be remedied, cured, corrected, alleviated, or changed?

Personality Reorganization. Perhaps the most ambiguous of all is the attempt to construct a nonmedical definition of psychotherapy as being the process of personality reorganization.

Those authorities who refer to psychotherapy as being personality reorganization seldom explain what they have in mind when they use this label. Though personality reorganization consists of two words it seems to be used as if it were a one-word synonym for psychotherapy. As in many instances where a word is defined by using a synonym (e.g., courtesy is kindness and courage is bravery), the synonym may be as foreign as the word it supposedly defines. To say, "You are courteous" and respond to the question, "What do you mean by 'courteous'?" by saying, "I mean you are kind" invites another question, "What do you mean by 'kind'?"

> The objective of vocational counseling is problem solution while that of psychotherapy is personality reorganization. (13)

This differentiation of vocational counseling and psychotherapy reveals an immediate need to examine the concept of "personality reorganization." This is complicated by the fact that there are many theories regarding personality and as many different definitions of the word. Let us assume that personality means every trait, aptitude, interest, strength, or weakness which combine into unique individuality which can be identified as Sally Wilson, Tom Archer, Max Brentano, or Sue Cordigan. The names are simply parental labels which identify the individual as an individual, just as "elm" identifies a certain kind of tree.

If the personality is the self, the totality of all the elements and ingredients which combine to create an individual, the reorganization of the personality would involve a rearrangement of interdependent parts of the self, such as interests, needs, and values, each of which has a special function with respect to the whole.

Johnson, Stefflre, and Edelfelt (6) have an interpretation of the difference between counseling and therapy which involves the concept of personality reorganization:

> ... counseling deals largely with conscious processes and is aimed at helping an individual make more realistic appraisal of his present situation and plan his future accordingly. Therapy might be defined as a more total reconstruction of the personality based

on an understanding of unconscious processes and motivation. (6, p. 141)

Again there is an ambiguity connected with the concept of personality reorganization. There is the implication that counseling and therapy differ only in the scope of personality reconstruction, with an involvement of the conscious and unconscious processes as discriminating between counseling and therapy. Since psychoanalysis has been defined as being the science of the unconscious, as a particular theoretical school of thought in psychology and as an art in the practice of psychoanalysis, this adds further semantical, legal, and ethical factors for serious reflection by those professionals who practice or plan to practice psychotherapy.

Personality Modification. If psychotherapy means helping an individual to change his personality or to alter a particular trait of his/her personality, there are some difficulties in semantics to overcome in relation to one interpretation of learning.

"Learning is shown by a change in behavior as a result of experience." (3, p. 71) Using this definition of learning and the foregoing interpretation of psychotherapy would mean that whenever a teacher assisted a student in changing his behavior from rudeness to courtesy, the teacher would be simultaneously engaging in teaching and psychotherapy. To carry this further, when the teacher helped a student type accurately and rapidly instead of inaccurately and slowly, learning would have occurred. There would be no psychotherapy because the personality or a personality trait was not altered, unless one wished to argue that the characteristics of inaccuracy and slowness, in the process of typing, had been changed to accuracy and speed, representing an alteration of characteristics. If this argument succeeded, one would then be acknowledging again that the teacher was simultaneously engaged in teaching and psychotherapy.

To suggest that teaching and psychotherapy are synonymous makes one of the terms probably obsolete at the most and each word confusing at the least.

Will the issue resolve itself if another definition of learning is accepted? "Learning is the acquiring of understanding or skills.

Understanding is comprehending the meaning of something. Skill is doing something well." (5, p. 25)

Within the framework of the understanding-and-skills concept of learning, the question could be raised as to whether or not it is possible to have the teacher teach, assisting the student in the acquiring of understanding or skills, while someone else does psychotherapy by helping the individual modify his personality. Within the concept, is it possible for the teacher to help a student acquire the skill of courtesy which, if and when acquired, replaces the skill of rudeness? Is there a difference between the teacher working with the rude youngster, attempting to assist in the acquirement of the skill of courtesy, while the psychotherapist works with the rude youngster to change the responses from rude to courteous?

An analysis of the above paragraph could yield the interpretation that teaching and psychotherapy are synonymous whenever any personality alteration is being attempted, and only differ when the teacher moves away from personality change to other fields.

Let's pursue the thinking of some of the authorities who prefer the "personality modification" concept of psychotherapy.

> I have limited the meaning of counseling to one kind of process – that of helping a person attain a clear sense of personal identity. Such a concept of what counseling is ... distinguishes it from psychotherapy. Therapy is aimed essentially at change in developmental structures rather than fulfillment. Personal identity covers what and whom one belongs to as well as what one is. (16)

> The aim of therapy is generally considered to be personality change of some sort. Let us use counseling to refer to a helping process the aim of which is not to change the person but to enable him to utilize the resources he now has for coping with life. The outcome we would then expect from counseling is that the client do something, take some constructive action on his own behalf. (15, p. 12)

> Therapy generally has as its goal personality change; counseling attempts to bring about the best possible utilization of what the person already has. (14)

If one may accept for the moment the last of the foregoing statements, and transpose it to the preceding teaching-psychotherapy semantical difficulty, we may conclude that teachers and counselors should refrain from any activity designed to produce personality change, that they may help individuals in realizing self-potential, but refrain from attempting any alterations of what exists. In this role, the teacher would help the rude student to understand what he is and what his behavior means to others, including the various social ramifications, but the process would be instructional and the goal self-understanding, not personality modification. If the understanding resulted in behavior change – from rude to courteous – it would be a by-product, not a goal achievement.

> Counseling involves decision making and personal problems not embedded in the personality structure. Counseling as contrasted with psychotherapy is surface-level, involving a present problem and a future plan of action. It involves the normal person with a normal problem. Psychotherapy, on the other hand, is a treatment involving the inner life through depth psychology. It deals with attitudes which it endeavors to change. In the analytical context, it explores the unconscious in an attempt to uncover the hidden impulses that have been brought about by repressed hostilities of childhood. (10, p. 213)

In the foregoing interpretation, the concept of personality modification is contained in the expression "attitudes which it endeavors to change." In addition, the treatment factor appears again, together with another ingredient that also has its basis in medicine, "the exploration of the unconscious," which in practice is psychoanalysis.

> Psychotherapy differs from counseling on two major counts: the degree of pathology and the focus of the therapist toward personality change instead of solely attitudinal change. Problems dealing with attitudes or situational factors are considered amenable to counseling. (8, p. 10)

"Pathology" appears again in the quotation above, along with the implication that counselors may deal with the pathological individual up to the point at which the pathology becomes too severe; then the individual should see a psychotherapist. In addition, it is pointed out that the therapist focuses on personality change while the counselor confines himself to problems dealing with attitudes or situational factors.

☞ The Meaning of Psychotherapy

After wading through these several interpretations of psychotherapy and counseling, the reader may at this point be (1) exhausted, (2) confused, (3) angry, or (4) overwhelmed. However, he/she might have selected for himself one of the theories proposed by the authorities cited in this chapter or from those listed in Suggested Readings at the end of the chapter. For the benefit of those students and/or practitioners who still seek an explanation more satisfying than any of those yet discovered, we will propose yet another definition of psychotherapy.

Returning to the concept of counseling as the one-to-one relationship between counselor and client, in which the counselor tries to help the client in making wise choices and adjustments, this process consists of helping the client improve his/her self-understanding and his/her understanding of his/her present and probably future environment so that he/she can reach the point where he/she can make his/her own choices and "be satisfied or happy." (5, p. 5)

To accept this interpretation of the meaning of counseling is to postulate that the counselor is engaged in an educative process which involves several disciplines, for the counselor has to be an educator who knows education, psychology, sociology, economics, and the other disciplines needed to contribute to his competency in helping his clients to greater self-understanding as well as present, and probably future, environmental understanding.

Let it be said most emphatically: the counselor is an educator, a highly specialized professional whose knowledge and skills qualify him/her to deal in greater depth and more extensively in the adjustment problems of individuals than most educators are qualified to do. Accordingly, if one accepts the meaning of "learning" to be " …acquiring understanding or skills," (5, p. 25), one may proceed on the basis that counseling assists the individual in making wise choices and adjustments by helping the person acquire the understanding and skills needed to make these choices and adjustments.

It is not the function of the counselor to change the individual, but to help him/her learn in the most personalized and unique learning setting there is: the one-to-one relationship of expert and learner, with the subject matter being the self and the environment.

Now for the psychotherapist – keeping firmly in mind that the meaning proposed herein is strictly nonmedical and for use by nonmedical professionals, just as the nonmedical interpretation of "diagnosis" is utilized and practiced by educators. (The medical professionals may, of course, define psychotherapy as they choose.)

Psychotherapy is a one-to-one relationship between psychotherapist and his client in which psychological techniques are used to effect a change in one or more personality traits of the client.

A personality trait is a characteristic pattern of actions or reactions by an individual. For example, the person who does the kindest thing in the kindest way, uses polite phrases such as thank you, please, may I, or pardon me, and avoids hurting others, will be labeled courteous; from possession of these responses emerges the concept of courtesy. If an individual acts or reacts – most of the time – according to this behavior pattern, he/she may be said to possess the personality trait of courtesy.

If an individual has the trait of rudeness, it is the counselor's function, in the process of developing self-understanding, to help the person to comprehend that he is rude. If the individual being assisted wishes to change this trait of rudeness to courtesy, it becomes the function of the psychotherapist to work with the client to help him/her make this change.

☞ *References*

1. Albert, Gerald. "If Counseling is Psychotherapy – What Then?" *Personnel and Guidance Journal,* October 1966, pp. 124–129.

2. Blum, Milton L. *Counseling and Psychology.* New York: Prentice-Hall, 1951.

3. Cronbach, Lee J. *Educational Psychology.* New York: Harcourt, Brace & World, 1963.

4. Dunsmoor, C. C. "Counselor – Or What?" *Personnel and Guidance Journal,* October 1964, 135–138.

5. Grant, Bruce, George D. Demos, and Willard Edwards. *Guidance for Youth.* Springfield, Illinois: Charles C. Thomas, 1965.

6. Johnson, Walter F., Bufford Stefflre, and Roy A. Edelfelt. *Pupil Personnel and Guidance Services.* New York: McGraw Hill Book Company, 1961.

7. Levinson, Harry. *Emotional Health in the World of Work.* New York: Harper and Row, 1966.

8. Lifton, Walter. *Working with Groups.* New York: John Wiley and Sons, 1961.

9. Lynch, Thomas A., and Clarence S. Brown. "Opinion." *Marriage Counseling Quarterly,* November 1966, pp. 1–5.

10. Moser, Leslie E., and Ruth Small Moser. *Counseling and Guidance: An Exploration.* Englewood Cliffs, New Jersey: Prentice-Hall, 1963.

11. Patterson, C. H. *Counseling and Psychotherapy: Theory and Practice.* New York: Harper and Brothers, 1959.

12. Reaves, Gayle C., and Leonard E. Reaves, III. "The Counselor and Prevention Psychiatry." *Personnel and Guidance Journal,* March 1965, pp. 661–664.

13. Thompson, Albert S. "Personality Dynamics and Vocational Counseling." *Personnel and Guidance Journal,* 38, 1960, pp. 350–357.

14. Tyler, Leona. "Minimum Change Therapy." *Personnel and Guidance Journal,* 38, 1960, pp. 475–479.

15. Tyler, Leona E. *The Work of the Counselor.* New York: Appleton-Century Crofts, 1961.

16. Tyler, Leona E. "Theoretical Principles Underlying the Counseling Process." Journal of Counseling Psychology, 5, 1958, pp. 3–10.

17. Vance, Forrest L., and Theodore C. Volsky, Jr. "Counseling Psychotherapy: Split Personality or Siamese Twins." *American Psychologist,* August 1962.

☞ *Suggested Additional Readings*

Aubrey, Roger F. "Historical Development of Guidance and Counseling and Implications for the Future." *Personnel and Guidance Journal* 55, no. 6 (1977), pp. 288–295.

Fenske, Robert H. "Historical Foundations." In *Student Services,* edited by Ursula Delworth and Gary R. Hanson, pp. 3–24. San Francisco: Jossey-Bass, 1980.

Gallagher, Phillip J., and George D. Demos. *The Counseling Center in Higher Education.* Springfield, Illinois: Charles C. Thomas, 1970.

Garcia, Eugene, & Nunez, Jose, Bilingualism and Cognition, APA, 2011.

Giroux, Roy F., Donald A. Biggs, Alan M. Hoffman, and John J. Pietrofesa, eds. *College Student Development Revisited: Programs, Issues, and Practices.* Rev. ed. Falls Church, Virginia: American Personnel and Guidance Association, 1979.

Glasser, William. *Reality Therapy: A New Approach to Psychiatry.* New York: Harper and Row, 1965.

Gysbers, Norman C. "Career Guidance at the Crossroads." In *New Imperatives for Guidance,* edited by Garry R. Walz and Libby Benjamin, pp. 1–29. Ann Arbor, Michigan: ERIC Counseling and Personnel Services, 1978.

Herr, Edwin L. *Guidance and Counseling in the Schools.* Falls Church, Virginia: American Personnel and Guidance Association, 1979, pp. 1–24.

Hollis, Joseph W. "Guidance and Counseling in Schools: An Historical Approach." In *The Status of Guidance and Counseling in the Nation's Schools,* American Personnel and Guidance Association, pp. 1–16.

Washington, D. C.: American Personnel and Guidance Association, not dated.

Miller, Carrol H. *Foundations of Guidance.* New York: Harper and Bros., 1961.

Patterson, C. H. *Theories of Counseling and Psychotherapy.* New York: Harper and Row, 1966.

Rappaport, Julian. *Community Psychology.* New York: Holt, Rhinehart and Winston, 1977, pp. 12–16.

Stephens, W. Richard. *Special Social Reform and the Origins of Vocational Guidance.* Washington, D. C.: National Vocational Guidance Association, 1970.

Wrenn, C. Gilbert. "Personal Perspectives – Past and Present." In *New Imperatives for Guidance,* edited by Garry R. Walz and Libby Benjamin, pp. 456–491. Ann Arbor, Michigan: ERIC Counseling and Personnel Services, 1978.

Zytowski, Donald G. "Four Hundred Years Before Parsons." *Personnel and Guidance Journal* 50, no. 6 (1972), pp. 443–450.

Chapter 4

ETHICS OF COUNSELING

A code of ethics must emerge from any activity or vocational pursuit to deserve the designation "profession." So, if counseling asserts its right to be identified as a profession, it must naturally construct a code of ethics for counselors. Fortunately, this has been done competently by the American Personnel and Guidance Association through its introduction in 1961 of *Ethical Standards*. (4) So valuable is this contribution that it is included in its entirety in this chapter.

> ... the word profession implies ... a code of ethics governing the conduct of its members. We cannot expect those who employ us or the communities in which we work to decide for us what ethical counseling practice is. The central core of the counselor's code is concerned with the safeguarding of the counseling relationships. (6, p. 250)

Perhaps as a welcome change from the diversity of interpretations of "psychotherapy," with which the preceding chapter was concerned, the reader may relish savoring the term "ethics." While there may be slight deviations in terminology from the following definition, most authorities would agree that, in essence, ethics is the science of right and wrong conduct. In addition, morality, or ethical behavior, may be referred to as the practice of right conduct, and immorality, unethical behavior, as the practice of wrong conduct.

Schmidt (3) discusses the concept of ethics by offering a dictionary meaning of ethical as "in accordance with formal or professional rules of right and wrong." He further says that ethical also relates to "standards of right and wrong," and defines ethics as "the standards of right and wrong, that part of science and philosophy dealing with moral conduct, duty, and judgment." He concludes by designating (for purposes of his article) "'ethical' as relating to what the counselor, morally, philosophically, and otherwise, expects from himself as a counselor or limits himself to in his work with clients."

It may be said that the concept of an "ethical counselor" would explicitly denote an individual who – most of the time and within the limitation prescribed by human error – would act "as he should," both professionally and personally.

When the term "ethical" is used, it usually refers to proper professional conduct. For example, to say that "the counselor is ethical" is the same as saying "his conduct is beyond reproach." To say, "John is a moral person," says he is practicing "right conduct." To use the phrase "wrong conduct," or refer to its practice, is equivalent to saying, "Tom is unethical," or "Tom is immoral."

☞ *What is Right Conduct for the Counselor?*

While the meaning of ethics may not be a matter of even minor concern, the determination of what is right and what is wrong conduct, either professionally or personally, is not resolved so easily. "One of the major problems in counseling involves ethical consideration." (2) Some of the issues are enumerated below:

1. In case of conflicting interest, which takes precedence, the individual or society?

2. Should the counselor suppress information derived from the counseling relationship which would be helpful to his principal or his boss?

3. Who should have access to the client's file?

4. What information is confidential and what is not?

5. How does the counselor discriminate between "discussing a client with a professional colleague in order to clarify his own thinking" from "gossiping"?

6. When, how, and why should referrals be made?

7. To what extent should the interview be confidential?

Fortunately, the counselor may be guided in his/her establishment of a code of professional ethics by the work already done by the counseling authorities who evolved the *Ethical Standards*. Utilization of this code is recommended, and perhaps some consideration can be given to adding to or modifying its criteria using other sources of standards and individual preferences for ethical guidelines. But care should be taken not to deviate significantly from the concepts presented in the *Ethical Standards*.

When considering criteria applicable to personal conduct (as distinguished from professional conduct) it is a matter of a person's own preferences as prescribed by his own value system, providing there is no serious conflict between the professional and personal codes.

It should be a truism that a counselor's personal value system is compatible with his/her professional code of ethics, but because of the fallibility of humans, it is better to think in terms of a reasonable degree of friction, which appears to be irreconcilable, between the professional and personal codes. If the friction amounts to more than a reasonable degree, the individual has evidence of a serious weakness in his/her choice of counseling as a career. This illustrates how important it is for a potential counselor to determine his/her value system and relate it to the occupation of counselor – it is a vital ingredient in the individual's consideration of the wisdom of choosing a counseling career.

To aid the counselor in evolving satisfactory professional guidelines, the contents of the APGA's *Ethical Standards* are presented verbatim. The reader is urged to read and reread them, making marginal notes on points of agreement and disagreement, followed by profound reflection on the rationale concerning each point accepted or rejected.

Following these *Ethical Standards,* the authors propose some "ethical principles" for counselors. It is suggested that the reader study these principles to critically compare them with the *Ethical Standards,* determining points of agreement and disagreement with a rationale for each, and then attempt to evolve a code of ethics which has its basis in authority yet is acceptable to and defensible by the reader in reference to his own value system. (See 1974 Attachment)

APGA
ETHICAL STANDARDS
Adopted by the Board of Directors
1974

Preamble

The American Personnel and Guidance Association is an educational, scientific, and professional organization whose members are dedicated to the enhancement of the worth, dignity, potential, and uniqueness of each individual and thus to the service of society.

The Association recognizes that the role definitions and work settings of its members include a wide variety of academic disciplines, levels of academic preparation, and agency services. This diversity reflects the breadth of the Association's interest and influence. It also poses challenging complexities in efforts to set standards for the performance of members, desired requisite preparation or practice, and supporting social, legal, and ethical controls.

Reprinted by permission from the American Personnel and Guidance Association, Washington D.C., 1974, pp. 78–112.

The specification of ethical standards enables the Association to clarify to present and future members and to those served by members the nature of the ethical responsibilities held in common by its members.

The existence of such standards serves to stimulate greater concern by members for their own professional functioning and for the conduct of fellow professionals such as counselors, guidance and student personnel workers, and others in the helping professions. As the ethical code of the Association, this document establishes principles which define the ethical behavior of Association members.

☞ *Section A: General*

1. The member influences the development of the profession by continuous efforts to improve professional practices, teaching, services, and research. Professional growth is continuous throughout the member's career and is exemplified by the development of a philosophy that explains why and how a member functions in the helping relationship. Members are expected to gather data on their effectiveness and to be guided by the findings.

2. The member has a responsibility both to the individual who is served and to the institution within which the service is performed. The acceptance of employment in an institution implies that the member is in substantial agreement with the general policies and principles of the institution. Therefore the professional activities of the member are also in accord with the objectives of the institution. If, despite concerted efforts, the member cannot reach agreement with the employer as to acceptable standards of conduct that allow for changes in institutional policy conducive to the positive growth and development of counselees, then terminating the affiliation should be seriously considered.

3. Ethical behavior among professional associates, members and nonmembers, is expected at all times. When information is possessed which raises serious doubt as to the ethical behavior of professional colleagues, whether Association members or not, the member is obligated to take action to attempt to rectify such a condition. Such action shall utilize the institution's channels first and then utilize procedures established by the state, division, or Association.

The member can take action in a variety of ways: conferring with the individual in question, gathering further information as to the allegation, conferring with local or national ethics committees, and so forth.

4. The member must not seek self-enhancement through expressing evaluations or comparisons that are damaging to others.

5. The member neither claims nor implies professional qualifications exceeding those possessed and is responsible for correcting any misrepresentations of these qualifications by others.

6. In establishing fees for professional services, members should take into consideration the fees charged by other professions delivering comparable services, as well as the ability of the counselee to pay. Members are willing to provide some services for which they receive little or no financial remuneration, or remuneration in food, lodging, and materials. When fees include charges for items other than professional services, that portion of the total which is for the professional services should be clearly indicated.

7. When members provide information to the public or to subordinates, peers, or supervisors, they have a clear responsibility to ensure that the content is accurate, unbiased, and consists of objective, factual data.

8. The member shall make a careful distinction between the offering of counseling services as opposed to public information services. Counseling may be offered only in the context of a reciprocal or face-to-face relationship. Information services may be offered through the media.

9. With regard to professional employment, members are expected to accept only positions that they are prepared to assume and then to comply with established practices of the particular type of employment setting in which they are employed in order to ensure the continuity of services.

☞ Section B: Counselor-Counselee Relationship

This section refers to practices involving individual and/or group counseling relationships, and it is not intended to be applicable to practices involving administrative relationships.

To the extent that the counselee's choice of action is not imminently self-or-other-destructive, the counselee must retain freedom of choice. When the counselee does not have full autonomy for reasons of age, mental incompetency, criminal incarceration, or similar legal restrictions, the member may have to work with others who exercise significant control and direction over the counselee. Under these circumstances the member must apprise counselees of restrictions that may limit their freedom of choice.

1.   The member's *primary* obligation is to respect the integrity and promote the welfare of the counselee(s), whether the counselee(s) is (are) assisted individually or in a group relationship. In a group setting, the member-leader is also responsible for protecting individuals from physical and/or psychological trauma resulting from interaction within the group.

2.   The counseling relationship and information resulting therefrom must be kept confidential, consistent with the obligations of the member as a professional person. In a group counseling setting the member is expected to set a norm of confidentiality regarding all group participants' disclosures.

3.   If an individual is already in a counseling/therapy relationship with another professional person, the member does not begin a counseling relationship without first contacting and receiving the approval of that other professional. If the member discovers that the counselee is in another counseling/therapy relationship after the counseling relationship begins, the member is obligated to gain the consent of the other professional or terminate the relationship, unless the counselee elects to terminate the other relationship.

4.   When the counselee's condition indicates that there is clear and imminent danger to the counselee or others, the member is expected to take direct personal action or to inform responsible authorities. Consultation with other professionals should be utilized where possible. Direct interventions, especially the assumption of responsibility for the counselee, should be taken only after careful deliberation. The counselee should be involved in the resumption of responsibility for his actions as quickly as possible.

5.   Records of the counseling relationship including interview notes, test data, correspondence, tape recordings, and other documents are to be considered professional information for use in counseling,

and they are not part of the public or official records of the institution or agency in which the counselor is employed. Revelation to others of counseling material should occur only upon the express consent of the counselee.

6.   Use of data derived from a counseling relationship for purposes of counselor training or research shall be confined to content that can be sufficiently disguised to ensure full protection of the identity of the counselee involved.

7.   Counselees shall be informed of the conditions under which they may receive counseling assistance at or before the time when the counseling relationship is entered. This is particularly so when conditions exist of which the counselee would be unaware. In individual and group situations, particularly those oriented to self-understanding or growth, the member-leader is obligated to make clear the purposes, goals, techniques, rules of procedure, and limitations that may affect the continuance of the relationship.

8.   The member has the responsibility to screen prospective group participants, especially when the emphasis is on self-understanding and growth through self-disclosure. The member should maintain an awareness of the group participants' compatibility throughout the life of the group.

9.   The member reserves the right to consult with any other professionally competent person about a counselee. In choosing a consultant, the member avoids placing the consultant in a conflict of interest situation that would preclude the consultant's being a proper party to the member's efforts to help the counselee.

10. If the member is unable to be of professional assistance to the counselee, the member avoids initiating the counseling relationship or the member terminates it. In either event, the member is obligated to refer the counselee to an appropriate specialist. (It is incumbent upon the member to be knowledgeable about referral resources so that a satisfactory referral can be initiated.) In the event the counselee declines the suggested referral, the member is not obligated to continue the relationship.

11. When the member learns from counseling relationships of conditions that are likely to harm others, the member should report

the condition to the responsible authority. This should be done in such a manner as to conceal the identity of the counselee.

12. When the member has other relationships, particularly of an administrative, supervisory, and/or evaluative nature, with an individual seeking counseling services, the member should not serve as the counselor but should refer the individual to another professional. Only in instances where such an alternative is unavailable and where the individual's condition definitely warrants counseling intervention should the member enter into and/or maintain a counseling relationship.

13. All experimental methods of treatments must be clearly indicated to prospective recipients, and safety precautions are to be adhered to by the member.

14. When the member is engaged in short-term group treatment/training programs, e.g., marathons and other encounter-type or growth groups, the member ensures that there is professional assistance available during and following the group experience.

15. Should the member be engaged in a work setting that calls for any variation from the above statements, the member is obligated to consult with other professionals whenever possible to consider justifiable alternatives. The variations that may be necessary should be clearly communicated to other professionals and prospective counselees.

☞ *Section C: Measurement and Evaluation*

The primary purpose of educational and psychological testing is to provide descriptive measures that are objective and interpretable in either comparative or absolute terms. The member must recognize the need to interpret the statements that follow as applying to the whole range of appraisal techniques including test and nontest data. Test results constitute only one of a variety of pertinent sources of information for personnel, guidance, and counseling decisions.

1. It is the member's responsibility to provide adequate orientation or information to the examinee(s) prior to and following the test administration so that the results of testing may be placed in proper

perspective with other relevant factors. In so doing, the member must recognize the effects of socioeconomic, ethnic, and cultural factors on test scores. It is the member's professional responsibility to use additional unvalidated information cautiously in modifying interpretation of the test results.

2.   In selecting tests for use in a given situation or with a particular counselee, the member must consider carefully the specific validity, reliability, and appropriateness of the test(s). "General" validity, reliability, and the like may be questioned legally as well as ethically when tests are used for vocational and educational selection, placement, or counseling.

3.   When making any statements to the public about tests and testing, the member is expected to give accurate information and to avoid false claims or misconceptions. Special efforts are often required to avoid unwarranted connotations of such terms as IQ and grade equivalent scores.

4.   Different tests demand different levels of competence for administration, scoring, and interpretation. Members have a responsibility to recognize the limits of their competence and to perform only those functions for which they are prepared.

5.   Tests should be administered under the same conditions that were established in their standardization. When tests are not administered under standard conditions or when unusual behavior or irregularities occur during the testing session, those conditions should be noted and the results designated as invalid or of questionable validity. Unsupervised or inadequately supervised test-taking, such as the use of tests through the mails, is considered unethical. On the other hand, the use of instruments that are so designed or standardized to be self-administered and self-scored, such as interest inventories, is to be encouraged.

6.   The meaningfulness of test results used in personnel, guidance, and counseling functions generally depends on the examinee's unfamiliarity with the specific items on the test. Any prior coaching or dissemination of the test materials can invalidate test results. Therefore, test security is one of the professional obligations of the member.

Conditions that produce most favorable test results should be made known to the examinee.

7. The purpose of testing and the explicit use of the results should be made known to the examinee prior to testing. The counselor has a responsibility to ensure that instrument limitations are not exceeded and that periodic review and/or retesting are made to prevent counseling stereotyping.

8. The examinee's welfare and explicit prior understanding should be the criteria for determining the recipients of the test results. The member is obligated to see that adequate interpretation accompanies any release of individual or group test data. The interpretation of test data should be related to the examinee's particular concerns.

9. The member is expected to be cautious when interpreting the results of research instruments possessing insufficient technical data. The specific purposes for the use of such instruments must be stated explicitly to examinees.

10. The member must proceed with extreme caution when attempting to evaluate and interpret the performance of minority group members or other persons who are not represented in the norm group of which the instrument was standardized.

11. The member is obligated to guard against the appropriation, reproduction, or modifications of published tests or parts thereof without the express permission and adequate recognition of the original author or publisher.

12. Regarding the preparation, publication, and distribution of tests, reference should be made to:

a. *Standards for Educational and Psychological Tests and Manuals,* revised edition, 1973, published by the American Psychological Association on behalf of itself, the American Educational Research Association, and the National Council on Measurement in Education.

b. "The Responsible Use of Tests: A Position Paper of AMEG, APGA, and NCME," published in *Measurement and Evaluation in Guidance* Vol. 5, No. 2, July 1972, pp. 385–388.

☞ *Section D: Research and Publication*

1.   Current American Psychological Association guidelines on research with human subjects shall be adhered to (Ethical Principles in the Conduct of Research with Human Participants. Washington, D.C.: American Psychological Association, Inc., 1973).

2.   In planning any research activity dealing with human subjects, the member is expected to be aware of and responsive to all pertinent ethical principles and to ensure that the research problem, design, and execution are in full compliance with them.

3.   Responsibility for ethical research practice lies with the principal researcher, while others involved in the research activities share ethical obligation and full responsibility for their own actions.

4.   In research with human subjects, researchers are responsible for their subjects' welfare throughout the experiment, and they must take all reasonable precautions to avoid causing injurious psychological, physical, or social effects on their subjects.

5.   It is expected that all research subjects be informed of the purpose of the study except when withholding information or providing misinformation to them is essential to the investigation. In such research, the member is responsible for corrective action as soon as possible following the research.

6.   Participation in research is expected to be voluntary. Involuntary participation is appropriate only when it can be demonstrated that participation will have no harmful effects on subjects.

7.   When reporting research results, explicit mention must be made of all variables and conditions known to the investigator that might affect the outcome of the investigation or the interpretation of the data.

8.   The member is responsible for conducting and reporting investigations in a manner that minimizes the possibility that results will be misleading.

9.   The member has an obligation to make available sufficient original research data to qualified others who may wish to replicate the study.

10. When supplying data, aiding in the research of another person, reporting research results, or in making original data available, due care

must be taken to disguise the identity of the subjects in the absence of specific authorization from such subjects to do otherwise.

11. When conducting and reporting research, the member is expected to be familiar with and to give recognition to previous work on the topic, as well as to observe all copyright laws and follow the principle of giving full credit to all to whom credit is due.

12. The member has the obligation to give due credit through joint authorship, acknowledgement, footnote statements, or other appropriate means to those who have contributed significantly to the research, in accordance with such contributions.

13. The member is expected to communicate to other members the results of any research judged to be of professional or scientific value. Results reflecting unfavorably on institutions, programs, services, or vested interests should not be withheld for such reasons.

14. If members agree to cooperate with another individual in research and/or publication, they incur an obligation to cooperate as promised in terms of punctuality of performance and with full regard to the completeness and accuracy of the information provided.

☞ Section E: Consulting and Private Practice

Consulting refers to a voluntary relationship between a professional helper and help-needing social unit (industry, business, school, college, etc.) in which the consultant is attempting to give help to the client in the solution of some current or potential problem. When "client" is used in this section it refers to an individual, group, or organization served by the consultant. (This definition of "consulting" is adapted from "Dimensions of the Consultant's Job" by Ronald Lippitt, *Journal of Social Issues,* Vol. 15, No. 2, 1959.)

1. Members who act as consultants must have a high degree of self-awareness of their own values and needs in entering helping relationships that involve change in social units.

2. There should be understanding and agreement between consultant and client as to the task, the directions or goals, and the function of the consultant.

3. Members are expected to accept only those consulting roles for which they possess or have access to the necessary skills and resources for giving the kind of help that is needed.

4. The consulting relationship is defined as being one in which the client's adaptability and growth toward self-direction are encouraged and cultivated. For this reason, the consultant is obligated to maintain consistently the role of a consultant and to avoid becoming a decision maker for the client.

5. In announcing one's availability for professional services as a consultant, the member follows professional rather than commercial standards in describing services with accuracy, dignity, and caution.

6. For private practice in testing, counseling, or consulting, all ethical principles defined in this document are pertinent. In addition, any individual, agency, or institution offering educational, personal, or vocational counseling should meet the standards of the International Association of Counseling Services, Inc.

7. The member is expected to refuse a private fee or other remuneration for consultation with persons who are entitled to these services through the member's employing institution or agency. The policies of a particular agency may make explicit provisions for private practice with agency counselees by members of its staff. In such instances, the counselees must be apprised of other options open to them should they seek private counseling services.

8. It is unethical to use one's institutional affiliation to recruit counselees for one's private practice.

☞ Section F: Personnel Administration

It is recognized that most members are employed in public or quasi-public institutions. The functioning of a member within an institution must contribute to the goals of the institution and vice versa if either is to accomplish their respective goals or objectives. It is therefore essential that the member and the institution function in ways to: (a) make the institution's goals explicit and public; (b) make the member's contribution to institutional goals specific; and (c) foster mutual accountability for goal achievement.

To accomplish these objectives it is recognized that the member and the employer must share responsibilities in the formulation and implementation of personnel policies.

1. Members should define and describe the parameters and levels of their professional competency.

2. Members should establish interpersonal relations and working agreements with supervisors and subordinates regarding counseling or clinical relationships, confidentiality, distinction between public and private material, maintenance and dissemination of recorded information, work load, and accountability. Working agreements in each instance should be specified and made known to those concerned.

3. Members are responsible for alerting their employers to conditions that may be potentially disruptive or damaging.

4. Members are responsible for informing employers of conditions that may limit their effectiveness.

5. Members are expected to submit regularly to review and evaluation.

6. Members are responsible for inservice development of self and/ or staff.

7. Members are responsible for informing their staff of goals and programs.

8. Members are responsible for providing personnel practices that guarantee and enhance the rights and welfare of each recipient of their service.

9. Members are expected to select competent persons and assign responsibilities compatible with their skills and experiences.

☞ Section G: Preparation Standards

Members who are responsible for training others should be guided by the preparation standards of the Association and relevant division(s).

The member who functions in the capacity of trainer assumes unique ethical responsibilities that frequently go beyond that of the member who does not function in a training capacity. These ethical responsibilities are outlined as follows:

1. Members are expected to orient trainees to program expectations, basic skills development, and employment prospects prior to admission to the program.

2. Members in charge of training are expected to establish programs that integrate academic study and supervised practice.

3. Members are expected to establish a program directed toward developing the trainees' skills, knowledge, and self-understanding, stated whenever possible in competency or performance terms.

4. Members are expected to identify the level of competency of their trainees. These levels of competency should accommodate the paraprofessional as well as the professional.

5. Members, through continual trainee evaluation and appraisal, are expected to be aware of the personal limitations of the trainee that might impede future performance. The trainer has the responsibility of not only assisting the trainee in securing remedial assistance, but also screening from the program those trainees who are unable to provide competent services.

6. Members are expected to provide a program that includes training in research commensurate with levels of role functioning. Paraprofessional and technician-level personnel should be trained as consumers of research. In addition, these personnel should learn how to evaluate their own and their program effectiveness. Advanced graduate training, especially at the doctoral level, should include preparation for original research by the member.

7. Members are expected to make trainees aware of the ethical responsibilities and standards of the profession.

8. Training programs are expected to encourage trainees to value the ideals of service to individuals and to society. In this regard, direct financial remuneration or lack thereof should not influence the quality of service rendered. Monetary considerations should not be allowed to overshadow professional and humanitarian needs.

9.   Members responsible for training are expected to be skilled as teachers and practitioners.

10. Members are expected to present thoroughly varied theoretical positions so that trainees may make comparisons and have the opportunity to select a position.

11. Members are obligated to develop clear policies within their training institution regarding field placement and the roles of the trainee and the trainer in such placements.

12. Members are expected to ensure that forms of training focusing on self-understanding or growth are voluntary, or if required as part of the training program, are made known to prospective trainees prior to entering the program. When the training program offers a growth experience with an emphasis on self-disclosure or other relatively intimate or personal involvement, the member should have no administrative, supervisory, or evaluative authority regarding the participant.

13. Members are obligated to conduct a training program in keeping with the most current guidelines of the American Personnel and Guidance Association and its various divisions.

Chapter 5

EVALUATION OF COUNSELING

Evaluation, as it is used here, means the process of determining the strengths and weaknesses of counseling. Accordingly, any evaluative activity is an attempt to discover the assets and liabilities involved in or accruing from counseling.

A superficial reflection might yield the false assumption that it should be relatively simple to determine the quality of counseling and its beneficial or disadvantageous results. However, quite the contrary is true.

> There are five major stumbling blocks to evaluating guidance services: 1) Guidance workers in the schools often lack the time, training and/or facilities necessary to conduct research studies of this type. 2) Many outcomes of guidance are intangible and are, therefore, exceedingly difficult to evaluate. 3) Many outcomes of guidance cannot be determined for a long period of time. 4) Even intermediate outcomes of guidance are measured by criteria themselves. 5) There are many variables outside the control of the guidance program which may influence the student's adjustment or development. (5, p. 237)

Subsequent comments in this chapter will refer again to the difficulties involved in evaluating counseling. It is hoped that these obstacles will be regarded as a challenge to improve the evaluative task, rather than causing the student and/or practitioner of counseling to "throw up his hands in despair" in a rejection of any attempt to improve counseling.

It should be held firmly in mind that the major reason for evaluating counseling is to discover strengths, which should be exploited and developed, and weaknesses, which should be eliminated, alleviated, or nullified as much as possible. From this treatment of strengths and weaknesses an improvement of counseling should emerge. If counseling is not improved as a direct result of the evaluation, then the evaluative process has been merely an academic exercise which can hardly be justified in terms of the time, energy, and cost involved in the investigation.

In any evaluative process pertaining to professional men and women such as lawyers, dentists, counselors or physicians, there is the ever-present, delicate factor of top-level people with graduate degrees being judged in terms of competency or rated against colleagues. This type of judgment is made of factory workers who may not relish any more than the professional worker this evaluative process. There is one critical difference: the factory worker is being evaluated by a supervisor, foreman, or boss who, at least theoretically, is a superior individual, with more education and/or experience; the professional being rated may have his doctorate and more years of experience than the individual who is trying to evaluate him. As a department chairman in a college once remarked about a newly employed professor who came to the institution with a national reputation (far beyond the reputation acquired by the department chairman), "Who am I to judge him?"

On the other hand, there have been numerous examples of the less talented being able to lead, teach, and evaluate the more talented. Some major-league baseball team managers have done outstanding jobs as managers even though they were not sufficiently talented to be big-league ball players, or, if they played in the majors, never were outstanding players. As one big-league star allegedly said about a manager who did not select him for the all-star game, "Where does that bum get off not picking me? He never even played regularly in the big leagues."

While it may be a fact of life that "those who can't do can evaluate," the people being judged frequently react with hostility, suspicion, resentment, and bitterness to any evaluation, particularly from a person who has never proved himself to be outstanding in the very factors he is involved in evaluating. The foregoing statement is especially applicable to the professional.

Even when the frame of reference is changed from an evaluation of the individual, as a worker, to the evaluation of a division, a department, a section, an office, or a counseling center, the threat to ego is not entirely removed; the suspicion remains when the traditional is questioned, and the resistance to change continues unabated.

The teaching profession for many years has tried to solve the problem of rating teachers. Giving raises on the basis of merit has clashed with the automatic increments of seniority. Each system has its protagonists and supporters; neither has escaped the scathing rebukes of dissidents. Suffice it to say that at this time there is no general agreement on the best basis for rating teachers. This generalization carries over into the other professions.

It is, certainly, a matter for counselors and counselor educators to proceed with the utmost caution in the evaluation of counseling, to continue to seek ways of evaluating without inciting the antagonism, resistance, rebellion, and/or alarm of counselors, and to approach the goal of enhancing counseling in as scientific and humane a manner as possible.

☞ *The Counselor*

The most sensitive area in the evaluation of counseling is the evaluation of the counselor as a counselor.

1. Employ only individuals who have completed their counselor education and are qualified counselors prior to beginning employment.

2. Sharpen the selection techniques to a degree possible to permit the exclusion of people who, without supervision, continue to develop professionally, for a lifetime.

3. Strive to effect the transfer or reassignment of parasites and mediocre staff members who, professionally speaking, possess tenure but little else.

4. Provide each counselor with the time to develop strengths and utilize, to the utmost, his special talents.

5. Avoid any negative ratings that aren't based on behaviors.

6. Treat professionals as professionals.

If a physician were to be judged by his/her peers in terms of the percent of success he/she obtained with patients for whom he/she prescribed "stop smoking," it would be a most erroneous inference to conclude that a given physician was not an effective medical counselor because only 10 percent of his patients actually stopped smoking. It must be remembered that a physician is a physician, he/she is not God, he/she is not empowered to initiate miracles, he/she must not be expected to overcome hereditary weakness, and he/she should not be castigated for his/her patients' character defects, etc. Certainly, the word "counselor" may be substituted appropriately for "physician" in these statements.

With the foregoing cautions in mind in reference to judging counselor competency, the reader is referred to two monumental studies dealing with the effectiveness of counseling. Campbell (2) and Rothney (7) certainly have made massive contributions in significant counselor evaluations. It must be remembered that the true value of each counselor, as a counselor, may be virtually impossible to determine.

Perhaps the best hope for the enhancement of counseling lies in the evaluation of the counseling center, counseling service, counseling agency, or whatever label is used to depict the organization assigned the counseling responsibility.

☞ *Evaluating the Counseling Center*

To assist in the determination of the strengths and weaknesses of the counseling center, evaluative criteria have been developed and published for usage. There may be sections of the evaluative instrument devoted to counselor evaluation, or such could be inferred from some oblique portions of the instrument. But the purpose of the evaluative instrument is not, nor should it be so construed, to evaluate the counselor per se, but rather the organization within which and for which he works.

Any evaluation of a counseling center should be made by the counselors themselves. The first paragraph in the introduction of one of these evaluative instruments expresses this nicely.

> The *Evaluative Instrument* provides criteria and techniques that make possible the individual participation of each counselor in a group process which is dedicated to the proposition of individual and group professional growth in the enhancement of the counseling service. (3)

Over a period of many years, each of the authors has been involved in using evaluative instruments, and on one occasion had the opportunity of participating together with others in the construction of *one – Improving Counseling: An Evaluative Instrument for Improving Counseling Centers.* (3) From these experiences has emerged a set of reactions which are noted in the following presentation of the possible disadvantages and advantages in the use of evaluative instruments. We are giving the disadvantages a priority over the advantages in order of presentation because of our conviction that unless these liabilities can be eliminated, or alleviated to a significantly workable degree, the use of an evaluative instrument is not recommended.

Possible Disadvantages of Using an Evaluative Instrument. When one individual, (e.g., the director of the counseling center, an outside consultant, or a professor) makes the evaluation, the typical reactions of the counselors are hostility, fear, resentment, indifference, or a rejection of the findings. One or more of these adverse responses almost inevitably accrues from the "one individual evaluator" type of evaluation. Even when the counselors receive a proper explanation concerning the rationale for making the evaluation and the qualifications of the evaluator, some negative reactions usually occur.

If the counselors themselves do the evaluating, this circumvents the preceding disadvantage, but it may create a new problem linked to counselor participation in the evaluating: the resentment of counselors who do not wish to spend their time evaluating. If the evaluating is done on the counselor's own time, this is a critical disadvantage; it if takes place on school or agency time, the difficulty may be substantially alleviated unless there are counselors who begrudge giving up client time for an auxiliary activity.

After the strengths and weaknesses of the counseling center have been determined, action should be taken to exploit the strengths and to eliminate or alleviate the weaknesses. If these steps are not taken, this is the most devastating weakness of all! If counselors have been exposed too often to the fiasco of "ignoring the results of the study by making no improvements," they may react with indifference or cynicism. In any event, once an evaluative study has been made by the counseling staff, and it is not considered and put into application but considered to be merely an academic exercise, any subsequent evaluations proposed to or made by these counselors usually will be strongly resisted and possibly fraught with hostility, sarcasm, belittlement, ridicule, contempt, or disgust.

Advantages in Using an Evaluative Instrument. If the study is properly introduced and explained to the counseling staff members who are to do the evaluating themselves, with an instrument of their own choosing and at a time mutually agreeable, the evaluative process can be an effective in-service training experience.

If the determined strengths are exploited on a continuing basis after the evaluation has been completed, this obviously contributes to the effective functioning of the counseling center. If the determined weaknesses are eliminated or alleviated as soon as possible after the evaluation has been completed, this easily can be the most important result evolving from the evaluative study.

In those instances in which a weakness cannot be eliminated or even alleviated in the predictable future, the counselors should be given evidence of the impossibility of effecting a change. Even though the counselors do not accept this situation as being right or logically justifiable (e.g., too few counselors to handle the client load), they need to know that the administrators and executives involved will do everything possible to correct the matter when factors currently beyond their control become amenable to remedial action. Unless the determined weaknesses elicit some constructive recognition or response, the damages and ill effects resultant from such a situation may well destroy the evaluative study as an improvement technique. Furthermore, the lowering of the counselors' morale and the growth of their professional disillusionment often are additional devastating by-products.

When counselors are presented with the evidence that the seeds of their evaluative labors are germinating – through the elimination or alleviation of weaknesses – into a better counseling center, the morale of the counselors certainly rises, and the worth of evaluative studies becomes a fact.

Counselors may become self-motivated to self-improvement as a by-product of the strengthening of the counseling center. When the counselor, of his own volition, proceeds to keep abreast of developments in his field, participates in research and creativity, writes, sharpens his methodology, and continuously strives to extend and intensify the knowledge which contributes to his effectiveness as a counselor, this certainly epitomizes the best possible approach to the enhancement of the counseling profession.

Evaluative Instruments. There are some evaluative instruments available for purchase. The authors recommend that a copy of each of the appropriate instruments be obtained for examination by the counselors so that they may select the one that seems best to them.

If the counselors cannot agree on an instrument for their evaluation, or if the one they choose is out of print or unavailable, it is suggested that consideration be given to the development of their own instrument. This is what occasioned the development of *Improving Counseling: An Evaluative Instrument for Improving Counseling Centers*, (3) a project in which each of the authors participated with eleven other counselors. While such a project has its values, it is time consuming. The construction of *Improving Counseling* took a seemingly endless succession of meetings over a two-year period. In addition, after devoting the time needed to develop the instrument, there still remain the tasks of (1) evaluating the counseling center in terms of the criteria and (2) carrying out a program of exploiting the discovered strengths and eliminating or alleviating the discovered weaknesses.

It takes an unusually dedicated individual to continue through these processes. Consequently, the risks are great that the project may burn itself out due to a too-prolonged period of time. Certainly, the final and most important step – exploitation of strengths and elimination or alleviation of weaknesses – may be omitted or superficially treated.

When an evaluative instrument is developed, it may be a sound instrument representing the best thinking relative to improving a counseling center. But, unless it is revised according to new concepts and the growth and development of a progressive profession, it, or portions of it, easily can become obsolete in a few years.

For the counseling center which does an evaluative study and applies its findings in an improvement program, there is the problem of how to further improve once the criteria have been met. In those instances in which this occurs, the counselors would do well to consider the development of their own evaluative instrument, constructing standards sufficiently high and challenging to stimulate a continuous program of improvement.

☞ *References*

[1.] Benson, Arthur L. *Criteria for Evaluating Guidance Programs in Secondary Schools, Form B.* Washington, D.C.: Federal Security Agency, Office of Education, 1949.

[2.] Campbell, David P. *The Results of Counseling: Twenty-Five Years Later.* Philadelphia: W. B. Saunders Company, 1965.

[3.] Grant, Bruce, George D. Demos, and Richard Oldenburg. *Improving Counseling: An Evaluative Instrument for Improving Counseling Centers.* Columbia, Missouri: Lucas Brothers, 1965.

[4.] Kitch, Donald E., and William H. McCreary. *Improving Guidance Programs in Secondary Schools.* Sacramento, California: California State Department of Education, 1950.

5. Miller, Frank W. *Guidance - Principles and Services*. Columbus, Ohio: Charles E. Merrill, 1961.
6. Rackham, Eric N. *Student Personnel Services Inventory*. Kent, Ohio: Kent State University, 1963.
7. Rothney, John W. M. *Guidance Practices and Results*. New York: Harper & Brothers, 1958.

☞ Suggested Additional Readings

Buckner, Eugene T. "Accountable to Whom? The Counselor's Dilemma." *Measurement and Evaluation in Guidance* 8, no. 3 (1975), pp. 187–192.

Burck, Harman D., Harold P. Cottingham, and Robert C. Reardon. *Counseling and Accountability: Methods and Critique*. New York: Pergamon Press, 1973.

Carlin, Leslie O. "Negative Responses to Counseling." *Vocational Guidance Quarterly*, Summer, 1965, pp. 287–290.

Coopersmith, Stanley. *The Antecedents of Self-Esteem*. San Francisco: W. H. Freeman, 1967.

Cramer, Stanley H., Edwin L. Herr, Charles N. Morris, and Thomas T. Frantz. *Research and the School Counselor*. Boston: Houghton Mifflin, 1970.

Gelso, Charles J. "Research in Counseling: Methodological and Professional Issues." *Counseling Psychologist* 8, no. 3 (1979), pp. 7–36.

Glass, Gene V. "Educational Putdown Men." *Phi Delta Kappan* 50, no. 3 (1968), pp. 148–151.

Goldman, Leo. "A Revolution in Counseling Research." *Journal of Counseling Psychology* 23, no. 6 (1976), pp. 543–552.

Hays, Donald G., and Joan K. Linn. *Needs Assessment: Who Needs It?* Washington, D. C.: American School Counselor Association, 1977.

Joint Committee on Standards for Education Evaluation. *Standards for Evaluations of Educational Programs, Projects, and Materials*. New York: McGraw-Hill, 1981.

Kelz, James W. "The Development and Evaluation of a Measure of Counselor Effectiveness." *Personnel and Guidance Journal,* January, 1966, pp. 511–516.

Kerr, Robert A. "Evaluating the Services." In *Student Services,* edited by Ursula Delworth and Gary R. Hanson, pp. 421–438. San Francisco: Jossey-Bass, 1980.

Krumboltz, John D. "An Accountability Model for Counselors." *Personnel and Guidance Journal* 52, no. 10 (1974), pp. 639–642.

Lasser, Barbara R. "An Outcomes Approach to Counseling Evaluation." *Measurement and Evaluation in Guidance* 8, no. 3 (1975), pp. 169–174.

Linden, James D., Shelley C. Stone, and Bruce Shertzer. "Development and Evaluation of an Inventory for Rating Counseling." *Personnel and Guidance Journal,* November, 1965, pp. 267–276.

Miller, Frank W., James A. Fruehling, and Gloria J. Lewis. *Guidance Principles and Services.* 3rd ed. Columbus, Ohio: Charles E. Merrill, 1978.

Miller, Theodore K., and Judith S. Prince. *The Future of Student Affairs.* San Francisco: Jossey-Bass, 1976.

Mitchell, Anita M. *Ways to Evaluate Types of Career Education Activities: A Handbook of Evaluation Models.* Palo Alto, California: American Institutes for Research in the Behavioral Sciences, 1978.

Rappaport, Julian. *Community Psychology.* New York: Holt, Rinehart and Winston, 1977.

Shertzer, Bruce, and Shelley C. Stone. *Fundamentals of Guidance.* 4th ed. Boston: Houghton Mifflin, 1981.

Sternberg, Robert J., & Swerling, Louise S., *Teaching For Thinking,* APA, 1996.

Sullivan, Howard J., and Robert W. O'Hare, eds. *Accountability in Pupil Personnel Services: A Process Guide for the Development of Objectives.* Fullerton: California Personnel and Guidance Association, 1971.

Tolbert, E. L. *Research for Teachers and Counselors.* Minneapolis: Burgess Publishing Company, 1967.

Volsky, Jr., Theodore, Thomas M. Magoon, Warren T. Norman, and Donald P. Holt. The Outcomes of Counseling and Psychotherapy: Theory and Research. *University of Minnesota Press, 1965.*

Wrenn, C. Gilbert. *The Counselor in a Changing World*. Washington, D.C.: American Personnel and Guidance Association, 1962.

Zax, Melvin, and Gerald A. Specter. *An Introduction to Community Psychology*. New York: John Wiley and Sons, 1974.

☞ *Activities Which the Counselor Should Perform*

One approach to ascertaining the functions of the counselor is to identify on a broad basis his qualifications. Failor lists these general points:

> First of all, the counselor is an educator, usually a person who has had successful teaching experience, and is proud to be an educator to the point where one does not attempt to ape other disciplines.
>
> In the second place, one should have a personality and an ability to relate himself to others, and usually is a superior person.
>
> In the third place, the counselor has the equivalent of a master's degree in pupil personnel and guidance services, or is progressing in this direction. (2)

Farwell identified the counselor's functions through pointing out the role he should play:

> The role of the school counselor can be identified as (1) Is a school staff member committed to education and the educational process; (2) It is a function to study human lives and the contingent environment in which they live; (3) The school counselor should devote a two-thirds majority of time to counseling with individuals; (4) Is a consultant to teachers, administrators, and parents. (3, p. 159)

The fourth point above might seem to conflict with the authors' expression of this chapter regarding counselors not counseling teachers and other colleagues. However, observe that Farwell's word is "consultant." Functioning as a consultant means offering professional help in one's specialty to a colleague, not counseling. The teacher who confers with the counselor regarding what should be done in a guidance situation involving a student, or how to proceed in such a situation, is not seeking help for oneself as an individual but as a professional.

☞ *Counseling Functions*

I. **Counseling Services.** Individual, Group, Educational, Occupational, Social, Personal.

Goal: Counselor must be able to develop and maintain effective individual and group counseling relationships and to provide assistance in educational, vocational, and personal needs and concerns of students.

II. **Consultation.** Guidance Services Staff, Instructional Staff, Administrative Staff, Parents & Parent Organizations, Community Referral Agencies/Resources.

Goal: Counselor must possess the ability to serve as resource person relative to the guidance needs and concerns of individuals and groups.

III. **Coordination.** Materials, Human Resources, Educational Program, Facilitation of Human Development.

Goal: Counselor must be able to coordinate the various aspects of the total guidance program resulting in a continuous and meaningful sequence of services to students, staff, and community.

IV. **Career Development Services.** Educational, Occupational, Social & Personal, Environmental.

Goal: The Counselor must be able to assist students, parents, and the instructional and administrative staff in developing healthy attitudes toward the world of work, understanding the role of work in the life of man, and encouraging students to become mature life planners, responsible jobholders, and responsible contributors to productive and service enterprises.

V. **Planning and Development.** Need Assessment Data, Instructional Staff Input, School/Community Data.

Goal: Counselor must possess the ability to develop guidance program goals, objectives, and activities, using both school and community personnel. Program goals and objectives should be written and made readily available to appropriate constituencies.

VI. **Individual Assessment and Inventory.** Test Instruments and Data, Nontest Instruments and Data Collecting, Recording, Interpreting, Implementing.

Goal: Counselor must be able to appraise the characteristics of students, describe the needs and potentialities of individual students, identify individual differences, and provide for recording the resultant data.

VII. **Research and Evaluation.** Guidance Services Program, Guidance Services Staff, School Environment and Population, Community Agencies and Community Resources.

Goal: Counselor must possess the ability to interpret clearly the implications of research data to staff, parents, students, and community resources and also possess the ability to use the results of such research in guidance program development and revision.

VIII. **Placement and Follow-up.** Educational, Occupational, Classroom Training, Part Time, Full Time, Systematic Follow-up and Evaluation.

Goal: Counselor must be able to anticipate in long range student planning and to assume responsibility for periodic review and revision of such plans. Revision will be based on changes in the curriculum, student appraisal data, school achievement, educational and occupational opportunity, the student's maturity, and new life goals.

IX. Referral. Institutional, Psychosocial, Agency.

Goal: Counselor must possess the ability to assist students, instructional and administrative staff, and parents in accepting referral to other specialists within the school district and within the community.

Part II

FUNCTIONS OF THE COUNSELOR AND OTHER GUIDANCE SPECIALISTS

Chapter 6

COUNSELING

The concept of counseling is the rationale for the existence of the counselor. Whatever else he/she may do, if he/she stops counseling, he/she automatically becomes something other than a counselor. If he/she continues to counsel, even though engaged in a diversity of auxiliary functions, he/she is still a counselor. When these activities become something else besides supporting or helping, then to a corresponding degree, the counselor becomes less and less a counselor and more and more "a something else."

In *Part II: Functions of the Counselor and Other Guidance Specialists,* four auxiliary functions to the prime and major function of the counselor are discussed. In this chapter which, by label, refers to the main function of counseling, the matter of the counselor's function is examined as a whole, with a recurring emphasis upon "the one-to-one relationship" as the most important function. "Counseling is the primary function of the school counselor." (3, p. 159)

Activities Which the Counselor Should not Perform. It should be advantageous to examine some of the functions counselors have been asked or assigned to perform which they should not do.

High school principals have too often solved the problem of an absent teacher by having a counselor serve as a substitute teacher for one period or for the entire teaching day.

There are situations in which counselors have been removed from the counseling office to patrol the school yard in a policing capacity; to serve as guards at athletic contests; to enforce regulations at school dances; to investigate stolen property; to discipline students; to influence students to select certain vocations, behave in a prescribed manner, or choose a certain major, course, or subject; to act as a buffer between an irate parent and a teacher or the principal; to impose a code of ethics on the unethical student; or to convince parents of the efficacy of the guidance department, the school, or the school district.

In high schools, counselors have been asked to teach classes, which in itself is not lamentable, if the counselor wishes to teach a class or two, and if a principal who is conscious of costs can justify placing a highly trained specialist in a classroom when there are teachers qualified to teach (while in most high schools, there is a serious shortage of qualified counselors).

There is an old fallacy, which still persists in some schools, that a counselor should do some teaching so as not to lose touch with the students, become unsympathetic to the teachers' problems, or to forget what it is like to manage a class. That this proposition often is advanced by a principal who does not teach, or by teachers who envy or resent counselors, is beside the point. The fact remains that it is a poor business practice that permits diverting a specialist from his specialty. The counselor can hardly lose touch with students if he/she has a more intimate relationship with them than the teacher. He/she is not apt to be unsympathetic to teachers, any more than the nonteaching principal, the dean of girls, or the superintendent, just because he/she is not teaching. If time erodes his/her memory of what it is like to manage a classroom, what difference does this make? The public school counselor exists to serve the students, not to alleviate the neuroses of teachers, to salvage mediocre teachers, or to feed the ego of principals. If the school board wishes to employ a counselor for teachers, principals, deans, and superintendents, then, of course, such a counselor would serve this group, not the students. Until this unique possibility becomes a fact, all concerned need to keep reminding themselves that the public school counselor has the responsibility to serve the welfare of the students in the same manner that a lawyer is obligated to serve his clients. The client should not be subordinated to the wishes of others, nor should anything adverse to the client's welfare be acceptable, tolerable, or permitted.

With the exception of a few highly talented individuals who should be given the time to exploit their talents, the college counselor ought to avoid (as should his/her colleague, the college professor) spreading himself/herself too thin by engaging in too many noncounseling functions, regardless of how supportive these functions may be. As a practitioner – just as the physician or lawyer – the college counselor should counsel. Even though his/her auxiliary activities usually contribute to enriching his/her effectiveness as a counselor and certainly enhance his/her professional development, he/she must be careful not to relegate counseling to a minor role in his/her professional life. At the same time, if he/she is capable of contributing to the profession of counseling, he/she has an obligation to do so; for, in general, he/she is a member of the most highly trained and experienced group of counselors. If professional leadership and innovations do not emanate from him/her, the profession faces a serious weakness.

"Junior college counselors are not psychiatrists, nor clinical psychologists, nor depth psychotherapists, and those who overtly or covertly hold to such pretensions should be disabused of them." (1) This statement, made by Charles C. Collins, a junior college dean of instruction, and concerning junior college counselors, certainly is most appropriate for college counselors, some of whom have taken to regarding themselves as junior psychiatrists. The most psychologically oriented or biased individual would pause to reflect before claiming that psychiatric or psychotherapeutic (in the medical sense) counseling should be integrated into the concept of counseling. Collins goes on to emphasize his point: "Even if every junior college counselor were a certified clinical psychologist, by what authority should the counseling center be converted into a clinic? The college has circumscribed functions established by the state legislature and by the local board of trustees. Operating an out-patient clinic is not one of them."

Activities Which the Counselor Should Perform. One approach to ascertaining the functions of the counselor is to identify on a broad basis his qualifications. Failor lists these general points:

> First of all, the counselor is an educator, usually a person who has had successful teaching experience, and is proud to be an educator to the point where he does not attempt to ape other disciplines.

In the second place, he has a personality and an ability to relate himself to others, and usually is a superior person.

In the third place, the counselor has the equivalent of a master's degree in pupil personnel and guidance services, or is progressing in this direction. (2)

Farwell identifies the counselor's functions through pointing out the role he should play:

The role of the school counselor can be identified as (1) He is a school staff member committed to education and the educational process; (2) It is his function to study human lives and the contingent environment in which they live; (3) The school counselor should devote a two-thirds majority of his time to counseling with individuals; (4) He is a consultant to teachers, administrators, and parents. (3, p. 159)

The fourth point above might seem to conflict with the authors' expression in this chapter regarding counselors not counseling teachers and other colleagues. However, observe that Farwell's word is "consultant." Functioning as a consultant means offering professional help in one's specialty to a colleague, not counseling. The teacher who confers with the counselor regarding what he should do in a guidance situation involving a student, or how to proceed in such a situation, is not seeking help for himself as an individual but as a professional. The authors agree with Farwell that this function could be assigned to counselors, but it is not listed or treated as such in this section since counselors usually do not perform this responsibility except in a superficial, unorganized, spasmodic manner which places it in the category of miscellaneous activities, carried out without any consistency. Most counselors have not specialized to an extent that makes them eligible to be considered as consultants to other counselors. With more specialization and additional training, plus talented people and sufficient time, the consultative process may develop to the point at which enough counselors are utilized as consultants to warrant including consulting as a function of the counselor.

Another approach to getting at the counselor's functions is to note what he currently is doing.

> A survey involving nearly one-fourth of the school counselors in California indicates that over half their working time is spent with students. Staff consultation with teachers, pupil personnel specialists (psychometrists, psychologists, welfare and social workers, and psychiatrists), health agencies, and probation departments takes up a fourth to a third of their time. The remainder of their workday is spent consulting with parents or participating in community activities. (5, p. 1)

The foregoing breakdown does not indicate what percentage of the time spent with students is counseling or group guidance. It implies, by omission, that the counselors do not have any clerical responsibilities, which in public schools is most unrealistic, because clerical activities often are so time-consuming as to be a major function of the counselor. Again the word "consulting" appears, but without any delineation regarding the way the word is used. One may assume it encompasses any and all contacts the counselor has with individuals other than his clients, but this is not consulting and is too ambiguous as a frame of reference to be of much help.

One director of a college counseling center was overheard remarking that "the counseling center attempts to maintain relative obscurity," based on the theory that the students who need help either find the department on their own or are guided there by faculty members. What kind of help was not specified. The implication is that the problem had better be massive, critical, overwhelming, or at minimum most pressing.

It is only fair to comment in reference to this statement that if a counseling center advertises or conducts a publicity campaign soliciting all students, there would be the very real risk of inundating the counselors with a massive number of clients. The number would extend far beyond any possibility of professional service being given due to the number of counselors available and the time each is allotted for counseling.

This brings into focus the matter of the ratio of counselees to counselor. Recommendations have been made for the secondary level of 300:1, and at the college level, 500:1. Unfortunately, these ratios are too often dictated by budgetary limitations. According to the California Junior College Bureau, junior colleges have circumscribed budgets which set student loads of 400 to 500 per counselor. (7)

To the authors, each of whom has been both a secondary and a college counselor, even the best of these ratios (e.g., 200:1 for high school counselors and 400:1 for college counselors) never ceases to be a source of amazement, for simple arithmetic provides evidence that there just aren't enough hours in the day for a counselor to provide counseling for 200 high school students or 400 college students. Human beings being what they are, a few aggressive individuals or those who are persistently referred by faculty members, are going to usurp the counselor's time, and whenever this happens other potential clients are certain to either miss counseling or get less help than they need.

Within the three major areas of guidance – educational, vocational (or career), and personal-social – it is pertinent to recognize the significance of the vocational. This is brought out forcibly by Collins in regard to the junior college counselor, and his statement pertains equally to high school and college counselors.

> The function of vocational counseling has too frequently been downgraded, minimized, or sidestepped by junior college counselors yet vocational counseling and its corollary, educational guidance, have a centrality, which makes all other functions pale in significance. (1)

Another viewpoint is expressed by Stewart and Warnath, who suggest that the functions of the counselor should include teaching clients to change their environment to make it more amenable to the achievement of their goals and that the counselor should attempt to develop a more hospitable environment for his clients. (6)

Most people in the ghettos would be more than willing to change their environment and society would be delighted to have this happen. Lamentably, little progress has been made in realizing this dream, even though most of the helping professions such as civic organizations, city governments, churches, and other social institutions have worked for generations toward environmental improvement. Even if counselors could "develop a more hospitable environment for their clients," it would be a philosophical issue as to whether or not they should engage in this manipulative activity. The point remains academic, for there is little the counselor can do to change his client's environment unless, of course, moving Tommy from Miss Watson's history class to Mr. Harford's is construed as "developing a more hospitable environment."

Striving towards effecting those changes which would eliminate the environments of delinquency, poverty, unsanitary conditions, poor housing, culturally deprived homes, language barriers, racial prejudice, or religious prejudice is the responsibility of all citizens, including the counselor as a citizen. The counselor as a counselor is not included, except indirectly in whatever progress is made by his clients resulting from what they are able to accomplish through the self-enhancement that accrues from the counselor-client relationship.

It is fitting and necessary to consider the functions of the counselor as reported in evaluative instruments. Eleven functions which are presented in one of these instruments are given here:

A. Does interviewing

B. Writes interview records

C. Conducts group guidance activities when appropriate

D. Utilizes referral services and resource materials

E. Participates in the evaluation of the Counseling Center

F. Assists the Director of Counseling in development of policies and procedures

G. Participates in research, service studies, or projects as assigned by the Director of Counseling

H. Participates in in-service training activities

I. Participates in community and professional activities

J. Assists in controlling access to and use of counseling records and files in Counseling Center

K. Works cooperatively with faculty in interpreting and developing services of the Counseling Center (4, pp. 8–9)

In the foregoing, "Does interviewing" is listed as A not accidentally, but purposely. Again, this is *the* function of the counselor. Some of the other functions exist only in terms of being integrated with A, such as B, D, and J. C is pertinent when it serves the purposes detailed in *Chapter 2, Counseling and Group Guidance,* and *Chapter 9, Group Guidance.* E may be justified as explained in *Chapter 5, Evaluation of Counseling.* F exemplifies a democratic and wise administrative approach in the enhancement of the Counseling Center. G can only be justified if the counselor is able to contribute to the improvement of the profession and to his own professional development. H may be defended on the grounds of contributing to the professional development of the counselors involved. I is warranted if it has a good public-relations impact on the community or stimulates community or professional development. K is justifiable as a matter of public relations with colleagues and as a process of democratic professional development.

It is most important to adhere firmly to the realization that counseling, using the one-to-one relationship, is the one all-important function of the counselor. All of the other functions should contribute to the enhancement of counseling.

Part III: The Art of Counseling is devoted to the performance of "counseling," and *Part IV: The Science of Counseling* deals with the knowledge needed by the counselor in order for him "to counsel."

🖜 *References*

1. Collins, Charles C. "Junior College Counseling: A Critical View." *Personnel and Guidance Journal,* February 1965, pp. 546–550.

2. Failor, Clarence, W. "Who Should Counsel in the Schools?" *News and Views,* School of Education, University of Colorado, January, pp. 4–5.

3. Farwell, Gail F. "The Role of the School Counselor." From *Guidance for Guidance: Readings in the Philosophy of Guidance,* edited by Carlton F. Beck. Dubuque, Iowa: W. C. Brown, 1966.

4. Grant, Bruce, George D. Demos, and Richard Oldenburg. *Improving Counseling: An Evaluative Instrument for Improving Counseling Centers.* Columbia, Missouri: Lucas Brothers, 1965.
Grossberg, Blythe, Asperger's Teens, ADA, 2014.

5. *Occupational Guide: School Counselor.* Southern California: State of California, Department of Employment, 1967.

6. Stewart, Lawrence H., and Charles F. Warnath. *The Counselor and Society: A Cultural Approach.* Boston: Houghton Mifflin, 1956.

7. *Student Personnel Programs in California Public Junior Colleges.* Sacramento, California: California Junior College Bureau, State Department of Education, 1959.

Chapter 7

THE COUNSELING RECORD

When the term "counseling record" is used in this text, it refers to what the counselor reports in writing concerning the one-to-one relationship. While this chapter is primarily concerned with the Counseling Record, attention is directed toward the Personal Data Form, the Cumulative Record, and *The California Pre-Counseling Self-Analysis Protocol Booklet.* (3)

Record-keeping has been the bane of many professional workers. Most lawyers, physicians, and counselors accept the fact that they must have a file on each client or patient. Fortunately for the lawyers and physicians, the bulk of their paperwork is processed by their clerical personnel. Unfortunately, too many counselors are confronted with doing much or all of the clerical work which accrues from the functions of the counselor.

One of the differences between counseling in a secondary school and a college is the massive amount of record-keeping which often is thrust upon the high school counselor. Frequently, he/she is expected to maintain a cumulative record for each student assigned to him/her that includes the recording of personal identification data, test results, as well as personal data. The college counselor usually faces only the reporting of interview data; however, even this task can be too time-consuming, particularly when it includes wordy discourses of doubtful value.

In this chapter the authors propose an approach to record-keeping which makes it possible to reduce counselor clerical work to an absolute minimum.

☞ *A Philosophy of Record-Keeping*

It is timely and pertinent to observe that educators need to sharpen their business acumen so that they will not commit the grievous error of having their professional workers doing clerical work. Whenever this mistake is not eliminated, an educational administrator is guilty of condoning a bad business practice.

What is jotted down, precisely noted, or extensively written in reference to the one-to-one relationship varies from counselor to counselor and from school district to school district.

" ...most counselors agree that it is necessary to keep some type of record regarding each counseling interview and related activities." (1, p. 322) However, they tend to operate from positions of extreme, ranging from almost no records at all to a massive accumulation of details. The latter deviation is illustrated in the following anecdote relating to all alleged differences between college undergraduate and graduate students. "A professor greeted his undergraduate class, 'Good morning, students.' Whereupon they replied, 'Good morning, Professor.' Later in the day he/she met with a class of graduate students, saying, 'Good afternoon, students.' Whereupon they wrote down what he said."

It is hoped that as the counselor becomes more and more of an expert in his/her profession, he/she will not feel compelled to write down more and more about his/her clients. Conversely, it is hoped that he/she doesn't reach the point at which he/she regards record-keeping as not being worthwhile.

The goal should be to achieve a workable compromise between the extremes. The authors lean more in the direction of brevity than length. Length usually results in verbosity, making too many entries, or filling a record with too many details and trivia. Our viewpoint has been conditioned by observations of how little most of the written record is ever used. Sometimes students have been asked to complete a personal data sheet containing many items which the counselor looks at superficially or ignores; in a few instances, lack of time prohibits him from even glancing at this form. Whatever records are kept, they should be organized in a manner conducive to easy recording and use.

Prior to dealing with the Counseling Records, a brief mention should be made of auxiliary records which the counselor may use.

☞ *Personal Data Form*

When the counselor wants a minimal amount of information about his/her client prior to the start of counseling, or after one interview when additional interviews are planned, a one-page structured form to be completed by the client often serves as a useful auxiliary to the Counseling Record.

Exhibit 1: *Personal Data Form,* is offered as a functional tool for the purpose described above. When more detailed facts are desired, or when the counselor wishes to obtain a history, *The California Pre-Counseling Self-Analysis Protocol Booklet* (3) is recommended. This rather frightening, verbose title might better be reduced to *Self-Analysis Inventory* or *Self-Understanding Instrument.* In addition to soliciting the usual identification information, it provides for obtaining a record of education, work history, background of experiences, needs, interests, talents, personality traits, goals, values, problems, and health. It is designed to be completed by the client, representing another time-saver for the counselor. In the obtaining of a history the counselor may use it as a structured organizer for getting diversified and extensive data concerning his/her client.

☞ *Cumulative Record*

The Cumulative Record has been widely used. Its extensive usage has been focused on the need for records to supply " ...a developmental picture of the individual." (2, p. 12) It is unfortunate that too frequently, it has been "more bother than good." The time required for filing items and making entries has led to the previously noted clerical yoke inflicted upon counselors.

When a Cumulative Record contains too much data, too many entries, or too many items filed in the folder, the counselor tends to be superficial in his examination or review of it; in some instances the location of a needed bit of information becomes too time-consuming or it even becomes "lost," as if it were misfiled.

To move in the direction of alleviating this difficulty, the authors have devised a Cumulative Record which is a radical departure from the ones now in use. Exhibit 2: *Cumulative Record,* shows this proposal.

This Cumulative Record may be filed in a regular file folder which serves as a container for the Cumulative Record, test booklets and answer sheets, test profiles, letters, and other accumulated data. It is recommended that the file folder be used as a custodian of items of data, rather than attempting to make it serve as a four-page recorder of information. This departure from usual practice means that the contents of the file do not have to be emptied onto the desk in order to read the entries or to make an entry; the irritation of having to cram a diversity of data into small spaces is eliminated; and the continuation of the structured folder beyond the point at which improvement is indicated, because it is too costly to abandon until all of the remaining folders have been used up, is no longer a problem.

A few identifying items are included, which may be completed by the student. Then, whenever a test is taken, the name of the test, the date and the test results can be recorded by a student assistant. However, the use of student assistants to do this recording always involves a possible violation of confidentiality and therefore raises a question regarding the ethics of such a practice. It is a difficult policy to defend, and since the school district seldom can supply the clerical employees necessary to record these data, the counselor usually is the person who must do this record-keeping.

To circumvent this difficulty, it is suggested that the client himself/herself record the names of the tests, dates, and results of tests at the time they are being interpreted to him by the counselor. If the test results are not going to be interpreted, then the tests should not be administered, unless the results are desired for administrative purposes to be used as an aid in determining homogeneous grouping, in which instances the recording of test results should be handled by the administrative staff or their clerical workers instead of by the counselor or anyone functioning in a guidance capacity. This proposal would free the counselor from clerical work in the interpretation of tests, which most secondary counselors should welcome with an enthusiasm appropriate to their being relieved of an irksome burden.

Whether or not the student or practitioner of counseling can bring himself/herself to accept this dramatic change in the concept of the Cumulative Record and its maintenance, it is proposed that some progress must be made in the direction of reduced record-keeping if counselors are to function as professionals.

When more data on the client are desired than the proposed Cumulative Record provides – that is, besides the items filed in the folder, together with the Cumulative Record – it is recommended that the counselor obtain a history of the client using an instrument such as *The California Pre-Counseling Self-Analysis Protocol Booklet.* (3)

For an elaborate presentation of the case for collecting and storing information about students, the reader is referred to Traxler's and North's text, *Techniques of Guidance,* (4) which also contains a fine exposition on cumulative records. After studying this text, the reader may decide to move quickly away from the philosophy of brevity being expounded in this chapter.

☞ *Counseling Record*

It is only logical that if the one-to-one relationship is the most important function of the counselor, there should be some kind of a record of what transpires in this relationship.

The counselor's record of his/her interview with a client has varied as much as the individual differences among counselors themselves. On the surface, there appears to be little objection to such variation. More profound, however, is the realization that unless some degree of uniformity in the recording of interviews is maintained by a counseling staff, there may be misinterpretations and resentment arising from too much diversification in writing up an interview.

When one counselor takes over or receives a colleague's client as a referral, the receiving counselor is entitled to know the background of the previous interviews – namely, the kind of counseling, the problems, and the actions taken. These data should be recorded succinctly and organized in a manner that permits very rapid assimilation by the receiving counselor.

It is most annoying for a receiving counselor to have to wade through excess verbiage in the sending counselor's record of interviews. In addition, the receiving counselor should not be subjected to the sending counselor's opinion "concerning" him/her in the corridor or giving them a verbose explanation of why the client is being referred, or a discourse on an allegedly important background, or an attempt to present a case history. Most secondary school counselors have to endure too much of this from teachers; certainly it should not be too much to expect their counseling colleagues to avoid this unnecessary infringement on the counselor's time. (See Figure 1.)

Figure 1
I Have Acquired the Following Skills

	Date/Initial	
Level I		**Career** (Look what's available to all.)
1.1	____/____	I am familiar with the resources available in the Advisement Center.
1.2	____/____	I know how to use career exploration materials.
1.3	____/____	I can list community and school employment resources.
		Education (What's happening now?)
1.4	____/____	I know the school facilities and location of all resources.
1.5	____/____	I am familiar with the high school graduation requirements.
1.6	____/____	I can explain good study skills.
1.7	____/____	I have a high school plan.
1.8	____/____	I have discussed my progress report with my advisor and my parents.
	____/____	_____
	_____	_____
	_____	_____
	_____	_____

Leisure (Free time fun!)

1.9 ____/____ I can list some leisure activities available to me out of school.

1.10 ____/____ I can list some leisure activities available to me in school.

Personal/Social (Who am I? How do I fit in?)

1.11 ____/____ I have contributed as a member of my group.

1.12 ____/____ I have identified my social interests.

1.13 ____/____ I have recognized friendship skills in myself and others.

Level II		**Career** (Looking to the future!)

2.1 ____/____ I can name some occupations that reflect my work values and interests.

2.2 ____/____ I can demonstrate decision-making skills.

2.3 ____/____ I have my work permit and social security card # _____.

2.4 ____/____ I know the requirements for Work Experience and CROP.

2.5 ____/____ My work experiences are: _____

Education (How am I doing in school?)

2.6 ____/____ I can list my academic strengths: _____

2.7 ____/____ I have reviewed my educational goal(s) and have re-evaluated my plans.

2.8 ____/____ I have discussed my progress report with my advisor and my parents.

____/____ _____

____ ____ _____

____ ____ _____

____ ____ _____

Leisure (Look how I spend my time.)

2.9 ____/____ I participate in out-of-school activities that match my leisure interests.

2.10 _____/_____ I participate in school activities that match my leisure interests.

Personal/Social (I see how I am with other people.)

2.11 _____/_____ I have learned skills to change my behavior(s):

2.12 _____/_____ I know how groups function and how I communicate in them.

| Level III | **Career** (Creating my future) |

3.1 _____/_____ My career plans are:

3.2 _____/_____ I understand my skills and strengths as they relate to my career goal.

Education

3.3 _____/_____ I have selected courses that are consistent with my career goal.

3.4 _____/_____ My work experiences are:_____

3.5 _____/_____ I have re-evaluated my high school plan, keeping in mind the graduation requirements and my career plans.

3.6 _____/_____ I have a post high school plan.

3.7 _____/_____ I have discussed my progress report with my advisor and my parents.

_____/_____ _____

_____ _____

_____ _____

_____ _____

Leisure (It's fun: It's recreation)

3.8 _____/_____ I select activities that reflect my skills.

3.9 _____/_____ I participate in recreational activities in school
Out of school_____

Personal/Social (Sharing who I am!)

3.10 _____/_____ I have skills for participating in a group.

3.11 _____/_____ I can listen to myself and to others.

Level IV		**Career** (Preparing myself for the future.)
4.1	_____/_____	I have had an experience outside of school that relates to my career goal.
4.2	_____/_____	I have identified ways to prepare myself for my occupational goal.
4.3	_____/_____	My work experiences are:_____
		Education (What's next?)
4.4	_____/_____	After high school I will
4.5	_____/_____	I've taken action on my best high school plan.
4.6	_____/_____	I have re-evaluated my 4-year plan to meet all graduate requirements.
4.7	_____/_____	I have discussed my progress report with my advisor and my parents.
	_____/_____	_____
	_____	_____
		Leisure (Do it for life!)
4.8	_____/_____	I participate in recreational activities: In school:
4.9	_____/_____	I understand the value of leisure and how it relates to life-long sharing.
		Personal/Social (I know I am the best I can be!)
4.10	_____/_____	I can identify social groups that match my personality and goals.
4.11	_____/_____	I know my personal interests and how to pursue them.

References. Before you put a person's name here, you should ask him/her if it's O.K. You are encouraged to get these people to write a letter of recommendation for you and keep it in this folder.

Name   *Address*

_____   _____

_____   _____

_____   _____

Surveys/Inventories/Tests

Date	Name of Instrument	Comments/Results	Initial
_____ /	Proficiency Test: HBUMS District	/ Fr._____	/_____
_____ /	_____	/_____	/_____
_____ /	Aptitude Tests: CAPS, ASVAB, CATB	/_____	/_____
_____ /	_____	/_____	/_____
_____ /	_____	/_____	/_____
_____ /	HBUMS Career Planning Survey	/_____	/_____
_____ /	Interest Inventory: Syper's work	/_____	/_____
_____ /	Inventory, JOB-O, Kuder, COPS, SOS	/_____	/_____
_____ /	_____	/_____	/_____
_____ /	_____	/_____	/_____
_____ /	_____	/_____	/_____

Conferences I Have Had That Are Important to Me

Date	Participant(s)	Recommendation:
_____ /	_____	/_____
_____ /	_____	/_____
_____ /	_____	/_____
_____ /	_____	/_____
_____ /	_____	/_____
_____ /	_____	/_____
_____ /	_____	/_____
_____ /	_____	/_____
_____ /	_____	/_____
_____ /	_____	/_____

My Summary of My Year: You are encouraged to take a close look at yourself and the skills and experiences you have gained during the year. Look your folder over carefully *before* you write your comments. *Be sure* to give your impressions and your feelings of this year. You may ask your advisor to add a comment.

Year I

My Comments: _____

_____

_____

_____

_____

_____

_____

Advisor's Comments: _____
_____
_____
_____

Year II

My Comments: _____
_____
_____
_____
_____
_____
_____

Advisor's Comments: _____
_____
_____
_____

Year III

My Comments: _____
_____
_____
_____
_____
_____

Advisor's Comments: _____
_____
_____

Year IV

My Comments: _____

_____

_____

_____

_____

_____

_____

Advisor's Comments: _____

_____

_____

Other Comments: _____

_____

_____

_____

_____

_____

_____

_____

Chapter 8

REFERRALS

A referral is the action a counselor takes when he/she sends his/ her client (or potential client) to another individual or agency. The rationale of referring has its basis in ethics. This point was introduced in the previous chapter dealing with the ethics of counseling.

There are many individuals and agencies for the counselor to use in making referrals. Each professional should have at his fingertips a comprehensive list of referrals.

It is just as important for a counselor to select the appropriate referral as it is for him to choose wisely the action to be taken in helping those clients he/she retains. This means that more than a cursory glance at a list of referrals is required, as the counselor should know something about the individuals and agencies before he/she refers clients to them.

Careful discrimination should be exercised in choosing the most appropriate specialist among specialists. For example, when a physician is deciding to which surgeon he/she should refer his/her patient, an attempt should be made to choose (in addition to the appropriate specialist for the particular surgery required) a surgeon whose personality will blend with the patient's; the importance of this is manifested in the psychological factors involved in the preoperative and postoperative relationships of surgeon and patient.

☞ Who Receives Referrals?

To receive referrals, one or more conditions must usually be met. A specialist, whether in counseling, medicine, or law, needs to gain recognition among his/her colleagues, other professionals, and from the general public. It is imperative that he/she create an image of being a top man in his/her specialty.

Individuals who are considering making a referral need to feel assured that the professional to whom the referral is made is highly competent. "Referrals to the counselor will depend in large part upon the amount of confidence held in the counselors by the people who refer." (3, p. 241)

Teachers often make referrals to a particular counselor in the school's counseling office. While in some instances this may be the perpetuation of a habit, or one "old-timer" relating to another veteran, it also indicates that the teacher is referring to the counselor in whom he has the most confidence.

Since most of the counselors in secondary schools are counseling generalists rather than specialists, and since most referrals are from teachers, the counseling center must acquire a reputation among the teachers as being able to help students in all of the three areas of guidance: educational, career, and personal-social. In addition, teachers must believe that the counseling center will make referrals when referrals are necessary.

Counselors in private practice – as is true with lawyers and physicians – are not permitted by the ethics of their profession to advertise their services. In fact, one of the alleged marks of the "quack" is advertising. Because of this limitation imposed upon the professional practitioner, he/she must seek other ways of projecting himself/herself into public awareness so that people will know about him and solicit his/her help. The following techniques are offered as aids to the private practitioner as means of establishing and maintaining his practice.

1. As a counselor intern, socializing with other interns who are going to specialize in different areas.

2. Membership in professional organizations, supplemented by participation in the activities of these organizations.

3. Joining community organizations and participating in one or more of their projects.

4. Socializing with members of the other related professions.

5. Contacting, by letter, members of the other related professions, explaining the service offered and inviting referrals.

6. Speaking to civic, community, professional, and other organizations on topics related to the professional service offered.

7. Teaching a college course in one's specialty.

8. Making referrals to members of the other related professions.

9. Publishing books, articles, tests, etc., in one's specialty.

10. Serving as a consultant.

Obviously, the school counselor, particularly the high school counselor, does not have to be concerned as does the private practitioner about receiving sufficient referrals to keep busy – quite the contrary. It would be an ego-reinforcing factor, however, if the high school counselor could reach a level of professional effectiveness at which he/she could know that his/her clients use his/her services because they have confidence in his/her professional competency and accept him/her as a person worthy of their request for help.

A much-neglected aspect of referrals is those which could and should be made within the professional staff of one counseling center. Each counselor on the staff will usually be stronger and more experienced or knowledgeable in one or another of the areas of counseling; those without specializations should be listed as "generalists," with a comment regarding the type of cases they feel most competent in handling.

Every counseling center should consider having one or more "intake counselors" who see each new client briefly to determine the nature of the problem so that the client can then be assigned to the counselor most competent to help with this particular problem. In some cases, the disposition or resolution of the difficulty may be accomplished in the intake interview, in which instance no referral occurs, and the case is ended with the one interview.

After the intake counselor refers, the receiving counselor may not feel he/she is the most appropriate counselor for this particular client after all; if so, he/she then refers to still another counselor. Also, whenever the receiving counselor makes a judgment that one or more of the "when-to-refer criteria" applies, he/she would then make another referral.

"Effective interprofessional referrals typically involve mutual understanding and mutual respect." (1, p. 321)

☞ *When to Refer*

As we stated in Chapter 4, on the ethics of counseling (page 25), the time that a referral should be made is just as soon as the counselor realizes that he should refer. The program of counselor education and its resultant sharpening by experience are the necessary ingredients basic to making the time of "realization" occur when it should.

It is helpful for the counselor to have specific criteria to aid him/her in knowing when he/she should refer. A careful study of the ten points given in the chapter on the ethics of counseling, together with the other comments made there concerning referring (see pages 142–152), is pertinent at this time. Each of these factors is self-explanatory on the wisdom of referring whenever one or more of these criteria are met.

Reaves and Reaves offer another set of criteria regarding when to refer. They suggest that:

… the following counseling situations, among others that exist, demand prompt referral to the physician, psychologist, or psychiatrist, and/or appropriate consulting agencies:

1.   Unusual patterns of physical growth.

2.   Persons who have bodily complaints or exhibit physical signs suggestive of disease.

3. Behavioral disturbance with coexistent history of seizure or head trauma.

4. Incapacitating psychoneurosis. Suicidal ideation.

5. Personality disorders such as sexual deviation, marked withdrawal, paranoid reactions, addiction.

6. Suspicion of mental deficiency or organic disease.

7. Psychotic disorders.

8. Situational reactions that do not respond to normal counseling techniques.

9. The person whose diagnosis and/or treatment plan is in doubt. (5)

☞ *Referral Sources*

There are many excellent professional, civic, community, and lay organizations offering a diversity of services. Lists of these organizations are presented in this section, with the following caution: The counselor should know something about the individuals and agencies before he/she blithely refers from his/her list.

Certain organizations are noted first as being of paramount importance to the counselor. No intent of an adverse rating is either meant or implied for those organizations not singled out for this special mention.

1. State Employment Service

2. Veterans Administration

   The Veterans Administration program has perhaps done more to spur interest, research, and diversification in broad areas of counseling work than any other influence. (2)

3. Family Service

4. Catholic Welfare Bureau

5. Jewish Family Service

6. Bureau of Vocational Rehabilitation

7. College(s)

8. Child Guidance Clinic

> The Child Guidance Clinic is probably the best-known type of clinic in American communities today ... (It) is therapeutic in its design, emphasizes psychotherapeutic treatment concepts, and works exclusively with children having problems too 'deep' to be handled by the 'guidance services' in the schools. (3, p. 384)

When a counselor is in a metropolitan area with many organizations and services, sometimes a referral guide is available which provides a comprehensive listing. As an example, a partial listing of the multiple organizations and services existing in the greater Long Beach, California, area is given below.

1. Catholic Welfare Bureau

2. Family Service

3. Jewish Family Service

4. Juvenile Bureau

5. County Department of Charities, Bureau of Public Assistance

6. Bureau of Vocational Rehabilitation

7. County Probation Department (6)

Peters and Farwell present a comprehensive list of community resources which they obtained from John G. Odgers, Director, Division of Guidance and Testing, Ohio State Department of Education.

1. Parent-Teachers' Association

2. Adult Education Association

3. Service Clubs: Rotary, Kiwanis, Future Farmers of America, Lions, Altrusa, etc.

4. Professional Clubs and Associations

5. Chamber of Commerce: Junior and Senior

6. Labor Organizations and Employee Organizations

7. Private Vocational Schools and Institutions of Higher Learning

8. The Public Library: Occupational Information

9. Churches of the Community

10. YMCA, YWCA, K of C, YMHA, etc.

11. The Juvenile Courts and Courts of Domestic Relations

12. Public Hospitals, Clinics, and Other Medical Agencies

13. Guidance of Mental Hygiene Clinic (Public or Private)

14. Public Relief or Welfare Organizations

15. Public Employment Service

16. Employees of the Community

17. Public Schools (4, pp. 462–463)

There are also referral sources for emotionally disturbed students:

1. American Red Cross

2. Boy and Girl Scouts

3. County Child Welfare Boards

4. Juvenile Courts

5. State Division of Mental Health

6. Treatment service for psychotic children at the nearest mental health clinic (4, pp. 466–467)

A partial list of organizations serving physically handicapped children:

1. International Association of Lions Clubs

2. Kiwanis International

3. Rotary International

4. Shriners of North America

5. Benevolent and Protective Order of Elks

6. National Foundation for Infantile Paralysis

7. Cerebral Palsy Treatment Centers (4, pp. 468–469)

We might add some other organizations and services:

1. Child Welfare Service

2. Department of Industrial Relations, Division of Apprentice Standards

3. Welfare Information Service

4. Aid to Dependent Children

5. Salvation Army

6. Free Clinic

☞ *Limitations of Referral Sources*

After perusing the foregoing lists of referral sources, the reader may now be experiencing illusions regarding the uses he/she intends to make of these services. Unfortunately, in many instances, utilization is restricted by one or more of the following factors:

1. Long waiting lists: Some mental health clinics have a waiting list of several months.

2. Cost of services: Even if the fee for service is only $5.00 or $2.00 (in terms of what the client could be expected to pay), this sometimes deters the individual from utilizing the service.

3. Few agencies available: In the rural areas the number of agencies available often is minimal.

4. Lack of competent personnel: No matter how well-intentioned an individual may be, if he/she is not trained to do the job he/she is performing, clients usually cannot receive the professional help they are seeking.

☞ References

1. Callis, Robert, Edward Roeber, and Paul C. Polmantier. *A Casebook of Counseling.* New York: Appleton-Century Crofts, 1955.
2. Long, Louis. "The V. A. Guidance Program: An Evaluation." *Personnel and Guidance Journal,* November 1952, pp. 104–107.
3. Moser, Leslie E., and Ruth Small Moser. *Counseling and Guidance: An Exploration.* Englewood Cliffs, New Jersey: Prentice-Hall, 1963.
4. Peters, Herman J., and Gail F. Farwell. *Guidance: A Developmental Approach.* Chicago: Rand McNally, 1959.
5. Reaves, Gayle Clark, and Leonard E. Reaves, III. "The Counselor and Preventive Psychiatry." *Personnel and Guidance Journal,* March 1965, pp. 661–664.

☞ Suggested Additional Readings

American School Counselor Association. "The Role of the Secondary School Counselor." *School Counselor* 24, no. 4 (1977), pp. 228–234.

_____. "The Unique Role of the Middle/Junior High School Counselor." *Elementary School Guidance and Counseling* 12, no. 3 (1978), pp. 203–205.

_____. "The Unique Role of the Elementary School Counselor." *Elementary School Guidance and Counseling* 12, no. 3 (1978), pp. 200–202.

Carlson, Joe & Glasser, William, Consulting With Teachers, APA, 2014.

Capuzzi, Dave. "From the Editor's Desk." *School Counselor* 28, no. 3 (1981), pp. 158–159.

Counselor's Guide to Jobs – Careers for Young People 16–24. Welfare Information Service, Inc., Los Angeles, 1966.

Foster, Charles R., Paul W. Fitzgerald and Rubye M. Beal. *Modern Guidance Practices in Teaching.* Springfield, Illinois: Charles C. Thomas, 1980.

Goldman, Leo, Marguerite R. (Peg) Carroll, Louise B. Forsyth, James Muro, and Franklyn A. Graff. "How Are We Doing in School Guidance? The Moody Colloquium." *School Counselor* 25, no. 5 (1978), pp. 307–325.

Goodyear, Rodney K. "Counselors as Community Psychologists." *Personnel and Guidance Journal* 54, no. 10 (1976), pp. 512–516.

Herr, Edwin L. *Guidance and Counseling in the Schools: The Past, Present, and Future.* Falls Church, Virginia: American Personnel and Guidance Association, 1979.

Hoyt, Kenneth B. *An Introduction to Career Education.* Washington, D.C.: U.S. Government Printing Office, 1975.

Lewis, Judith A., and Michael D. Lewis. *Community Counseling: A Human Services Approach.* New York: John Wiley and Sons, 1977.

Mann, Philip A. *Community Psychology.* New York: The Free Press, 1978.

McComb, Bette. "Guest Editor's Introduction." *Elementary School Guidance and Counseling* 15, no. 3 (1981), pp. 180–181.

Miller, Frank W., James Fruehling, and Gloria J. Lewis. *Guidance Principles and Services.* 3ʳᵈ ed. Columbus, Ohio: Charles E. Merrill, 1978.

Miller, Theodore K., and Judity S. Prince. *The Future of Student Affairs.* San Francisco: Jossey-Bass, 1976.

Ostroth, D. David. "Competencies for Entry-level Professionals: What Do Employers Look for When Hiring New Staff?" *Journal of College Student Personnel* 22, no. 1 (1981) pp. 5–11.

Packwood, William T., ed. *College Student Personnel Services.* Springfield, Illinois: Charles C. Thomas, 1977.

Pietrofesa, John J., Bianca Bernstain, Jo Anne Minor, and Susan Stanford. *Guidance: An Introduction.* Chicago: Rand McNally, 1980.

Rappaport, Julian. *Community Psychology.* New York: Holt, Rinehart and Winston, 1977.

Ross, Robert R., and Paul Gendreau, eds. *Effective Correctional Treatment.* Toronto: Butterworth and Company, 1980.

Shertzer, Bruce, and Shelley C. Stone. *Fundamentals of Guidance*. 4th ed. Boston: Houghton Mifflin, 1981.

Stamm, Martin L., and Blossom S. Nissman. *Improving Middle School Guidance*. Boston: Allyn and Bacon, 1979.

Walz, Garry R., and Libby Benjamin, eds. *New Imperatives for Guidance*. Ann Arbor, Michigan: ERIC Counseling and Personnel Services Clearinghouse, 1978.

Chapter 9

GROUP ACTIVITIES

Group guidance occurs whenever a counselor or other guidance worker is assisting a group of individuals in making wise choices and adjustments.

The rationale for a counselor, the expert in the "one-to-one" situation, engaging in a group activity has been discussed in *Chapter 2, Counseling and Group Guidance,* under the headings of "An Interpretation of Group Guidance," "When Not to Utilize Group Guidance," and "When to Utilize Group Guidance." A careful review of that chapter at this time would be pertinent, prior to reading this chapter. In addition, an extensive sampling of the sources listed in the additional reading list at the end of this chapter is recommended for those students and practitioners who plan to use group procedures frequently. It would be wise for these individuals to take sufficient formal courses to attain that degree of sophistication and competency needed for making group practices yield the desired outcomes, within the framework of the counselor's philosophy.

Kemp's book of readings, *Perspectives on the Group Process: A Foundation for Counseling with Groups,* (9) offers an interdisciplinary approach to the functioning of groups, with fifty specialists dealing with group activity and relating it to biology, philosophy, religion, psychology, personal adjustment, group dynamics, and leadership.

The interest of the general public in group activity is apparent in the appearance in the *Los Angeles Times* of an article entitled, "The Great 'Group' Binge." (7) This report touches on some of the group innovations: marathon, sensitivity training, leadership training, human potential workshop, human relations workshop, basic encounter group, management development, Synanon games club, and transactional analysis.

Beckley indicates that group guidance (which he refers to as "group counseling") " ...applies the principles of group dynamics in group discussion, which means that most of the discussion, suggestions, questions, advice, and information come from the counselees." (2) The most basic of these principles are, as listed by Beckley:

1. Group counseling should be conducted by an experienced counselor with a good understanding of group dynamics.

2. Participants should be selected from individual counseling cases. The nature and advantages of group counseling should be explained to them, so that they know what is expected of them.

3. Participation should be voluntary.

4. Homogeneity, with respect to age, educational background, economic status, and similarity of problem is desirable.

5. Sessions should be approximately 1 hour in length.

6. There should be no more than 12 counselees in the group.

7. Group counseling sessions followed by at least one individual counseling session with each participant seem to be most beneficial and produce more lasting results.

It is worth repeating, and it must be constantly borne in mind, that it is the welfare of each member of the group that justifies the existence of the group. If and when "the group" supersedes the welfare of any individual or all individuals in the group, it should be abandoned.

☞ Group Procedures

What an individual gets out of being in a group situation is entirely dependent upon what he/she puts into it. However, what he/she assimilates from the other members of the group and the counselor, and the extent to which the resolution of his/her problem is aided, is also determined by the particular type of group methodology used by the counselor.

Sophistication in group methodology is basic if the counselor is to choose wisely the most appropriate procedures for aiding each individual in the solving of his/her problem in the group setting. An exhaustive treatment of group methodology and the pursuit of the attainment of competency in group skills is the objective of courses and texts devoted to group guidance. For our purposes, a cursory notation of some of the procedures should serve as a springboard in motivating those counselors who intend to make significant use of group guidance to proceed with the formal education needed to qualify themselves as experts in group activities.

One of the reasons that teaching in a regular classroom situation serves as an excellent background for counseling is the obvious experiential contribution the group work of teaching makes to the group activities which may be used by the counselor.

The literature on group guidance abounds with statements relative to group guidance procedures. Prior to focusing attention briefly on some of these, Beckley's presentation of procedures designed to enhance the effectiveness of the group guidance session should be noted:

1. Reiterate the purpose of group counseling at the first session, even though it was previously stated in the individual counseling session.

2. Remind the participants that whatever benefits they derive from group counseling will largely depend upon how deeply they invest in it.

3. Ask each member to identify himself/herself.

4. Start the session by asking a general question applicable to all members of the group. For example, "What do you feel is the greatest obstacle keeping you from securing suitable employment?"

5. Use the different personality types, of which the group is composed, to advantage. For example, the argumentative individual can be used to provoke discussion; the poor speaker to slow the tempo of verbal exchanges; the volatile person to stimulate controversy; and the logical individual to clarify issues.

6. The counselor must not only assess the personality types of which the group is composed, he/she must also become keenly aware of: (a) what is said, (b) the manner in which it is said, (c) at what point, (d) by whom, and (e) what purpose it seems to serve.

7. Once the counselor has become sensitized to the overtones, the undertones, the implications of the group discussion, he can engage in group building and maintenance tasks by: (a) encouraging participation – by being warm and responsive; (b) mediating – by being conciliatory, helping to effect compromises and establishing harmony; (c) following – by going along with the group; (d) gate-tending – by insuring that everyone gets a chance to express himself; (e) relieving tension – by jesting. (2)

In an additional elaboration of the foregoing, Beckley points out six group task functions for the counselor:

1. Initiating – suggesting different ways of viewing the problem under discussion.

2. Clarifying – probing for meaning or common understanding.

3. Elaborating – expanding upon ideas already expressed.

4. Coordinating – clarifying relationships or pulling ideas together.

5. Testing – checking the group to see if a consensus exists.

6. Summarizing – reviewing the previous discussion and verbally charting the progress achieved.

Organizational Units for Group Guidance. The counselor's conference room, assuming it is large enough to accommodate up to a dozen people in comfortable chairs – either around a conference table or away from the table in an informal circle – is an excellent place for the counselor to conduct group activities. This room should be in the counseling center, and there should be more than one such room if the number of counselors using it makes additional space necessary.

The counselor's office may be used for small groups of two to four, unless the office is too small.

If group guidance is being presented as a curricular offering, either in the form of a group guidance course or as a unit in a subject other than guidance, the classroom serves as the logical meeting place. It is essential that a classroom with movable desk-chairs be used to permit informal groupings (e.g., a large circle for the entire group or small circles for several small groups).

If a large number of students is being met by a counselor, as so often occurs in an orientation session, then the auditorium, gymnasium, or a theater-like room is necessary to accommodate everyone. This type of unit should seldom, if ever, be used unless it is soon followed by dividing the huge group into small groups for meetings with counselors.

Activities Which May Be Used as Vehicles of Group Procedures. The previously mentioned orientation session is one of the activities which may be provided for incoming students such as freshmen and transfer students. It may consist of an Orientation Day or Week; sometimes it occurs as a one-hour session.

College Day or Night – nearby four-year colleges are invited to send their representatives to meet with those high school students who indicate an interest in a particular college. This should be extended to include two-year junior or community colleges, technical, trade, business, and special schools. It may be further expanded to involve union representatives, in cooperation with trade school officials, in a combined program of information on apprenticeship programs as they can be integrated with formal school training.

The Career Day or Career Conference may be utilized to bring executives, professional men, tradesmen, clerical workers, or other occupational representatives into the school for a series of meetings with students who are exploring industries, companies, and occupations.

The field trip can inject realism into career guidance by going to industries and companies to study the world of work, and to observe and interview executives and workers in selected occupations.

Methods Which May Be Used. In addition to the methods of discussion, contrived experience, marathon, brainstorming, and group dynamics (which are touched upon briefly in subsequent sections of this chapter), there are several other methods in which the counselor who plans to practice group guidance should be adept.

The lecture-listen method, with the counselor doing the talking and the students doing the listening, has its value in certain situations. In spite of the many criticisms it has received from a variety of opponents, lecturing, even for a counselor, has a place in the presentation of facts which do not need interpretation, elaboration, or discussion, and which are usually so self-explanatory that questions are not forthcoming after the data are given. For example, suppose 300 high school seniors want to know what the deadline is for applying for admission to "X" College, "Y" College, etc.

Closely related to the lecture-listen method is the *question-answer* method. This serves well in groups of any size in which the members of the group have a common curiosity in a particular area and are seeking information or interpretation of facts. For example, this method might be used alone or in combination with the lecture-listen method by a senior high school counselor meeting with the graduating class of a junior high school. Giving the students the opportunity to ask questions helps to avoid the error of omitting comment on those items of most interest or urgency to the students.

In both of the above methods, each student who so desires should have the opportunity of seeing the counselor in the one-to-one situation.

Committee work, with each member accepting the responsibility of obtaining something or doing something which may be reported or given to the committee, is a useful adjunct to other methods. For example, those high school students who express the need for sharing experiences derived from visiting colleges, business schools, etc., could meet as a group to decide what each member should investigate, how to correlate the findings of the committee members, what to do with the data obtained, etc.

Discussion. One of the most widely used group-guidance methods is the discussion.

> The primary goal of the counseling group is the creation of an interpersonal helping climate (counseling atmosphere) which will allow each individual to develop insight into himself/herself and to achieve healthier personal adjustment. The vehicle for accomplishing this goal is the discussion of personal concerns at an affective level. (3)

As used herein, the term "discussion" means declaring considerations pro and con. In addition to the concept expressed in the quotation above, discussion consists of the verbal interactions of individuals dealing with an issue, a problem, or alternative decisions.

It is absurd to gather together a group of individuals to "discuss" questions which demand a factual response without any deviation. For example: "What is a GPA (grade point average)?" "What are the entrance requirements of 'X' College?"

In these questions there is nothing to discuss. The task is to obtain the information required to answer the question. Offering pros and cons, arguments, etc., about what a GPA is borders on the ridiculous.

Examples of discussion questions are: "Who should go to college?" "Should the MBA (master of business administration) be obtained prior to the onset of one's career or while working?"

One of the most effective ways of implementing a discussion (once the appropriate topic has been chosen) is to utilize the small group of four to eight persons. This size facilitates verbalizing by each member of the group, encourages a social intimacy in the interaction of group members, and stimulates each individual to participate. Small groups are easy to form. They lend themselves readily to a variety of situations, problems, and issues.

For many years, residents of fraternity houses, sorority houses, and college dormitories have had informal gatherings of small groups of students with common interests and mutual problems who need to verbalize with their peers. In this setting has emerged " ...the bull session, in which a group of students talk about any- and everything that is important to them." (6, p. 32)

For any kind of a discussion to be effective it is necessary that each individual in the group use a vocabulary that is meaningful to the others. The group members must communicate.

"If you are transferring your thoughts to others, you are communicating. However, *communicating* includes the implication of making your thoughts known to others. This is the hurdle that too often many persons fail to surmount in communicating." (5)

The major causes of faulty communication in the usual forms of verbal exchange are making semantic errors, speaking technique errors, listening errors, and psychological errors, as the authors have stated in the article quoted above. This article also points out techniques for eliminating these errors, and offers "two guiding principles for your consideration in seeking the improvement of communication techniques or skills:

1. Talk less; listen more.

2. Listen as if you were going to be required to respond verbatim to whatever is being said."

The counselor's role in the discussion group is to serve as the discussion leader, to delegate leadership to a group member, or "to throw the group on its own" without a leader. He/she serves as the expert on the group's rationale for discussing whatever subjects they have gathered together to discuss; he/she is available as a source of data, a mirror for feedback of emotions, a clarifier and a helper in whatever ways the group solicits assistance.

Contrived Experience. Whenever a group is unable to engage in a "real experience" in order to derive those insights necessary to making decisions, the contrived experience often serves as the next best approach.

"A contrived experience consists of a situation simulating reality in which you participate in the attempt to grasp the meaning of the reality without actually having to experience it." (6, p. 30)

For example, a group of college students who have been verbalizing the pros and cons of drinking in dormitories, fraternity, and sorority houses, decides to conduct a controlled experiment for a semester with certain houses permitting drinking on the premises and others forbidding drinking. Assume that this research is not permitted by the college officials. As a substitute, the group elects to observe the simulated experiences of dormitory drinking and the simulated results of the drinking.

A form of simulated experience that has considerable value as a learning technique, even though it primarily has been utilized as a therapeutic technique, is psychodrama or role-playing. "Role-taking is the basis for communication; it is the ability to take the position of another, understand his point of view, and see oneself as others do." (10, p. 89)

As the term "psychodrama" is used here within the frame of reference of "learning technique," it may be defined as role-playing of two or more individuals in which the persons involved are given a situation and "parts" to play, without any scripts or memorization of lines; the emphasis must be on the individuals, not on the group.

A high school student faced with the problem of how to apply for a job may well profit from playing the role of job applicant while another student, with the same problem, is playing the role of the employer; then the students may reverse their roles. Other students may observe the role-playing, and at its conclusion, the observers and role-players may join in an evaluative discussion, followed by other students taking the same parts.

A group may be discussing LSD when an individual suggests that the only way "to know it" is "to use it." Obviously, while direct experience might be a most effective teacher concerning the hazards involved in taking LSD, direct experience should no more be used in this situation than one should drive 100 miles per hour on thin tires until a blowout occurs to determine how to come out of such a situation alive. However, through contrived experience in the vehicle of psychodrama, individuals who have studied the effects of LSD can play the roles of LSD users for the observation of other group members. This again serves as a springboard for returning to a discussion of what was simulated by the participants in the role-playing.

The authors have used psychodrama over a period of years with gratifying results. Students enjoy it; zest and enthusiasm for learning often are noteworthy by-products of the role-playing technique.

Marathon. One of the innovations in group activity that has emerged in recent years is the marathon method, which consists of members of the group meeting for many hours or even days. Its usage as a method has been almost exclusively within the framework of therapy.

Bach points out, "like all effective group psychotherapeutic programs, the *Marathon* is a group practicum in intimate, authentic human interaction." (1) He notes that his " ...*Marathon* group therapy retreats take place in a private setting where a selected group of 10 to 14 participants can stay together for 2, 3, or 4 days."

Certainly, a group whose purpose for existence consists in contributing to the self-understanding of each member, without any psychotherapy either being included or desired, may utilize the marathon.

Individuals with the common purpose of wanting to understand their behavior, the real-life roles they play, and the rationale for their responses in a variety of situations over a prolonged period of group interaction should spend a weekend or longer together in pursuit of these "learning" goals, the actualization of which could be enhanced by the use of group dynamics (discussed in the next section of this chapter).

One of the authors presented a paper (4) on the marathon, which, while it was within the confines of marathon therapy, contains a concluding paragraph that may be transferred to the concept of the marathon as a learning method rather than a therapeutic one.

"The marathon can indeed be an *awakening* experience and one must experience it to understand its increasing potential as a therapeutic (learning) modality. I urge all of you in the helping professions to explore the potential of this new 'awakening' approach. Its possibilities appear enormous." (4, p. 18)

It is apparent that the marathon method of learning does not readily lend itself to use by student groups below the college level. Even with college students or adults there are difficulties to surmount in the organization and administration of an activity of this nature. An individual should never be required, coerced, or even subtly maneuvered into participating in a marathon. He needs to have a felt need, coupled with an intense motivation, for this type of learning prior to experiencing it.

Brainstorming. One of the criticisms of group activity has been the stifling of the participation by individuals who are sensitive to criticism or resent evaluation.

In brainstorming, each member of the group is encouraged to verbalize about any idea that "pops into his head," regardless of whether it appears to have merit or not. "Off the top of one's head," spontaneity in presenting ideas, solutions to problems, alternate solutions, suggestions, plans, and decisions, are the "modus operandi" in brainstorming with no evaluation of any kind being done by any member of the group, including the counselor.

This type of approach to attacking problems encourages a diversity of ideas and a freedom of expression unhampered by any form of criticism or appraisal. There is a dismantling of the shackles of conformity in approaching problems in an atmosphere which is conducive to creativity, exploration, and ingenuity.

Members of the group must be mature and intelligent enough not to integrate into their lives any of the expressed ideas without examining them in terms of reality and common sense criteria. In short, while evaluation is ruled out of the brainstorming session, it should be introduced later in another type of group session or by individuals.

For example, if in the brainstorming session a group member proposes the use of LSD to escape the adverse vicissitudes resulting from life's traumatic happenings, there should be no criticism, negative reaction, or any appraisal of the worth of this idea. But, after the group finishes the session in which this proposal was made, each individual in the group should accept and act upon his or her responsibility for evaluating the wisdom of the idea.

There is, of course, a danger that individuals who fear peer disapproval for failure to accept a "far-out" idea, or who are overly susceptible to suggestion, anxious to try anything, or who abide by the "non-conformity code" as an expression of adolescent rebellion against adults or authority, will not make the wisest choice in terms of accepting or rejecting ideas proposed in brainstorming.

Group Dynamics. For many years, the literature has included information about group dynamics. One of the by-products of these reports has been confusion regarding the meaning of the term, with the implication being that it is a group method – as, for example, discussion. In a sense it is, just as the marathon identifies a type of group activity. Primarily, group dynamics is the study of the responses of the individuals in a group in order to ascertain the behavior role of each individual. This study may be made by the counselor, or it may be done by the members of the group.

By learning the behavior role or roles in which he/she engages during his/her interactions with the other members of the group, each individual is aided in the process of self-understanding. Ingils (8) states that many educators have assumed that the process known as group dynamics is one of the best means of developing interaction between individuals. Regardless of the extent and quality of the interaction resulting from group dynamics, this is secondary to the determination of the behavior role or roles of each group member.

One type of study which emerged as a form of group dynamics is the sensitivity training group or the "T-Group" (training group). "The idea was developed after World War II by social psychologist Kurt Lewin, whose experimental work in 'group dynamics' convinced him that no amount of telling people what to do could compare with the results when people 'discover' things for themselves." (7)

The use of "sensitivity" has been applied loosely and with considerable deviation in interpretation, but in general it refers to a group process designed to assist each individual in acquiring or enriching his receptivity to the needs, concerns, problems, feelings, and thoughts of others. As each person achieves more skill in receiving behavioral clues which facilitate his understanding of others, he in theory may transfer this insight into his perception of his own reactions, leading to an enriched self-understanding.

Studying the roles of the members of the group affords each individual the opportunity of relating the responses of the others to self and the reactions of self to the others. He/she is aided by the others in seeing himself/herself as others see him/her. His/her self-concept may be incompatible with the image he/she projects to other group members. When he/she becomes aware of this, he/she is in a position to better understand the reactions his behavior incites in others.

☞ *Some Key Types for Identifying Counselor Behavior Roles*

1. **Harmonizer:** agrees with group; brings together opposite points of view

2. **Encourager:** friendly; responsive to others; supports others

3. **Clarifier:** restates problem; interprets; brings late or new members up-to-date

4. **Initiator:** suggests problem; proposes procedures; "idea man"

5. **Energizer:** urges group towards making decision; prods for action

6. **Questioner:** asks questions; requests clarification; constructive critic

7. **Listener:** talks little or not at all; shows interest and attention by listening intently

8. **Tension Reducer:** alleviates tension by being humorous; helps others to relax

9. **Denominator:** autocratic; interrupts others; over-positive; launches long monologues

10. **Negativist:** pessimistic; rejects ideas of others; argues frequently

11. **Deserter:** withdraws from group by daydreaming; whispers; strays from subject; leaves group

12. **Opinion Giver:** states own beliefs

13. **Aggressor:** tries to achieve importance in group; boasts; shows anger or irritation; deflates others; blames others

A perusal of the above list will make obvious the fact that some individuals can be placed in two or more behavior roles. In some instances it may be difficult to fit a group member into any of the foregoing categories.

Other classifications may be more acceptable, and the counselor who uses group dynamics often, particularly if he is creative, is not always satisfied until he has evolved his own system of behavior roles.

☞ Suggested Readings

Bowlsbey, Jo Ann Harris. "Careers by Special Delivery." In *New Imperatives for Guidance,* edited by Garry R. Walz and Libby Benjamin, pp. 327–374.

Foster, June C., Claire Olsen, Peggy M. Kapisovsky, and Leslie S. Kriger. *Guidance, Counseling and Support Services for High School Students with Physical Disabilities.* Cambridge, Mass.: Technical Education Research Centers, 1977.

Ganikos, Mary L., Kathleen A. Grady, and Jane B. Olson, eds. *Counseling the Aged.* Washington, D.C.: American Personnel and Guidance Association, 1979.

Herr, Edwin L., and Stanley H. Cramer. *Career Guidance Through the Life Span.* Boston: Little, Brown, 1979.

Isaacson, Lee E. *Career Information in Counseling and Teaching.* 3rd ed. Boston: Allyn and Bacon, 1977.

Jacobson, Thomas J. "Career Resource Centers." In *New Imperatives for Guidance,* edited by Garry R. Walz and Libby Benjamin, pp. 375–420. Ann Arbor, Michigan: ERIC Counseling and Personnel Services Clearinghouse, 1978.

Larmer, Mary E., Harm Reduction with High School Students, A.P.A., 2015.

Meerbach, John. *The Career Resource Center.* New York: Human Sciences Press, 1978.

Norris, Willa, Raymond N. Hatch, James R. Engelkes, and Bob B. Winborn. *The Career Information Service,* 4th ed. Chicago: Rand McNally, 1979.

Ohlsen, Merle M. *Group Process.* Boston: Houghton Mifflin Company, 1964.

_____. *Group Counseling.* New York: Holt, Rhinehart, and Winston, 1970.

Pietrofesa, John J., and Howard Splete. *Career Development: Theory and Research.* New York: Grune and Stratton, 1975.

Schutz, William C. *Joy: Expanding Human Awareness.* New York: Grove Press, Inc., 1967.

Shertzer, Bruce, and Shelley C. Stone. *Fundamentals of Guidance.* 4th ed. Boston: Houghton Mifflin, 1981.

Shippen, Samuel Joseph, and Raymond A. Wasil, eds. *Placement and Follow-Up.* Lexington, Massachusetts: Xerox Individualized Publishing, 1977.

Tolbert, E. L. *Introduction to Counseling.* 2nd ed. New York: McGraw-Hill, 1972.

Walz, Garry R., Robert L. Smith, and Libby Benjamin, eds. *A Comprehensive View of Career Development.* Washington, D.C.: American Personnel and Guidance Association, 1974.

Chapter 10

RESEARCH AND CREATIVITY

To expect counselors to do research or to create anything may be regarded by some as "wishful thinking." "It is impossible to find a counselor who would not keep himself/herself so fully occupied with the day-to-day tasks that no time would be available for research and evaluation." (3, p. 323)

It would seem that in spite of the foregoing negativism, those counselors who have the interest, aptitudes, and educational prerequisites to engage in research or creativity should be permitted and encouraged by administrators to do so. This would put an overwhelming burden upon an administrator who is faced with the dilemma of having to decide what to do when he has one or more counselors who should be researching or creating, but there aren't enough counselors to serve all the clients who need counseling. This is a pressing problem which every administrator who is so fortunate as to be blessed with counselors who could be researchers or creators should attempt to resolve.

Probably the college offers the most realistic hope for research or creative opportunities being made available to counselors. But even here, there is seldom a sufficient number of counselors to serve the student body. The college milieu, in which research is being carried on by the faculty, with more freedom in scheduling and less rigidity in conforming to the "usual" counseling program, offers a chance for the vigorous, ambitious, fast-working counselor to move into the areas of research or creativity. In addition, the college counselor should possess the doctorate and should become a specialist or be outstanding in some phase of counseling. Unless he/she engages in research or creativity, it becomes most difficult for him/her to establish himself/herself as being especially excellent in some particular kind of counseling.

There have been frequent references in the literature concerning the value of research, but unfortunately there have been relatively few statements regarding the worth of creativity in the profession of counseling which is unpardonable. Accordingly, in this chapter, it is being given equal importance with research, and it is hoped that in the future counseling authorities will focus attention on the need and value of counselors involving themselves in creativity.

It has been said of professors who do not research that all they have to bring into the classroom are the findings of others. This, of course, is not quite true, for the professor brings his/her own experiences into his/her field – unless by the very fact of being a professor who does no research he/she has no experiences to bring. He/she may, if he/she is an outstanding teacher, bring the gift of the teaching art at its highest level, but when he/she merely stands in front of a class to parrot the findings of others, he/she then offers neither the benefits of the researcher nor the arts of the master teacher.

The foregoing may be applied to the counselor. Let us assume for the moment that the busy practitioner must rely on others to do the needed research for his profession. Can we also assume that this same practitioner is justified in never coming up with a new or better way of practicing his profession? Must we settle for mediocrity in the majority of counselors, or is it essential that counselor educators and employers of counselors insist upon having counselors who, by their talents, contribute towards the enhancement of counseling? Would not this be a worthy research project?

☞ Research

While the rationale for counselors doing research may be open to attack by the counselors who entered the profession as practitioners, not researchers, there should be little to quarrel with in Patterson's statement:

> Practice, at least good practice, is based upon research.
> Research is the basis of professional activity, the source
> of knowledge which is characteristic of a profession.
> The counselor as a professional person must therefore

base his practice, insofar as possible, upon accepted knowledge based upon research. (9, p. 351)

For the counselor who cannot accept research as one of his/her functions, a subsidiary function could be "keeping abreast of research." "For the sake of greater effectiveness in his/her activities, the guidance worker should be familiar with past research." (7, pp. 227–228)

In addition, the nonresearching counselor should evaluate research findings and utilize those data judged to be worthy of integration into his practice. This should be done not only by counselors but by counselor educators and the counseling researchers themselves. "One of the criteria of a profession is the utilization made of its research by both the theoretician and the practitioner." (1)

Hill (5) offers an interesting exposition of the role of research and the status of research in guidance. And some of Patterson's meaningful comments (9) regarding research and the counselor are noted below:

The counselor is a consumer of research. (p. 351)

One of the best ways to understand research is to do it. (p. 353)

Research is not limited to experimentation. (p. 354)

Research is a way in which curiosity can be satisfied, and every counselor, if he is alive and growing, should be curious, should question traditional ways of doing things, should be willing to test the effects of what he is doing and to try new approaches and evaluate them. (p. 354)

Happily, there are and will be some counselors who choose to do research. The possibilities for research for the individual who comes up with a theory and wishes to test it are limitless. This is illustrated nicely in Holland's theory of vocational choice in which he did several studies as he examined " ...the usefulness of a theory of vocational choice by testing some of its general hypotheses." (6)

Those counselors who would like to do research but feel inadequate or afraid are encouraged to enroll in a formal course in research methodology and to consider continuing graduate studies which involve doing research. "Research competence is provided through courses in statistics and experimental design, through seminars in which students review, analyze and plan research studies in their field of interest, and through research assistantships." (8, pp. 13–14)

High school counselors, hesitant to proceed due to lack of training in research, may find considerable help in a little volume entitled *Research Guidelines for High School Counselors.* (10)

Sometimes those who wish to do research wonder about whether or not there are research problems available to them. The difficulty is not what to research, but being discriminating about the diverse problems in counseling – that is, what to investigate first.

Fullmer notes several categories for consideration in determining a research problem: dropouts, delinquents, underachievers, intelligent and creative youngsters, new problem areas, and counselor education. (4, p. 321)

As Davidson states in *Pulitzer*, " ...the highest good for man is the complete and habitual exercise of his full potentialities, the constant effort for usefulness." (11, p. 12) Davidson's concept of usefulness is proposed in the concept that the useful life involves " ...the dedication to betterment." (p. 15)

Davidson's theory certainly offers an exciting challenge to a researcher, who can proceed to test it and to relate the findings to ways in which counselors may utilize such data to become more capable of aiding clients in self-actualization.

As a stimulant to would-be researchers, the following list is offered to indicate the diverse possibilities for research in counseling:

1. Significant differences in effectiveness of counseling techniques

2. Problems of clients

3. Best preparation for counseling

4. Who should be a counselor educator?

5. Effectiveness of counseling tools

6. Who should counsel?

7. Selection of candidates for graduate education in counseling

8. Clarification of types of counselors

9. Ethical practices

10. Disparities between theory and practice

11. Resolution of semantical difficulties in jargon of profession

12. Principles of counseling

13. Objectives of counseling

14. Utilization of referral resources

15. Evaluation of counseling center

16. Gathering data for utilization in creating

17. Knowledge needed to counsel

18. Specialization versus generalization

19. Personality traits requisite to success in counseling

20. Functions of the counselor

21. Follow-up of graduates

22. Obtaining reliability and validity data on tests and instruments

23. Corroborating findings of previous studies

☞ *Creativity*

In spite of the almost overwhelming need for the introduction of better counseling tools, the improvement of methodology, and the development of new approaches to enhance the professions, there has been a regrettable lack of creative contributions from counselors. Even counselor educators, within the academic setting of colleges, have been remiss by their negligence in avoiding the obvious needs for ingenuity, originality, improvisation, and improvements in the profession.

While there have been many tests and tools published for counselor use, they usually have been in an area already exploited, such as vocational interests. Certainly there is value in the creation of another vocational interests instrument, providing it has something to offer that is not already available in one or several other similar tools. It also is important to continue striving for improved ways of measuring vocational interests.

A case in point, which has to do with the value of continuing to explore new avenues of measurement, is in vocational aptitude. The question is why such aptitude tests as the GATB (General Aptitudes Test Battery) and SATB (Specific Aptitudes Test Battery) of the U.S. Employment Service are not available for use in the public schools. What is desperately needed are new tests or instruments designed to measure factors or to provide data heretofore not available.

There long has been a pressing need for an aptitude test battery which could provide measurement of many more essential aptitudes than are usually considered. The authors made a move in this direction by constructing an instrument, *Rating Scale of Vocational Aptitudes* (2), which provides a basis for the client to make a judgment regarding his aptitudes; the results are reported in twenty categories through a comparison of his judgment with the normative group's appraisal of these aptitudes. This is a most useful tool in providing the client with a concept of multiple vocational aptitudes and with his rating in each of them as compared with others. The twenty categories of aptitudes included in the *Rating Scale of Vocational Aptitudes* are administrative, animal, artistic, athletic, clerical, commercial, computational, creative, dramatic, executive, literary, manual, mechanical, musical, organizing, plant, scholastic, scientific, service, and socializing.

Considerable work should be done in the development of instruments to measure personality traits, within the frame of reference of the "normal" individual, affording insights into personality strengths and weaknesses.

Tools should be created which will enable an individual to formulate his value system.

A client could profit from having a structured device which would assist him/her in evolving his/her life goals, including major, minor, short-term, and continuing goals.

In all of the foregoing there will be a need for research to yield the data necessary for the development of whatever is being designed.

Creative practitioners should find it next to impossible to avoid innovations in the art of counseling. Whenever a new technique is developed or an old technique is improved, there certainly is a professional obligation to impart the discovery to members of the profession.

The enhancement of methodology should be a life-long goal of every counselor. Even the counselor who is deficient in creativity can strive for self-improvement in his/her art, so that while he/she may not contribute anything new, he/she can hope to sharpen his/her competency in the performance of the skills which he/she must use as he/she counsels. While this is not creativity, it is a close relative, for improvement of any kind has a kinship to creativity.

☞ References

1. Demos, George D. "Every Guidance Worker a Researcher." *Education,* December 1964, pp. 234–237.
2. Demos, George D., and Bruce Grant. *Rating Scale of Vocational Aptitudes.* San Diego, California: Educational and Industrial Testing Service, 1966.
3. Froelich, Clifford P. *Guidance Services in Schools.* New York: McGraw-Hill Book Company, 1956.
4. Fullmer, Daniel W. *Counseling: Process and Content.* Chicago: Science Research Associates, Inc., 1964.
5. Hill, George E. *Management and Improvement of Guidance.* New York: Appleton-Century Crofts, 1966.
6. Holland, J. L. "A Theory of Vocational Choice." *Journal of Counseling Psychology,* 46, 1959, pp. 35–44.
7. Humphreys, J. Anthony, Arthur E. Traxler, and Robert D. North. *Guidance Services.* Chicago: Science Research Associates, Inc., 1960.
8. Jordaan, Jean-Pierre, Roger A. Myers, Wilbur L. Layton, and Henry H. Morgan. *The Counseling Psychologist.* New York: Teachers College Press, Teachers College, Columbia University, 1968.
9. Patterson, C. H. *Counseling and Guidance in Schools: A First Course.* New York: Harper & Brothers, 1962.
10. *Research Guidelines for High School Counselors.* Experimental Designs Committee, Association for Counselor Education and Supervision. Princeton, New Jersey: College Entrance Examination Board, 1967.
11. Swanberg, W. A. *Pulitzer.* New York: Charles Scribner's Sons, 1967.

☞ Suggested Additional Readings

Demos, George D. "Guidance and Research." *Education,* November 1963, pp. 141–143.

Fitzgerald, Laurine E., Walter F. Johnson, and Willa Norris. *College Student Personnel: Readings and Bibliographies.* Boston: Houghton Mifflin Co., 1970.

Gallagher, Phillip J., and George D. Demos. *The Counseling Center in Higher Education*. Springfield, Illinois: Charles C. Thomas, 1970.

Gowan, John Curtis, George D. Demos, and E. Paul Torrance. *Creativity: Its Educational Implications*. New York: John Wiley & Sons, 1967.

Kratochwill, Thomas R., and Levin, Joel R., Single-case Intervention Research, APA, 2014.

Volsky, Jr., Theodore, Thomas M. Magoon, Warren T. Norman, and Donald P. Holt. *The Outcomes of Counseling and Psychotherapy: Theory and Research*. Minneapolis: University of Minnesota Press, 1965.

Chapter 11

PROFESSIONAL AND COMMUNITY ORGANIZATIONS AND SERVICES

Every counselor should be a member of the APGA (American Personnel and Guidance Association). This is the professional association for counselors. "The American Personnel and Guidance Association was founded in 1952, in order to unite several different guidance and personnel associations, the oldest of which had been in existence since 1913." (2, p. 257)

In addition to belonging to the APGA, the counselor should join one or more of the individual associations which comprise the APGA; for example, National Vocational Guidance Association, American College Personnel Association, and Association of Counselor Educators and Supervisors. Other organizations include the American Association of Family Therapy, California Association of Marital, and Family Therapy.

An appropriate time to begin membership in the APGA is during graduate study when engaging in the program of preparation designed to qualify one as a counselor. Student membership is possible at a reduced rate. After the completion of formal education and at the onset of his professional career, the counselor should consider extending his membership into additional divisions within the APGA.

If the state has a personnel and guidance association, the counselor should seriously consider becoming a member of this organization. The same is true in large metropolitan areas in which there may be a local personnel and guidance association. Those counselors who are psychologists should join the APA (American Psychological Association), affiliating themselves with one or more of its divisions, for example, counseling psychology, clinical psychology, or educational psychology.

The journals received from membership in professional associations are of inestimable value to the counselor who regards it as mandatory to keep informed on the current research, creativity, and happenings in his/her field. Such publications as the following are necessary for the continuous education of the counselor: *American Personnel and Guidance Journal, Vocational Guidance Quarterly, School Counselor, Counselor Education and Supervision,* and *Journal of College Student Personnel.*

Even though the counselor is not a member of several associations that publish articles worthy of assimilation by the counselor, a skimming of the following periodicals to locate data relevant to the practice of counseling is suggested:

1. Journal of College Placement

2. Journal of Counseling Psychology

3. American Psychologist

4. American Sociological Review

5. American Educational Research Journal

6. American Journal of Sociology

7. Educational and Psychological Measurement

8. Journal of Applied Behavioral Science

9. Journal of Educational Psychology

10. Journal of Educational Research

11. The Clinical Psychologist

A neglected area of counselor participation is community organizations. Certainly the busy counselor cannot "spread himself/ herself so thin" that he/she tries to affiliate with several community groups – regardless of how worthy they are. The other extreme of not participating in any community activity or at least some community organizations is equally regrettable. "To be effective, the school counselor needs to work within an integrated educational structure consisting of a school administration, a staff, and cooperating community agencies." (1, p. 106)

In *Chapter 8, Referrals,* there are several lists of the organizations existing in the community, with the number of these organizations varying with the size of the community (see page 92, 93, 94). *The Referral Guide to Health and Welfare Services* (4) and *Guidance: A Developmental Approach* (3) provide comprehensive lists of the community organizations available in metropolitan areas.

While there can be value in the counselor participating in any community organization (and of course each individual is free to choose the group with which he/she desires to affiliate himself/herself), there are certain organizations in which it is recommended that every counselor participate as much as possible as a means of contributing to his/her continuing education. In addition, he/she should serve his/her community by functioning as a consultant.

From the following list of recommended organizations it is suggested that the counselor choose one with which to associate himself/herself as a *participating* member:

1. State Employment Service

2. Junior Association of Commerce or Chamber of Commerce

3. Family Service, Catholic Welfare Bureau, or Jewish Family Service

4. Veterans Administration

5. Child Guidance Clinic

6. Juvenile Bureau

7. Bureau of Vocational Rehabilitation

8. County Probation Department

9. AFL-CIO or other labor organization

10. Religious group

11. Hospital

12. YMCA or YWCA

13. Boy Scouts or Girl Scouts

14. Rotary, Kiwanis, Lions, Elks, or other service club

15. Businessmen's Association

16. American Red Cross

17. Masons, Knights of Columbus, or other religious affiliated group

18. Free clinic

An examination of the above list reveals instantly the diversity of opportunities for the counselor who has not yet decided on an organization with which to affiliate himself. Before making this decision, it is recommended that the counselor study each of these groups and make personal contacts with officials and workers. Along with these contacts, he/she should establish the relationships he/she needs for making referrals. And it bears repeating that the counselor should know something about the individuals and agencies before he/she refers from his list.

It is important for administrators to remember that not every counselor will be effective in community relationships; some will prefer not to participate in community activity; and even those individuals who are public relations-minded, highly motivated, and extremely competent in community activities may not be able to justify the dissipating of their valuable time by being away from their office. The counselor should not be "pressured" into community service, but he/she should be made aware of the inherent opportunities if and when he/she chooses to participate. And, as in the case of the counselor engaging in research or creativity, the administrator has the dilemma of releasing counselors for community service when there is a shortage of counselors to meet the client load.

For those counselors who see their way clear to proceed with community participation, the rewards will be many, not the least of which should be the continuous enrichment of their professional effectiveness through what they will learn as a by-product of community service.

☞ *References*

1. Fullmer, Daniel W. *Counseling: Content and Process.* Chicago: Science Research Associates, Inc., 1964.
2. Miller, Frank W. *Guidance – Principles and Services.* Columbus, Ohio: Charles E. Merrill Books, 1961.
3. Peters, Herman J., and Gail F. Farwell. *Guidance: A Developmental Approach.* Chicago: Rand McNally, 1959.
4. *Referral Guide to Health and Welfare Services.* Community Welfare Council, Long Beach, California: Seaside Printing Company (no date).

☞ *Suggested Additional Readings*

Gallagher, Phillip J., and George D. Demos. *The Counseling Center in Higher Education.* Springfield, Illinois: Charles C. Thomas, 1970.

Part III

THE ART OF COUNSELING

Chapter 12

INTRODUCTION TO PART III

Following this introductory chapter, Part III consists of the presentation of the art of counseling by devoting a chapter to all the seventeen techniques which, in action, are counseling.

To avoid any semantic confusion the following interpretations of related words are given:

1. "Policy" is what is to be done.

2. "Procedure" is what is done to carry out policy.

3. "Method" is how something is done.

4. "Technique" is that which is used to carry out method.

The literature of counseling methodology contains many statements about the "directive," the "nondirective," or "client-centered," and the "eclectic" methods of counseling. It is not the function of Part III to propose or advocate a particular methodology, but to be concerned with the ways in which any methodology must be carried out by techniques.

Readers who are interested in pursuing the rationale for and against each counseling methodology would find it beneficial to study the writings of authors who devote considerable space to espousing these methods. It should be especially valuable to examine the works of the two eminent authorities – Dr. E. G. Williamson and Dr. Carl Rogers – who have been widely acclaimed as the founders of the "directive" or counselor-centered (Williamson) and "nondirective" or client-centered (Rogers) methods.

Counseling Adolescents (22) is recommended reading on the "directive" methodology. *Counseling and Psychotherapy* (15), plus *Client-Centered Therapy* (14), are classics in delineating the "nondirective" method.

Since there are several authorities who lean towards the "eclectic" methodology, a particularly helpful text in exploring eclectic theory is Zeran, et al., *Guidance: Theory and Practice* (23). *Developmental Counseling* (2) offers a presentation of both counseling theory and procedure.

The following differentiation of the directive, nondirective, and eclectic methods should be helpful:

☞ *Directive*

1. Reliance on data gathered by counselor

2. Concern for intellect (reacting to intellectual content)

3. Scientific approach predominant

4. Primarily educational and vocational areas

5. Emphasis on problem of client

☞ *Nondirective*

1. Reliance on data offered by client

2. Concern for emotions (reacting to emotional content)

3. Art of human relations predominant

4. Primarily personal-social area

5. Emphasis on process of interviewing

☞ *Eclectic*

1. Reliance on data gathered by counselor or offered by client

2. Concern for intellect or emotions

3. Involves scientific approach or art of human relations

4. Includes educational, vocational, and personal-social areas

5. Emphasis on problem or process

It is the authors' contention that the mastering of the specifics, the techniques, is what will make an effective counselor. The counselor should not become concerned with accepting, advocating, exploiting, or defending what he does in the counseling interview in order to have it be compatible with a preconceived acceptance of a particular school of thought, philosophical learning, or methodological preference. In the final analysis, a counselor may have a nondirective philosophy while being directive, or a directive philosophy while functioning nondirectively, or any variation of the foregoing, until he meets himself "coming and going" in his practice. The important thing is "what he/she does specifically in the interview" in terms of what should be done.

The purpose of assigning a section of the next chapter to each counseling technique is to define it, discuss the meaning of the technique, include a few comments regarding it, and then proceed to show the technique in action by reporting from cases some excerpts that are examples of the application of the technique.

To the student of counseling and to the practitioner, the reporting of excerpts in order to show the technique in action should be more useful in the acquiring or enriching of insight into the technique than simply "talking about it."

The excerpts are succinct, for their function is to educate, not to anesthetize the reader. By lifting an example of the technique from an interview which may have included other techniques, the reader may experience some disappointment in not being able to study the entire interview. However, the objective of the excerpt is to aid the reader in understanding the technique, not to entertain him with an interesting interview.

Once a counselor is able to use several techniques, he/she should be free to select the ones he/she decides will be best in relation to the particular client and the client's particular problem.

The fluctuation of terms – from "technique" to "procedure" to "method" to "tool," etc. – from author to author may become a source of irritation to the student and the semanticist. However, the important goal is to acquire a thorough grounding in what the counselor does in an interview, regardless of the nomenclature attached to what he is doing. This is the reason for the authors presenting excerpts of, rather than "talking about," what goes on in the interview.

References and Suggested Additional Readings for Part III are listed at the end of this chapter in order to avoid a repetition that would be inevitable if they were reported for each of the seventeen sections in the following chapter.

Prior to studying the seventeen techniques, even the most sophisticated reader could profit from examining several of these sources, as a cursory perusal will reveal the variations in the interpretation of "techniques." For example, Traxler and North (21) extend the term to include "tools."

Shertzer and Peters (17) offer an approach that encompasses educational guidance techniques, vocational guidance techniques, personal-social guidance techniques, and integrative techniques and practices.

The *Handbook of Counseling Techniques* (9) presents techniques for both professional and laypeople, covering a wide range of types of counseling encompassing counseling in schools, child-care counseling, counseling techniques in child welfare, marriage counseling, religious counseling, techniques in psychiatric social work, etc.

Gruen's "The Counseling Interview" in Siegel's *The Counseling of College Students* (18) deals with techniques in college-student counseling.

The art of the counseling interview in elementary and secondary schools is treated in *The Student, the Interview, and the Curriculum: Dynamics of Counseling in the School.* (16) There are six interview typescripts, each about thirty minutes in length. Interpretation of the counselor-client interaction is made, and each interview is followed by a discussion selection.

Smith (19) divides counseling techniques into general and specific. He provides information about what he classifies as the general techniques: " ...clarifying the role of the counselor, structuring the counseling interview, encouraging counselee participation, encouraging counselee acceptance, responding to ambivalent feelings, and responding to unexpressed feelings." (pp. 110–116) Smith offers data on what he identifies as being specific techniques: " ...questioning, probing, suggesting, interpreting, listening, clarifying, approval, assurance, and observation." (pp. 116–124)

The following authorities have included a chapter on techniques: Erickson (7) – "Interviewing Techniques"; Brayfield (3) – "Techniques of Student Counseling"; Robinson (13) – "Dimensions and Techniques of Counseling"; and Strang (20) – "Orientation to Counseling Techniques."

In the treatment of counseling as an art (Part III) and as a science (Part IV), no attempt is made to propose or defend the position that counseling is more an art than a science, or the opposite, more a science than an art. For example, Bugental (4) contends that psychotherapy is more art than science. The authors believe that counseling is both an art and a science, and regard any attempt to rank art ahead of science or vice versa as a dissipation of intellectual energy which the counselor could more fruitfully direct toward the goal of becoming both an artist *and* a scientist. If the counselor can only justify being one or the other, artist or scientist, he/she should be willing to acknowledge the following:

1. As an artist, it is necessary to "know enough" to be able to function at this high level of skill and to possess adequate data so that when it is needed it is given.

2. As a scientist, it is imperative that there be communicative skill to impart the knowledge and sufficient skill in human interaction to permit maximal client benefits from having interacted with a scientist.

Certainly, some counselors may be more artist than scientist or vice versa. If their natural inclinations or training balance them more heavily on the side of either art or science, there is little doubt that they will function accordingly. The fact remains, regardless of particular preferences of counselors as to art or science, a professional counselor cannot function adequately and competently without the skill in the "doing," which comprises the counseling act, and without the knowledge required to be able to perform many of the techniques in the counseling act.

It is hoped that those readers who are in a counselor education program will realize that when they begin practicing as counselors, they will be engaging in what is primarily a mental art, just as the physician or lawyer. A physician does not diagnose a physical ailment by operating in an intellectual vacuum; nor does he prescribe therapy from a scientific void. In both of these (diagnosis and prescription of therapy) there is the act of doing, which must be effective or the patient may reject either or both the diagnosis and therapy – which would actually be a rejection of the physician.

Yes, it takes both art and science. That's what this book is all about!

No attempt is made to single out any one or more techniques as being superior to the others. Each technique has a contribution to make in any given situation. Unfortunately, some techniques have received an undue amount of publicity, to the extent that several counselors feel compelled to favor them. Equally regrettable are the instances of certain techniques being belittled by some authorities to the degree that many counselors shy away from their usage.

As a case in point: the impact of the nondirective methodology (due to its exposition by so many writers) helped some counselors to curtail their verbosity and to become better listeners – virtues of undoubted value. But unfortunately, " …little time and energy … is given to the value and meaning of expressive features of the body, facial expressions, bodily movements, and hand gestures." (1)

Probably the technique which has suffered the most belittlement is "informing." As Smith points out, "…a large proportion of the counseling carried on in high schools is with pupils who seek information." (19, p. 118) This makes the depreciation of the technique of informing a professional absurdity, which certainly applies just as accurately to any disparagement of closely related techniques such as interpreting, which " ...is probably the most common used of all those techniques employed by secondary-school counselors." (19, p. 118)

Hoyt attacks this disparagement by proposing an " ...increased use of information in the counseling process." (10) "I simply don't believe that counselors who help their clients 'feel' their way along in educational-vocational counseling can be as helpful to clients as those who help clients acquire new information pertinent to decisions the clients are trying to make. We have for too long had counselors and clients, both of whom are ignorant regarding pertinent characteristics and information regarding environmental opportunities, sitting down together, and sharing their ignorance. When this happens, no matter how clearly the client understands that the counselor accepts him and wants to help him, it seems to me that the major result must be accumulation of a considerable body of ignorance."

Another technique which has been looked upon with disfavor by some is inquiring. This technique is the antithesis to the proposition that the counselor should not seek data about the client, but only receive what the client volunteers; it is the active seeking of information about the client.

Counselors who practice in schools, colleges, agencies, and privately should find *The California Pre-Counseling Self-Analysis Protocol Booklet* (5) – an excellent aid to utilize in the inquiring process.

Part IV: The Science of Counseling, deals with the knowledge a counselor needs in order to be able to perform in several of the techniques treated in Part III. "If counselors are to become effective, they must study – they must know something." (10) There is, for instance, a vast difference between the knowledge required by a counselor to engage in "listening" as compared with "interpreting."

"The achievement of any degree of skill, especially that high level characteristic of an art is contingent upon the counselor successfully performing those steps which make possible the acquisition of skill." (8, p. 42) It is suggested that careful consideration be given to following these steps:

1. Observation of a skilled performance as a whole

2. Imitation of skilled performance as a whole

3. Observation of a technique of the skilled performance

4. Imitate the technique

5. Correct ... errors

6. Develop form and timing

7. Practice (21, pp. 42–44)

> Practice involves doing the whole activity over and over
> again. It means reverting to working on the specific
> techniques of the whole activity, eliminating errors, and
> working on form and timing. Practice is hard work ...
> Having once acquired the skill, the only way to keep it
> is through practice. If you abandon the activity in which
> you have acquired skill, the longer you remain inactive,
> the greater the possibility that the skill will be lost." (8,
> p. 44)

Since counseling is primarily a mental skill, rather than a physical
one, the development of "form and timing" would only apply to
"nonverbal responses," which include the physical mannerisms and
physical reactions – e.g., smiling, relaxed bodily posture, etc. – inherent
in all techniques.

A moment's reflection upon the steps in the acquirement of a skill
listed above will reveal how important *experience* is, and at the same
time, perhaps, cast some doubt on the value of *reading* about skills.
However, since at least a rudimentary knowledge of the technique is
prerequisite to performing it, the verbal explanation of the technique
followed by reading about it "in action" are certainly contributory factors

that should serve nicely as proper background before one proceeds with the steps outlined above.

Psychodrama is an excellent learning device for use in courses dealing with techniques in counselor education programs. The internship occurring in the final stage of counselor education serves as the best possibility for acquiring skill in counseling techniques. What Mazzini observed regarding teaching surely is applicable to counseling: people "learn while they teach." A helpful text in this area is *Supervised Counseling Experiences.* (11)

In the process of counselor-client interaction which is labeled counseling, the major bases of communication are talking and listening. It would be prudent here to review the comments made in *Chapter 9, Group Guidance,* in reference to communicating (see pp. 52–57). In addition, it is suggested that students and practitioners get a copy of "Sharpening Your Communicative Skills" (6) for careful study of factors that contribute to faulty communication and the recommendations made for eliminating these barriers to effective verbal interaction.

☞ *Brief Summary of Some Theories of Counseling*

Psychoanalysis, as viewed by many writers, is divided into two major sections. There is Freudian psychoanalysis and the neo-Freudians. This writer will attempt to describe, in a succinct manner, Freudian psychoanalytical counseling theory. In addition, the divergent theories of some of the major neo-Freudians such as Jung, Adler, Horney, Rank, and Sullivan will be presented.

Sigmund Freud first began to develop his psychoanalytic theory in his work with Breuer on hysteria. From this work and refined in his own latter studies, Freud postulated two fundamental hypotheses. The first hypothesis states that all psychic phenomena possess a causal factor and are determined by preceding events. The second hypothesis is that consciousness is of little importance. Unconscious mental processes are of primary significance and are the source of Man's actions. Essentially, these hypotheses state that Man is governed by unconscious, and relatively unknown motivations. Thus, in counseling, a Freudian analyst would view the counselee as a patient seeking help and guidance from an expert in the unconscious mental processes.

These unconscious mental processes contain the sources of mental disturbances in most psychoneuroses. Freud postulated that the sources of these disturbances were basically sexual in nature and began instinctively in infancy. In his theory of development, Freud states that the individual passes through four states of development: the oral, anal, phallic, and genital. Problems in any one of these stages result in a psychic "fixation" of energy and this energy or life force is entitled "libido." Included within the phallic stage is the Oedipal period in which an individual struggles with desire for the parent of the opposite sex and jealous feelings for the other parent. The successful resolution of this struggle results in the development of the "superego," which provides the internal social/moral restrictions on behavior.

The libido is the life force which drives the individual in search of pleasure. This force is basically sexual in nature and the individual is pushed by the libido toward achievement of mature sexuality. If the individual is thwarted or frustrated in any one of the developmental stages, the libido may fixate and later develop corresponding pathological problems.

Freud later expanded his concept of basic sexual drives or instincts to include an aggressive or death instinct. These instincts were physically represented and directed by the Id. Thus, the Id operates solely for the pleasure principle and its impulses are not controlled or disciplined. The mediator between the Id and external reality is the ego. When Id impulses discover frustrations by the external environment and are repeatedly thwarted from immediate gratification, the infant begins to differentiate between himself and reality. This differentiation and accommodation to reality constitute the ego. The Id, ego, and superego constitute Freud's theory of the structure of the mind.

In what might be termed a "normal" individual, the three forces, the Id, the ego, and the superego, are in a state of equilibrium. However, when tensions arise, the individual is caught between the anxiety of releasing instinctual tensions and impulses and punishment. The ego then develops defenses against the Id's impulses. These defenses include repression of the impulses material, rationalization, projection, introjection, regression, turning against the self, isolation, dissociation, reaction formation, and denial of reality. Thus, the practice of the psychoanalytic counselor includes the study of the activities of the ego and superego as well as the unconscious processes and psychosexual development.

Within this framework, Carkhuff states that the psychoanalytical counselor views the counselee as a victim of the interaction and conflict between instincts and social forces. His relationship to the counselee is in the role of uncovering, interpreting, and integrating unconscious, psychosexually repressed material.

Traditionally, this procedure employs some initial distance in the psychic relationship of the client and the counselor. The counselor is unseen beside the client who reclines on a couch. In this situation the client talks about anything. Everything stated is analyzed in a technique known as free association, whereby all statements or non-statements are viewed as clues to the submerged unconscious. Through this passive, permissive psychoanalytical situation, the client is encouraged to reveal stronger feelings as well as dreams. Eventually, transference occurs in which the client releases pent up feelings, which were suppressed or repressed since childhood. This release provides the client with insight or awareness of the workings of his psychic life. Whereas insight is significant, Fenichel also states that the corrective emotional experience of the therapy itself strengthens the individual's ego in handling the formerly repressed material in an integrative manner.

Classical Freudian psychoanalysis, according to Jones, is said to have made its greatest contribution by providing a comprehensive theory regarding the unconscious states of the mind and in describing the nature of psychoneurosis.

Rank's approach to psychoanalytic therapy was considered somewhat radical. As a practitioner, Rank experimented with short-term therapy, active as opposed to passive analytical situations, and the notion that the client should determine the method of achieving self-determination and self-direction. Rank encouraged and sought to strengthen the client's will and contended that the relationship between the client and the therapist should emphasize the unique and creative process. This implementation of the "will" psychology anticipated the later developments of client-centered therapy.

Karen Horney was another psychoanalyst who later broke with the psychoanalytic movement. Horney rejected both Freud's instinct theory and his structural theory of the mind categories – the id, ego, and superego.

Horney contended that security or insecurity was a principal determinant of human behavior rather than sex and aggression. Feelings of insecurity were basic anxieties which produced strategies in the disturbed individual to cope with these feelings. Irrationalities are proposed as neurotic which produce neurotic needs. These needs take the form of seeking affection and approval, seeking a partner or mate to take over his/her restricted, narrow life, seeking power, exploitation, prestige, personal admiration, personal achievement, self-sufficiency and independence, and perfection and unassailability. A developmental source of the needs are the inner conflicts and interplays of these same needs. As a group, these needs fall into three directions of moving toward people, moving away from people, and moving against people.

A neurotic person develops disturbances by creating an idealized image of self in which the contradictory image seemingly disappears but is only submerged or repressed. As the neurotic person seeks to actualize his idealized self, this idealized self comes into conflict with the actual self. The actual self is the whole personality of the individual as it actually exists. Another facet, the real self is the inner force of the person which is the source of free, healthy development of potential. This real self is the potential of the actual self and is the goal of therapy. Thus, this goal precludes the deflation of the idealized self. The client's release of the block allows the real self an avenue for constructive growth.

Like the previously mentioned Freudian dissidents, Horney also practiced a more directive and active therapeutic role.

Harry Stack Sullivan was considered a neo-Freudian who differed from Freud in many significant ways. As a working clinical psychiatrist, much of Sullivan's theory and knowledge was derived empirically from his work with schizophrenics and obsessional cases. From his experience, Sullivan theorized that a primary concern of therapy is to study interpersonal relations.

Sullivan introduced a particular kind of structure in his therapy sessions which he termed the "psychiatric interview." The interview consisted of four stages. These stages were:

1. the formal inception;

2. reconnaissance;

3. detailed inquiry;

4. the termination.

Sullivan states that during the inception of the interview, the interviewer should quietly observe and try to understand the nature of the patient's problems. However, this should not be so totally objective that the patient feels clinically "observed." The therapist should be attentive to all things about the patient. Speech pattern, intonations, rates and changes in volume of speech, nonverbal expressions should all be included in this observation.

The reconnaissance is the part of therapy whereby the therapist gathers, by intensive interrogation, biographical information about the patient.

The third stage of the interview, the detailed inquiry, consists of the therapist testing several hypotheses regarding the nature and source of the patient's problems. The therapist should be constantly aware of the two-way flow of time and communication, and when communication is blocked, the interviewer should be alert as to his own attitudes, which may impede progress.

Finally, Sullivan advocated a decisive and directive termination of the therapy. The therapist should summarize what was learned about the patient and the patient's interpersonal relations. With this knowledge, the therapist should be able to predict the possible effects of the patient's changed attitudes on future interpersonal relations.

Carl Rogers is considered by many writers to be representative of the phenomenological school of counseling and therapy. Rogers first termed his counseling non-directive and later called it client-centered.

Much of Rogers' theory was drawn from Goldstein, Snygg, Combs, Maslow, Harry Stack Sullivan, Otto Rank, and his own observations as the director of the Rochester Guidance Center. Rogers' theoretical construction of personality is based on a phenomenological point of view. Prior to Rochester, Rogers observed therapy which he felt was too authoritarian. The phenomenological outlook of Rogers proposes that each person possesses a phenomenal field which is a definition of events or phenomena as they appear to him. Behavior is determined by the field view of the person; thus, the only valid source of information is the client.

Rogers' constructs were held to be popular with many American psychologists during the Forties as they seemed to fit the American ethic of that era. The client was treated as an equal partner in therapy and possessed the power to cure himself. Consequently, the client did not need to lean on an "expert." The client's potential for change fitted the American ideal of optimism and constructive opportunity.

Rogers stated that each person's behavior is determined by their phenomenal field. However, the field is limited and is restructured according to the person's needs.

Self-concept is defined as those aspects of a person's phenomenal self which he had defined as definite and relatively stable attributes. Tension or anxiety occurs when the organism denies to awareness significant sensory and visceral experiences. Because of this denial, these experiences are not organized in the self-concept symbolically. The experiences that are not brought into awareness or organized symbolically into the self-concept are *disowned* by the individual. The organism and the self, according to Rogers, are double components of personality. The organism may have visceral and sensory experiences and the self may or may not allow itself to perceive these experiences if they are not harmonious or consistent with the self-structure.

As self-preservation and enhancement are the basic motivations of human behavior, therapy thus consists of providing a threat-free environment in which the client can work out a harmonious integration of self and the organism. Problems or tensions arise when the values attached to experiences and those which are part of the self concept might be either values experienced in the past or values taken over from others. These values might be perceived in a distorted manner, and may lead to confusion, unhappiness, and ineffectiveness. Within a client-centered therapeutic setting, the client may perceive, examine, and revise the self-structure to assimilate and include the experiences formerly avoided.

Rogers stresses that reality is the present. Past and future are relevant only if they are conceptualized by the client as constituting present tensions. Hence, behavior is goal-directed and needs and goals are an integral part of the present. Within this framework, Rogers' conception of personality is viewing the self-as-the-object. The presumption is that the client's reports are valid and reliable sources of information about his personality. These consciously experienced self-feelings can be honestly reported to a counselor.

An individual is ready for client-centered therapy when his organized self-structure no longer effectively meets the needs of the reality-situations in which he finds himself or when he feels a significantly large cleavage between what he wants to be and what he is.

When a client enters therapy he may:

1. have a critical negative view of himself;

2. have an idealized image of how he should be and is certain that he failed to measure up to this ideal;

3. later develop an awareness of contradictory attitude toward himself;

4. in the accepting environment, begin to accept himself as well as the contradictions;

5. begin objective observation of self;

6. shift goals to something more achievable and the discrepancy between ideal self-image and perceptions of real self becomes less;

7.   reduce or free tensions and anxieties.

Diagnosis, in client-centered counseling, is considered unnecessary, unwise, and detrimental. Rogers' attitude toward diagnosis stems from Otto Rank's views and influence concerning the client's "will." Rogers believes that diagnosis fosters the dependency of the client on the therapist as the "expert." He feels that the client should make the decisions about changes in his own behalf. Thus, the less the therapist's attitudes are biased by a predetermined point of view, the more he is able to accord the client acceptance and positive regard.

The following activities characterize the client-centered therapist:

1.   Consistent effort to understand the client's content of speech and feelings conveyed by words, gestures, expressions;

2.   An effort to communicate this understanding to the client by word or general attitude of acceptance;

3.   Occasional presentation of a synthesis of expressed feelings;

4.   Occasional statement of the nature and limits of the therapeutic relationship and the therapist's confidence in the client's ability to solve problems;

5.   Question-answering, information giving, are presented only when relevant in helping the client work through a problem. Otherwise, this is discouraged to prevent dependency;

6.   Few interruptions other than summarizing or clarifying the therapist's understanding of feelings expressed;

7.   The therapist does not give advice, praise, blame, teach, suggest programs of activities, suggest areas of exploration, or promote insight directly.

The central issue differing client-centered counseling from many other systems is that the responsibility for the course and direction of therapy is entirely up to the client.

Client-centered therapy is a process of disorganization and reorganization of the self-structure. The restructuring of the organization of the self is accomplished by the counselor's confidence and acceptance of the client's ability to work through problems in a threat-free environment.

In a threat-free environment, the client sees in himself more a pattern drawn from experience, rather than a pattern imposed upon experience. Consequently, the value system becomes based more upon actual experience. Because of this, the client feels more realistic, comfortable, and in harmony with the perceived self. Ideals are more achievable and overt behavior is more adjustive and socially more sound and realistic.

Rogers states that there are six psychological conditions which are necessary and sufficient to bring about constructive personality changes. These conditions are:

1. Psychological contact – the relationship of the therapist and the client in awareness of the presence of each other;

2. The client should be in a state of "incongruence." Incongruence is the anxious difference between the actual experience of the client and his self-image.

3. The therapist must be congruent or integrated in the relationship and is freely, genuinely himself.

4. The therapist must express unconditional positive regard for the client without compromise.

5. The therapist must experience an empathetic understanding of the client's awareness of his experience and feelings and should communicate this empathetic understanding to the client.

In other words, the therapist must sense and feel the client's emotions.

6. The client must perceive that the therapist empathizes and is accepting.

The merits of these conditions are that they are hypotheses which are testable. Although many psychological workers agree with Rogers that the above conditions are necessary, many disagree that they are sufficient.

A radical departure from Rogers' client-centered counseling is the *rational-emotive system* of **Albert Ellis.** This system was developed from his clinical practice. Ellis was a former marriage counselor who later turned to psychoanalysis, then learning theory, and finally settled into his own formulated operating system. This system was based on the premise that irrational, neurotic early learnings persisted in many clients because these individuals reindoctrinated themselves by not changing their thinking.

Ellis hypothesizes that emotion is significantly caused and controlled by thinking. This emotion, in many clients, is biased, prejudiced, and strongly evaluative in thoughts which take place in the form of thinking in language. Ellis states that a person feeling positive emotions may say to himself in a conscious or unconscious manner, "this is good." Conversely, in a negative situation, a person may be saying or thinking, "this is bad or terrible." Ellis believes that if the person did not think these thoughts, much of this emotion would cease to exist. It is Ellis' contention that an individual may control one's feelings by controlling one's thoughts. Thus, it is the role of the counselor to direct and teach the client to understand how they create their own emotional reactions and how they can create different emotional reactions by telling themselves other things.

Emotional disturbance, according to Ellis, arises when an individual mentally reiterates negative, unrealistic, illogical, self-defeating thoughts. As a result, these individuals are not aware that they are talking to themselves irrationally or illogically and are internalizing these thoughts in an unrealistic manner.

Ellis concedes that some irrationality is derived from biological limitations. However, most illogical ideas stem from societal upbringing. He feels that many clients receive irrational thoughts from parents, teachers, peers, the cultural milieu, and the mass media. Ellis contends that many of these beliefs are commonplace in our culture. Some of these commonly held irrational beliefs are as follows:

1. It is necessary to be approved by almost everyone for almost everything one does.

2. What others think is of utmost importance.

3. It is better to depend on others than on oneself to avoid being selfish and self-centered.

4. Things should be better than they are and it is terrible and catastrophic if they aren't.

5. Others should help one make life easier and one should not have to delay or put aside gratification.

6. It is easier to avoid than to face difficulties and self-responsibilities.

7. Inactivity or inertia is necessary and often pleasant and one should rebel against doing things, however necessary, if it is unpleasant.

These irrational beliefs, when internalized and reiterated in self-defeating sentences, develop into the client's self-defeat and neurosis. Hence, it is the task of the rational-emotive counselor to reveal and assail these basic ideas, philosophies, or values which underlie the neurosis.

Ellis employs the standard form of supportive expressive-emotive, relating, and insight-interpretative techniques. However, these are usually considered preparatory in his method. Thereupon, Ellis approaches the client's problem by assailing the client's general and specific irrational ideas, in several ways.

1. The counselor directly contradicts the self-defeating ideas and values which the client originally learned and is maintaining.

2. The counselor encourages, persuades, induces, and commands the client to perform in an activity which will counteract his illogical ideas.

3. Ellis focuses attention on current causes of emotional disturbance. Thus, the client is shown that it is not Oedipal attachment which is made and keeps him neurotic, but his self-perpetuated illogical ideas underlying the attachment. It is present attitudes toward these ideas that develop illogical fears about these events and situations.

Another focus of rational counseling is the focus on the client's self-interest in treatment procedures. Ellis believes that self-interest demands social interest. Hence, the rational-emotive client might be counseled that caring for others is in one's own best interest as this will produce a society which will be best for oneself.

Rational-emotive counseling, according to Ellis, appears to be most effective with clients who are not too psychotic, fairly intelligent, and reasonably young. Characteristic of his successful clients are intellectual curiosity, willingness to work, and a willingness to accept the counselor's direction. Within this framework, the counselor's task is to help the disturbed client become aware of his self-defeating verbalizations and adopt more rational perspective.

John Dollard and Neal Miller are two proponents of what is termed reinforcement counseling. Reinforcement counseling is an attempt to utilize the theoretical contributions of psychoanalysis, scientific studies on human behavior, and learning theories. Psychoanalysis provides some of the basic theoretical framework. However, learning theories and the studies of human behavior provide the nomenclature for the implementation of their techniques. Implementation is primarily concerned with neurosis as a product of learning.

Dollard and Miller describe a neurotic as miserable and inept in dealing with his emotional problems. The neurotic is capable of conducting activities in life, but is unable to function adaptively or enjoy life at its best. They state that some of the symptoms include sleeplessness, irritability, restlessness, sexual inhibitions, phobias, headaches, irrational fears, lack of clear personal goals, and a distaste for life. The neurotic condition is the result of conflicts produced by strong drives which leads to incompatible responses. These conflicts are often unconscious and repressed and the client is unaware of the forces within him. Dollard and Miller attribute the unawareness to the insufficient use of higher mental processes.

Dollard and Miller, like Freud, base neurotic behavior upon an unconscious emotional conflict which originated in early childhood. These conflicts are usually learned by children from their parents or their surrounding environment. Patterns or lack of patterns of child rearing contain many conflicts and inconsistencies and a child may be driven by unrealistic demands. These demands may stem from feeding, cleanliness, and sexual and aggression control training, which may be internalized before the child can verbalize. The conflicts that arise from any of these training situations are repressed and unconscious and later produce drives which lead to incompatible, learned experience responses.

Dollard and Miller propose four factors in accordance with learning theories, that are responsible for learning. Drive or motivation is a stimulus which leads to action. Some drives are primary or innate (pain, hunger, etc.), and others are secondary or learned drives. These are basically primary drives that have been elaborated and serve as the underlying factor. Fear or anxiety belongs in this category.

The second factor in learning is the stimulus or cue. Cues serve to determine when the drive is present, when, where and which response a person will produce. Both internal and external stimuli can function as cues. Fear has the property of possessing aspects of both internal and external stimuli.

Another factor in learning is the result of cues. Response is the consequent reaction to a cue and may present itself in a hierarchy of probable occurrence.

The last factor results from the response of a cue and is the reward or reinforcement of the cessation of the painful event.

In addition to the four main factors in learning, Dollard and Miller discuss the role of other aspects of learning. Extinction is a term applied to the decrease of a response without reinforcement. Spontaneous recovery is the recurrence of a response which has not been fully extinguished but inhibited. Generalization is the tendency of a response to spread to other stimuli and the variation of this tendency is called the gradient of generalization. Discrimination refers to the manner in which dissimilar stimuli are differentiated. Some responses are rewarded, some are not. The distance or time lapse of reinforcement to the response is termed the gradient of reinforcement. Lastly, there are anticipatory responses which occur before the actual response is carried out. Withdrawing a hand away from a fire after previously being burned is an anticipatory response.

Dollard and Miller divide behavior into two areas. The first area consists of automatic responses – eating, sleeping, etc. The second area includes the behavior which is mediated by the higher mental processes of thinking, imagery, and other internal responses. Labels act as higher mental process responses as they produce cues that are abstractly learned. Labels also provide distinction and facilitate discrimination as well as arouse drives. However, verbal or label-cued responses provide reasoning or planning for subsequent responses. Dollard and Miller contend verbal responses are learned in social interaction and a person who is poorly trained in verbal responses will possess a limited sense of reality as well as having a weak ego.

Dollard and Miller propose that a neurotic behavior is constituted of a set of responses that an individual has learned inappropriately to contend with certain problems. Their nomenclature of neurotic symptoms are similar to psychoanalytic descriptions. However, the responses or actions are described in terms of learning. Thus, the neurotic client in a counseling situation is provided with new conditions of learning which supplant as well as extinguish the more unfavorable responses.

The implementation of reinforcement counseling consists of several progressive steps which are similar to the psychoanalytic technique. However, reinforcement counseling differs from psychoanalytical counseling in that the former is more active and directive. Emphasis is also placed on the corrective and reinforcing values of experiences after the therapeutic sessions.

Reinforcement counseling begins with the counterconditioning or decreasing of anxiety associated with repressed feelings. The counseling situation provides a safe, accepting atmosphere where the client may, and is encouraged, to verbalize any and all feelings. This process encourages a generalization to thinking which weakens the drive's motivating repression. As the client becomes more reassured with the professional, benign attention of the counselor, this will also encourage the verbalization of more painful and deeper repressed material. A significant point in this process is the permissiveness of the counselor to the client's thoughts. The counselor's permissiveness does not extend to permissiveness of antisocial actions. In addition verbalization or free association is a requirement and a rule within the counseling session. Complete permissiveness of verbal material is totally allowed; however, it is the client's responsibility to volunteer his ideas and to do his utmost by talking. Thus, it is the client's responsibility to volunteer information, even in the presence of fear, in order to extinguish the fear. The verbalization situation is a slow process and the client experiences fear and anxiety. The counselor attempts to overcome this fear by rewarding the client with attentive listening, acceptance, understanding, calmness, and lack of punishment.

As the talking progresses, the client begins to emotionally react to the counselor. The ambiguity of the counselor stimulates transference reactions which arise from the client's decrease of anxieties generalized from the talking of hitherto forbidden material. The transference facilitates communication of information which the client is unable to provide directly. The transference coupled with the verbalization of fearful material also facilitates the avoidance response to the counselor. Although this material might be enlightening, it is the counselor's responsibility to inquire and identify the nature and origins of the responses. Dollard and Miller assert that transference responses, like many other responses, are learned, and that they are transferred inappropriately to the counselor. These responses provide a source of inference about the client's earlier condition. The counselor then directs the client's attention to the inappropriateness of these responses and their interference with the counseling situation. In addition, the counselor identifies the transferred responses as generalizations of previously learned, adaptive habits.

Once the generalizations or transference responses are manifested, the counselor then assists the client in naming or labeling these feelings. The labeling or insight consists of producing new verbal responses to correct emotional or situational cues. This is accomplished in three ways. The client may find or create new verbalizations himself; the counselor may encourage or discourage the client's responses by questioning, asking for clarification of labels or nonverbal cues; or the client might practice responses provided by the therapist's interpretations or promptings. Dollard and Miller advise against interpretive interventions unless the client ceases to make progress.

The following aspect of reinforcement counseling involves the client's learning discrimination. The client is instructed that present conditions do not justify the conflicts, repressions, and anxieties of the past and that they are dissimilar. The awareness of the dissimilarity also promotes the distinction of the former responses as well as encouraging new responses which are more realistic, sensible, appropriately adaptive, sociable, and prescient.

Another aspect of reinforcement counseling takes place in the client's outside environment. The counselor does not attempt to provide the client with unrealistic outside rewards. Thus, the life conditions or the client's environment is a strong consideration in the success of the counseling process. The counselor's main task is to then prepare the client to perform newly acquired responses to other people in what formerly was a threatening situation without fear, and with the result being extinction of the former response. In this regard, Dollard and Miller may be said to differ from Salter and Wolpe in that they emphasize discrimination, verbalization, and extinction compared to automatic conditioning and reconditioning. Furthermore, Dollard and Miller place the attitudes and feelings of the client as primary considerations, whereas Salter and Wolpe are first concerned with the symptoms.

An approach to counseling that is gaining popularity in America is the philosophy of *existentialism*. Existentialism represented a movement of ideas which opposed functionalism, instrumentalism, and pragmatism. The latter ideas were consistent with the scientific point of view whereas existentialism, through Martin Heidegger, Jean Paul Sartre, Adrian van Kaam, and Rollo May, represented a philosophy of crisis. Consequently, existentialism did not achieve considerable support in this country until the last decade. Since then, awareness of isolation, depersonalization, and desperation occurred and aroused a concern for the individual's or man's existence.

Existentialism is a philosophy which is specifically concerned with the nature of man, his existence in the modern world, and with the meaning of this existence to individual man. As defined by Rollo May, it is

> ... an endeavor to understand man by cutting below the cleavage between subject and object which has bedeviled Western thought and science since shortly after the Renaissance ...

Moreover, man is not a thing or mechanism but is defined as an emergent or existing being. Thus, existentialism concentrates on the nature of man's being, his spontaneous existence and his existence in the world. Importance is placed on the individual's values, goals, and the understanding of one's personal world, experiences, and inner values. The emphasis on being distinguishes existentialism in its regard for ontological aims.

The existentialist counselor viewing a client approaches the client and the situation in this framework. The term, "approach" should be noted as a significant dimension in the counseling situation, rather than as an operating method. Many of the practitioners within existentialism were influenced by the phenomenological movement which, besides the concerns for man and his world, focused on the individual's immediate experience – his own existence. However, due to this same emphasis on existence and being, existentialistic counseling itself exists as a philosophical assumption and dimension underlying the counseling situation. Carkhuff, Patterson, and Arbuckle concur that a systematic existentialist approach has not been formulated and presented and the nature of the philosophy seemingly precludes a disposition to delineate methods or techniques.

Rollo May has suggested some aspects of the philosophical assumptions which may be perceived in an existential counseling situation. These aspects are the following:

1. Man possesses a related awareness of his own presence which is self-conscious, referent, and experimental. This awareness or "Dasein" is a product of experience which leads to existence. Subsequently, man determines his own existence and is responsible for the decision to be free.

2. Man lives in a gestalt existence and the individual and the world are not separate.

3. The individual is not a static phenomenon and is constantly growing, emerging, and becoming. This state is a process of actualization and evolves toward the fulfillment of man's potentialities. The process in itself is a state of "being" and includes man's participation and awareness in a cosmology of things, events, interrelationships with people, and self.

4. Man's awareness of being and existence also recognizes nonexistence or death. This awareness of the certainty of death confronts the individual with the choice of participating and actualizing his life. Life has meaning only for the living. The concession to nonexistence results in nothingness, loss of individual significance and identity, emptiness, alienation, or death.

5. The threat of nonexistence is a source of fear, anxiety, and aggression. These feelings are normal inasmuch as all individuals share them alike. Anxiety is viewed as an ontological characteristic resulting from the concomitant diminution of one being and the emergence of the evolving, becoming, being. The

inability to allow the emergent being to realize itself further results in guilt.

6. The idea of being involves a sense of self-identity which is based on a sense of existence that is unique, irreplaceable, significant, and in its own inner world.

7. Each individual has the ability to transcend himself. Man possesses the capacity to abstract and symbolize time, events, and himself. This capacity allows man to view himself both as subject and object, and thus provides a basis for freedom, choice, and greater awareness.

8. The individual in society is confronted with the problems of modern living. Whether normal or neurotic, the individual now exists in a removed or distant technology which increases his awareness of depersonalization, detachment, and alienation. This awareness also heightens man's realization that he is alone.

These aspects of existentialism typify a concern with understanding the nature of human existence. It is the concern which also differentiates the existentialist approach from other counseling theories. Existentialism operates as an attitude or a presupposition underlying an approach rather than providing a particular methodology. Within this context, the existentialist counselor acts under certain modes or manners. Rollo May and Adrian Van Kaam suggest some of these characteristics:

1. The existential counselor views the client from the client's own unique point of view or existence which varies with each client. Consequently, the approach is different for each client and must be flexible and versatile.

2. Existentialist counselors might refer to psychoanalytic concepts of transference, repression, and other Freudian concepts. However, those are strictly viewed within the client's own

immediate existence or in the more personal meaning of the experimental situation.

3. The concept of "presence" is always omnipresent within the existential counseling situation. Thus, the counselor does not merely view and perceive the client's existence, as he is aware of and also participating in an experimental relationship called "presence." Both the counselor and the client become and are involved in the presence.

4. The existential counselor consistently supports the relationship of "full presence." A view of the client as an object of remediation impedes the full presence of the relationship. This might result in the production of anxiety because a full, open interaction with another person can evoke defensive behavior.

5. The effects of existential awareness is to experience the fullness of human existence, potentialities, and realizations, as well as act upon them. To view oneself in a strictly objective manner is to thus give credence to oneself as an object rather than an emerging, evolving human being.

6. Action upon one's existence and being is the outcome of existential counseling in developing an attitude toward commitment. Commitment transpires when a decision to act upon life occurs. Insight is then possible as an attitude deriving from the permission of a commitment or decision.

An essential characteristic of existential counseling is the emphasis on the "here and now" in an "I and Thou" relationship. The counseling situation is a participation in the life of each other. The goal is in the realization and acceptance of self-responsibility in its loftiest definition. Thus, to achieve a state of acceptance of responsibility to self-existence is to achieve a state of freedom undisturbed by external or other-being criteria. This achievement also aspires to stimulate a higher degree of individual freedom as well as a loftier meaning of existence and self-determination.

Aside from these theoretical, philosophical considerations, existentialistic counseling, according to Binswanger, rejects any systematic technique. A systematized approach tends to categorize and presume values into a relationship and thus jeopardizes the openness of that relationship. However, Rollo May has noted a similarity between existentialism and client-centered counseling. This similarity is rooted in both their concern for the dignity of the individual and his experience and existence.

☞ Behavior Modification (Behavior Therapy)

Application

Behavior modification is the clinical application of laboratory-based (as opposed to theoretically-based) principles to problems of the world outside the laboratory. Behavior Therapy is characterized by both the systematic application of experimentally derived principles and the attitude of the Behavior Therapist. For the most part his theoretical orientation is learning theory; he views a client as a person who is presenting problems, which he calls the *target behavior,* that are a function of either deficient learning (e.g, failure to have learned the appropriate behavior for the situation) or having learned a maladaptive behavior. He does not assume an underlying cause of the problem.

Review of major differences between Behavior Modifiers and "Traditional" therapists: emphasis on what *maintains* the target behavior versus emphasis on *underlying* cause of symptom (note the difference in labeling). The Behavior Therapist refers to a target behavior – he rejects the term *symptom.* The traditional therapist refers to a symptom which by definition requires an underlying cause. The Behavior Therapist emphasizes the maintaining of consequences to the problem behavior. The trend in behavior therapy is away from Pavlovian conditioning and to operant reinforcement principles (most recently operant cognitive process). In behavioral therapy the therapeutic relationship is that of the consultant/client vs. doctor/patient relationship. Behavior therapists do not view the relationship between themselves and their clients as critical to the outcome of therapy. No attempt is made to develop a transference process. Interpretation of unconscious processes is not attempted. Basic style of therapy utilized by the behavior therapist is very different from the traditional therapist.

Behavior therapists do not diagnose or label clients but rather perform a behavior analysis in which the functional relationship between the target behavior and environment is precisely defined. Traditional therapists usually give diagnoses. Behavior therapists stress outside of office "home work" assignments for client and detailed record keeping. He begins with baseline data and following intervention maintenance of regular records to evaluate effectiveness or lack of effectiveness of the behavior change program. Record keeping may show a gradual improvement or trend that may be missed on verbal self-report. Record keeping is seen as therapeutic in and of itself as a mild aversive tool (contingent behavior) for a client who is on a program to record all food eaten or cigarettes smoked, etc. Also, if there are no results after a reasonable trial, the Behavior Therapist will scrap the ineffective program and institute a new program. Improvement is data-based rather than self-report-based as in traditional therapy.

Therapy work, behavior therapist: behavior analysis of target behavior, matching whenever possible laboratory tested techniques to the problem, assigning homework tasks to implement change, precise recording of baseline and change, if any, to evaluate effectiveness. He or she does not use dreams, projective tests, client insight, and/or interpretation as does the traditional therapist in therapy sessions.

Behavior therapy procedures require that the problem behavior can be clearly specified. The patient who comes in complaining of an existential crisis – "Who am I? Where am I going?" – is usually not an appropriate candidate for behavior therapy. A careful behavioral analysis of the presenting problem may reveal however some specific behavioral deficits that may be functionally related to his existential difficulties. The key to using behavior therapy should be based on findings from the behavioral analysis of the presenting problem.

History of Behavioral Therapy

The origins of behavior therapy are found in the laboratory animal learning and conditioning studies of Pavlov and Bechterev in the Soviet Union, and Thorndike in the United States. These early investigations provided the first systematic basis for conceptualizing the behavioral interactions between organism and environment within the framework of an orderly and self-consistent body of scientific knowledge based on observation and experiment. Virtually all forms of behavior therapy have been derived more or less directly from the foundations of conditioned reflex (Pavlovian) studies and operant conditioning (Skinnerian) research on learning.

The distinctive manner in which the behavior therapist approaches a functional analysis of presenting symptoms in relation to the observable aspects of antecedent events and current environmental conditions, can be seen to have much in common with the experimental approach to the analysis of behavior. Indeed, the objective recording and quantification of clinical data in the evaluation of adjustment problems and specification of treatment goals represent procedures that adhere closely to the methodology characteristic of the laboratory foundations of behavior therapy.

Early Behavioral Research. The range of basic science studies underlying behavior therapy extends well beyond reflex conditioning. Included in the scientific roots of behavior therapy are many sophisticated studies of *verbal behavior, cognitive learning,* and *modeling.*

Several streams of development intervened between the emerging "behaviorism" of Russian and American experimental psychology early in the century, and the current applications of behavior analysis procedures in the treatment of human adjustment problems. During the 1920's and 1930's, for example, the writings of Watson and Rayner Jones, and Mowrer and Mowrer, among others in the United States, were indicative of the trend toward using learning and conditioning principles in approaching various problem behaviors in both educational and clinical settings. In the same era, Soviet psychophysiologists adhering closely to conceptualizations derived directly from laboratory research, became increasingly involved in psychological treatment and, by the 1940's, the experimental work of Gantt, Liddell, and Masserman had begun to establish a laboratory base for Pavlovian psychiatry in America.

Systematic attempts to reformulate psychoanalytic treatment practices in learning theory terms appeared in academic psychology by the mid-1940's. The work of Shoben, Mowrer, and Dollard and Miller, among others, set the stage for the development and rapid expansion of behavior therapy in the 1950's and 1960's.

Later Developments. Current applications of behavior analysis methods have emerged over the past twenty-five years principally as the result of three somewhat independent developments on three continents. These derive from the work of Wolpe and his associates begun in South Africa, from the work at Maudsley Hospital in London, and from the work identified with American applied operant conditioners. These three influences emerged independently but almost simultaneously, and provided refinements that have now begun to coalesce in the development of behavior therapy as a systematic and comprehensive clinical treatment approach.

The clinical and experimental innovations of Wolpe and his colleagues Lazarus and Rachman in South Africa during the early 1950's were based in part on laboratory research within the framework of Hullian learning theory, a theory based on Pavlov's conditioned reflex notions. Starting with an analysis of the role of conditioned emotional responses in the acquisition and maintenance of maladaptive behavior patterns in laboratory experiments with cats, Wolpe developed and extended the Sheringtonian principle of reciprocal inhibition to encompass counteracting response effects on anxiety-evoking stimulus bonds. He extrapolated these generally neurophysiological concepts to the human neuroses, and introduced systematic desensitization procedures that stressed classical conditioning effects involving the identification of symptom-eliciting antecedent stimulus events and respondent extinction of neurotic patterns. The subsequent move by Wolpe and Lazarus to the United States, and Rachman's decision to join the group at Maudsley Hospital in England not only provided the occasion for dispersal of these early conditioning therapy developments but also facilitated the interchange of ideas, techniques, and applications with other approaches.

A second source of direct influence in the development of behavior therapy was a group of psychologists and psychiatrists in London around 1950 who were following Evsenck's and Shapiro's lead in attempting to bridge what they perceived to be a distressingly wide gap between laboratory-based learning principles and clinically-oriented psychotherapeutic practices. Emphasizing experimental analysis and hypothesis-testing in individual case studies, this basically empirical approach to clinical assessment proved readily adaptable to treatment situations. Systematic attempts to change maladaptive behavior by carrying out controlled experiments in the clinic resulted in a focus on explicit operational descriptions of the psychiatric entity.

The third major impetus to the application of behavior analysis principles to clinical treatment emerged in the United States during the 1950's based on the earlier work of Skinner. This innovative experimental approach to behavior emphasized the study of the individual interacting with the environment, and focused attention on the effects or consequences of operant or "voluntary" performances as the principal determinant of behavior. Unlike other approaches prominent in American psychology, which was preoccupied at the time with the average behavior of groups of persons, Skinner and his students (notably Ferster, Lindsley, and Azrin, among others) emphasized the control of behavior in the individual as a basis for behavioral science.

The earliest operant experimental studies of *psychotics* were reported by Lindsley and Skinner and by Ferster and DeMyer. These laboratory studies showed that the behavior of severely disturbed persons was subject to the same learning principles as that of normal persons. In 1961 Allyon and Azrin, working with chronic adult psychotics, began to develop the ward management procedures that have come to be known as the token economy. Operant treatment programs for mildly disturbed preschool children and retardates were begun at this same time by Wolf, Baer, and their collaborators.

Over the past decade, a broad range of applications within the operant conditioning framework has extended behavior modification procedures to numerous individual and institutional settings, both clinical and educational. Although work with children continues to be emphasized, the precise measurement techniques and careful arrangement of environmental contingencies of the operant approach have produced reliable behavioral change in a variety of target populations.

Behavior Therapy Methods

Following a behavior analysis of the target behavior the clinician is in a good position to formulate one or more clinical hypotheses about the *origin* and *maintenance* of the client's target behavior.

Behavior therapy permits the testing of clinical hypotheses by the systematic manipulation of behavioral and environmental variables thought to be functionally related to the client's target behavior.

Systematic Desensitization. The first and most thoroughly researched method used by behavior therapists established the treatment of choice for phobia, and the first hard evidence that a therapeutic intervention for mental distress could reliably and effectively cure a client. (Gordon Paul, 1966)

Wolpe maintains "if a response antagonistic to anxiety can be made to occur in the presence of anxiety-evoking stimuli, so that the stimuli are accompanied by a complete or partial suppression of the anxiety response, the bond between these stimuli and the anxiety will be weakened." Wolpe further contends that mere exposure to a feared situation is unlikely to extinguish the fear unless responses that will compete with the anxiety response are simultaneously elicited.

Two principles are brought together, (1) a competing response to anxiety, primarily used is a relaxation state, (you can't be anxious and relaxed at the same time), (2) a fear hierarchy – an ordering of the patient's fears in a hierarchy with relatively small gradations between successive fear items. A typical hierarchy for scenes desensitizing maladaptive anxiety in the treatment of sexual inhibition (female) would be:

Low to high:

1. My boyfriend kissing me.

2. My boyfriend kissing me with an open mouth.

3. Breasts fondled while fully clothed.

4. Boyfriend's hands underneath blouse.

5. Undressing in front of him.

6. Seeing him with erection.

7. Kissing while both nude.

8. Breast fondling, nude, and lying down.

9. As above with clitoral stimulation.

10. As above immediately before intromission.

11. The act of penetration.

12. Hard vigorous vaginal thrusting.

Following training in relaxation, Jacobson's Deep Muscle, progressive relaxation is frequently used – the client proceeds through the hierarchy using imagery until she reports the ability to visualize the most difficult items on her hierarchy with minimal anxiety. Next the couple is instructed to begin at the beginning of the hierarchy en vivo and to proceed step by step, making sure to maintain relaxation or sexual excitement which also competes with anxiety, in ascendancy. The entire procedure is typically completed in fifteen to twenty-five sessions over three to four months' duration.

Success rates with phobias go over 80 percent with five-year follow-up.

Flooding. Like systematic desensitization, this is a procedure to extinguish maladaptive anxiety. In this approach the client maintains exposure or contact with the highest items on the hierarchy until a lowering of anxiety is felt by the client in the feared situation. Recent research indicates flooding to be the most efficacious treatment for *agoraphobia* with extinction of anxiety in six to eight sessions when client remains in situations two or more hours. Much experimental evidence exists for this procedure but it should not be used if client is a psychotic risk.

Implosive Therapy. Developed by Stampel in 1963, Implosive Therapy is based on psychoanalytic theory and items for client exposure come from the dynamic areas thought to be the basic problem of the patient. This procedure is not based on laboratory studies and is generally in disfavor by behavior therapists.

Token Economies. Developed by Stadt in the late 1950's in an educational setting, and by Allyon in a psychiatric inpatient hospital shortly afterwards, token economics is the application of operant reinforcement learning principles to develop and maintain appropriate behaviors. Inappropriate behaviors are inhibited by the removal of positive reinforcers (moving the person from reinforcement environment is called *time out*, technically a form of punishment).

The rationale of *token economy* program is based on studies which have shown that many behavioral problems with students and psychiatric inpatients were maintained by staff reinforcing the inappropriate behavior through attention.

Allyon sought to reinforce behavior incompatible with the problem behavior using a token as a conditional reinforcer in the form of points, or credits. The token is used to bridge the delay between the disordered response and the availability of the reinforcing stimulus. Rather than encouraging dependency the Token Economy operates much like the economy of the real world and encourages independent behavior in terms of a work-payment incentive system.

The greatest challenge of Token Economy is transfer. Some questions remain to be answered on this point when used in educational settings.

Token Economies have, with psychiatric inpatients:

1. improved performance within hospitals

2. improved patient socialization

3. reduced extreme or bizarre behavior

Approximately 10 percent of chronic schizophrenic patients are non-responsive (do not engage in any behaviors for which they can earn tokens).

Assertion Training or Personal Effectiveness Training or Pro-social Skills Training. A major behavior therapy program, second in frequency of use, very probably, to systematic desensitization. A small group (six to eight) approach to behavior change for those clients either too anxious or too unskilled to effectively speak up for themselves in a wide variety of social situations. Inclusion into an assertion group again follows a careful behavioral analysis of the problem. Eschewing dynamic group practices the therapist of an assertiveness training group uses modeling, (as described by Bandura in shaping techniques and behavioral rehearsal to assist a client to change his or her behavior from nonassertiveness to assertive behavior).

Alberti and Emmons, drawing upon the earlier work of Wolpe, were the first to publish on assertion. Earlier works go back to Andrew Salter (1940's) and Albert Ellis. This rather brief, eight-to-twelve week program seems to be a highly efficient therapy technique. Very promising research results are now appearing in the behavioral journals. The plethora of workshops and books flooding the country put it in an almost fad category. However, properly led assertion groups will very likely survive the rigor of outcome evaluation and prove to be a trend for more effective brief intervention methods at the group level.

Covert Sensitization. A form of aversion therapy to reduce the frequency of maladaptive behavior. Developed by J. Cautela in the early 1960's, the therapist would present noxious imagery to the client following the client's imagined performance of the problem behavior. A very promising technique with the client possessing vivid imagery, avoiding the thorny issues of physical aversive stimuli, and superior in transference and generalization properties due to the closer chosen similarity of stimulus elements from imagery to the actual setting (vs. aversion techniques in the office or laboratory).

Thought Stoppage. A brief inhibitory technique to reduce the frequency of undesirable self-generated verbalizations based on the stimulus control properties of words like "stop" and "out." The client is asked to begin to think the undesirable thought (e.g., I can't pass the test) at which time the therapist loudly shouts "STOP!" The highly conditioned word is supposed to interrupt the client's negative verbalizations and then turn to a series of competing verbalizations. Almost no research results to date.

Contingency Contracting. An operant reinforcement learning program in which a structured quid pro quo arrangement between client and therapist (or teacher, parent, etc.) is *jointly* worked out. Based on the concept of Skinner's positive control vs. society's usual aversive control, the client is informed, for example, upon completion of one chapter of history by 8:00 p.m. you may watch TV for thirty minutes. It is similar to Token Economy in the use of reinforcement as behavior control but differs in its specificity of both the behavior which must be performed and the contingent reinforcer.

Written agreements specifying the what and when method of evaluating satisfactoriness of the desired behavior and the what and when of the contingent reinforcer are the usual ingredients of a Contingency Contract.

☞ *References*

1. "ACES Corner: Sensitization to Non-Verbal Communications." *Counselor Education and Supervision*, Spring 1968, pp. 315–316.
2. Blocher, Donald H. *Developmental Counseling.* New York: The Ronald Press Company, 1966.

3. Brayfield, Arthur H. *Readings in Modern Methods of Counseling.* New York: Appleton-Century Crofts, 1950.

4. Bugental, James F. T. *The Search for Authenticity: An Existential-Analytic Approach to Psychotherapy.* New York: Holt, Rinehart & Winston, 1965.

5. Demos, George D., and Bruce Grant. *The California Pre-Counseling Self-Analysis Protocol Booklet.* Los Angeles, California: Western Psychological Services, 1965.

6. Demos, George, and Bruce Grant. "Sharpening Your Communicative Skills." *Education,* November 1966, pp. 174–176.

7. Erickson, Clifford E. *A Basic Text for Guidance Workers.* New York: Prentice-Hall, Inc., 1947.

8. Grant, Bruce, George D. Demos, and Willard Edwards. *Guidance for Youth.* Springfield, Illinois: Charles C. Thomas, 1965.

9. Harmes, E., and P. Schreiber. *Handbook of Counseling Techniques.* Long Island City, New York: Pergamon Press, 1964.

10. Hoyt, Kenneth B. "High School Guidance and the Specially Oriented Student Research Program." *Vocational Guidance Quarterly,* Summer 1965, pp. 229–236.

11. Kelz, James W., and Edward L. Trembley. *Supervised Counseling Experiences.* Boulder, Colorado: Pruett Press, 1965.

12. Packard, Vance. *The Pyramid Climbers.* New York: McGraw-Hill Book Company, 1962.

13. Robinson, Francis P. *Principles and Procedures in Student Counseling.* New York: Harper and Brothers, 1950.

14. Rogers, Carl. *Client-Centered Therapy.* Boston: Houghton Mifflin, 1951.

15. Rogers, Carl. *Counseling and Psychotherapy.* Boston: Houghton Mifflin, 1942.

16. Sachs, Benjamin M. *The Student, The Interview, and the Curriculum: Dynamics of Counseling in the School.* Boston: Houghton Mifflin, 1966.

17. Shertzer, Bruce, and Herman J. Peters. *Guidance Techniques for Individual Appraisal.* New York: The Macmillan Company, 1965.

18. Siegel, Max. *The Counseling of College Students.* New York: The Free Press, 1968.

19. Smith, Glenn E. *Counseling in the Secondary School.* New York: The Macmillan Company, 1955.

20. Strang, Ruth. *Counseling Techniques in College and Secondary Schools.* New York: Harper and Brothers, 1949.

21. Traxler, Arthur E., and Robert D. North. *Techniques of Guidance.* New York: Harper and Row, 1966.

22. Williamson, E. G. *Counseling Adolescents.* New York: McGraw-Hill Book Company, 1950.

23. Zeran, Franklin R., John E. Lallas, and Kenneth W. Wegner. *Guidance: Theory and Practice.* New York: American Book Company, 1964.

☞ *Suggested Additional Readings*

American Personnel and Guidance Association Policy Statement, "Responsibilities of Users of Standardized Tests." *Guidepost* 21, no. 5 (1978), pp. 5–8.

American Psychological Association. *Standards for Educational and Psychological Tests.* Washington, D.C.: American Psychological Association, 1974.

Association for Measurement and Evaluation in Guidance. "The Responsible Use of Tests: A Position Paper of AMEG, APGA, and NCME." *Measurement and Evaluation in Guidance 5,* no. 2, (1972), pp. 385–388.

Atkinson, Donald R., George Morton, and Derald Wing Sue, eds. *Counseling American Minorities.* Dubuque, Iowa: William C. Brown and Company, 1979.

Barclay, James R. "The Revolution in Counseling: Some Editorial Comments." *Personnel and Guidance Journal* 58, no. 7 (1980), p. 457.

Benjamin, Libby, and Garry R. Walz, eds. *Counseling Exceptional People.* Ann Arbor, Michigan: ERIC Counseling and Personnel Services Clearinghouse, 1980.

Betz, Ellen. "The Counselor Role." In *Student Services,* edited by Ursula Delworth and Gary R. Hanson, pp. 175–190. San Francisco: Jossey-Bass, 1980.

Blimline, Carol A., ed. *Innovations in Counseling Services.* Washington, D.C.: International Association of Counseling Services (not dated).

Callis, Robert, Edward Roeber, and Paul C. Polmantier. *A Casebook of Counseling.* New York: Appleton-Century Crofts, 1955.

Carroll, Marguerite R. "Introduction." *School Counselor* 20, no. 5 (1973), p. 333.

Carkhuff, Robert R. *Helping and Human Relations.* New York: Holt, Rinehart and Winston, 1969.

Cottle, William C., and N. M. Downie. *Procedures and Preparation for Counseling.* Englewood Cliffs, New Jersey: Prentice-Hall, 1960.

Corsini, Raymond, ed. *Current Psychotherapies.* Itasca, Illinois: F. E. Peacock, 1973.

Fullmer, Daniel W. *Counseling: Content and Process.* Chicago: Science Research Associates, Inc., 1964.

Ganikos, Mary L., Kathleen A. Grady, and Jane B. Olson. *Counseling the Aged.* Washington, D.C.: American Personnel and Guidance Association, 1979.

Goldman, Leo. *Using Tests in Counseling.* 2nd ed. New York: Appleton-Century-Crofts, 1971.

Hahn, Milton. *Psychoevaluation: Adaptation-Distribution-Adjustment.* New York: McGraw-Hill Book Company, 1963.

Harmon, Lenore W., Janice M. Birk, Laurine E. Fitzgerald, and Mary Faith Tanney, eds. *Counseling Women.* Monterey, California: Brooks/Cole Publishing Company, 1978.

Hennessy, Thomas C. "Introduction to the Special Issue, 'Values and the Counselors'." *Personnel and Guidance Journal* 58, no. 9 (1980), pp. 557–558.

Herr, Edwin L., and Stanley H. Cramer. *Career Guidance Through the Life Span.* Boston: Little, Brown, 1979.

Kell, Bill L., and William J. Mueller. *Impact and Change: A Study of Counseling Relationships.* New York: Appleton-Century Crofts, 1966.

Lee, James L., and Charles J. Pulvino, eds. *Group Counseling: Theory, Research and Practice.* Washington, D.C.: American Personnel and Guidance Association, 1973.

Leopard, Judy Gaines, and Dale Wachowiak. "Introduction to Coupling." *Personnel and Guidance Journal 55,* no. 9 (1977), p. 503.

Miller, Frank W., James A. Fruehling, and Gloria J. Lewis. *Guidance Principles and Services.* 3rd ed. Columbus, Ohio: Charles E. Merrill, 1978.

Miller, Theodore K., and Judith S. Prince. *The Future of Student Affairs.* San Francisco: Jossey-Bass, 1976.

Moser, Leslie E., and Ruth Small Moser. *Counseling and Guidance: An Exploration.* Englewood Cliffs, New Jersey: Prentice-Hall, 1963.

Patterson, C. H. "A Current View of Client-Centered or Relationship Theory." *Counseling Psychologist* 1, no. 2 (1969), pp. 2–25.

Shertzer, Bruce, and Shelley C. Stone. *Fundamentals of Guidance.* 4th ed. Boston: Houghton Mifflin, 1981.

Thoresen, Carl E., and Thomas J. Coates. "What Does It Mean to Be a Behavior Therapist?" *Counseling Psychologist* 7, no. 3 (1978), pp. 3–21.

Traxler, Arthur E., and Robert D. North. *Techniques of Guidance.* New York: Harper and Row, 1966.

Walz, Garry R., and Libby Benjamin, eds. *New Imperatives for Guidance.* Ann Arbor, Michigan: ERIC Counseling and Personnel Services Clearinghouse, 1978.

Weinrach, Stephen G. "Reviews." *Personnel and Guidance Journal* 55, no. 9 (1977), pp. 556–559, and 55, no. 10 (1977), pp. 612–618.

Wilkenson, Lee A., Autism Spectrum Disorder in Children & Adolescents, A.P.A., 2014.

Williamson, E. G. *Counseling Adolescents.* New York: McGraw-Hill Book Company, 1950.

Zeran, Franklin R., John E. Lallas, and Kenneth W. Wegner. *Guidance: Theory and Practice.* New York: American Book Company, 1964.

Chapter 13

COUNSELING STRATEGIES

🖝 *Advisement*

The first in sequence of the seventeen techniques of counseling is *informing*. This is defined as the giving of facts. A fact is anything that happens or exists. Accordingly, whenever a counselor is engaged in giving a client a report on a happening or something in existence, he/she is informing.

It is regrettable that some practitioners, authorities, and counselor educators have seen fit to belittle informing as a counseling technique. It is absurd to propose that when a counselor is informing, he is not counseling. The time has come to state unequivocally that there are many occasions when all that a client needs from a counselor is information – not even interpretation of data – just the facts. When data are requested or when the counselor decides that facts should be given, it obviously is appropriate to inform or to refer if the counselor does not possess the required knowledge.

Having teaching experience can be a valuable asset to the counselor in achieving that high level of skill identified as art. One deleterious practice that is characteristic of many teachers may unfortunately persist as the individual begins counseling – verbosity. The teacher finds it necessary to repeat "over and over and over again" in order to get through to some students. After so much of this, it is a rare teacher who can talk in any social situation without "overtalking."

Every effort should be made by the counselor to verbalize succinctly. The reader is invited to scrutinize carefully each of the excerpts in this and the following chapters to determine if the counselor adheres to this principle of brevity.

Another caution to be observed in informing is to avoid straying from the information requested or needed into a related or even unrelated area of thought. There must be as little redundancy as possible.

The examples of the informing technique which follow are not to be regarded as being perfect illustrations or models of the best of the technique, but simply as revealing the technique in action.

These excerpts given below and those following in subsequent chapters should provide ample bases for discussion concerning the strengths and weaknesses of each technique.

☞ Excerpts

Client: What is the deadline for applying for admission next fall to a state college?
Counselor: September 1.
Client: Is English I a required course for graduation?
Counselor: Yes.
Client: What GPA (grade point average) must a transfer student have to be considered for admission to the university?
Counselor: 2.0.

☞ Interpreting

Whenever the counselor is involved in presenting the meaning of something, he/she is *interpreting*. The frequent use of this technique is evidence of its importance in the counselor's repertory of skills.

As in the case of informing, brevity is important. However, while verbosity should be curbed, more latitude in verbalizing is permissible in interpreting than in informing. Indeed, to be too brief could be hazardous to the central purpose – giving an adequate explanation.

The counselor should strive to determine what meaning the client needs to acquire, how extensive or intensive the explanation should be, and the probability that the client will be able to comprehend the proposed interpretation.

Having resolved these questions, the counselor should proceed to interpret briefly, yet in sufficient detail and length to provide the client's needed insight. While giving the meaning of something may range from a simple definition to a detailed explanation, a wise admonition herein to all counselors in all interpreting is: "Say what must be said, then *shut up*." This colloquial expression might well be framed in big block letters to rest on the counselor's desk, serving as a continuous reminder whenever he is informing, interpreting, or clarifying.

One of the "tricky" aspects of interpreting is that usually there is more than one possible explanation whenever an interpretation is to be given. A fact is a fact just as a law is a law. But it is not any startling bit of news to report that many lawyers make a very fine living and carve a career out of the fabric of differing interpretations. Judges and juries are concerned with making decisions after being exposed to a multiplicity of opposing interpretations of facts.

Because a client may find the same fact explained to him/her differently every time he changes counselors, it certainly behooves all counselors, but especially guidance counselors, to avoid a distortion of facts by fuzzy interpreting, to be alert to exuding opinion under the guise of fact, to avoid professional jargon unless it is also explained, and to generally progress, rather than retrogress, in the process of interpreting.

As to the variation of meanings and the disagreement (even among authorities) on explanation of facts, it is important for the counselor to exercise caution in postulating, proclaiming absolutes, depicting extremes, or exhibiting rigidity. The client should be made aware of the relativity, fluidity, and looseness of the explanations he or she receives.

Another point to be noted in interpreting is the fact that occasionally what is being explained is not a fact but an opinion, belief, or idea. There is nothing wrong with explaining nonfacts if they are so labeled, but with the time factor being as critical as it is in most counselor-client situations, there seldom will be much opportunity within the interpretation for straying away from facts, unless there is a client need for such excursions.

☞ *Clarifying*

The last in the triumvirate of techniques focusing sharply on information is *clarifying*. Whenever the counselor is in the process of bettering the client's understanding of something, he/she is clarifying.

When an explanation of something – interpreting – is not sufficient to assure the client's understanding, or his/her reaction shows confusion, or he/she requests or obviously needs an elaboration, or there appears to be a degree of fuzziness, obscurity, or misunderstanding, then the process of clarifying becomes necessary. Once again the possession of a teaching background becomes an asset to the counselor, for so often the teacher must clarify previously explained items.

Actually, of course, clarifying is a form of interpreting, but it is included as a separate technique to reinforce the necessity of the counselor "interpreting his/her interpretation."

If the counselor interprets courtesy as "kindness," the client may reveal bewilderment about this explanation. Clarification would then be needed. This is demonstrated in the excerpts below.

Clarifying often is needed because the interpreting was inadequate. A cardinal error in interpreting is to define by giving a synonym, as in the paragraph above. Telling the client that courtesy is kindness accomplishes nothing unless kindness already has meaning for him/her.

But when counselor-client intellectual interaction is meant to enrich the client's understanding by enabling him/her to gain more profound or accurate insight into something, this is the process of clarifying at its finest. Clarifying can be a "depth approach" to refining a client's understanding. It is an elaboration of the interpretive process, an extending and intensifying of a basic explanation.

As with other techniques, however, some of the pitfalls of clarifying are "overdoing of a good thing," an introduction of redundancy, a tendency toward too much abstraction, or a belaboring of what could become the obvious.

The important fact in clarifying is not for the counselor to say to himself/herself, "I wonder if I am interpreting or clarifying," but for him/her to know that further interpretation – or, as it is labeled herein, clarifying – is necessary at strategic points in the process of helping his/her clients.

☞ *Evaluating*

Evaluating means determining the strengths and weaknesses of something. This always demands the use of criteria in order that a judgment may be made to ascertain the strengths and weaknesses of whatever is being evaluated.

Actually, there is no such thing as one separate technique of evaluation – as there is in informing, interpreting, and clarifying – for evaluating consists of a variety of techniques. Furthermore, it is ultimately the client who should do the evaluating, so that the counselor's role is to introduce this "technique" as a process for the client to use whenever he/she is trying to determine the value of something.

Having selected or developed criteria, the client is ready to determine strengths and weaknesses by relating facts about whatever is being evaluated to the criteria. When this comparison is completed, the client then studies the revealed strengths and weaknesses until he/she is ready to formulate conclusions from them.

This section does not deal with the client engaging in the evaluative process, but with the counselor initiating the client's use of evaluating at a time when this – as a technique of the client – is an appropriate and effective way to acquire insight into the value of something. Accordingly, from the counselor's standpoint, he/she is not evaluating; instead, he/she is using other techniques to make it possible for the client to evaluate.

☞ *Reviewing*

Even though the counselor has adequately informed and/or interpreted, and then clarified the information, there still remains for some clients a need to go over the same things again. This repeating of information is *reviewing.*

Once again the value of a counselor having had experience as a teacher is apparent, for repeating while teaching is a necessity if some individuals are to learn. Equally obvious is the pitfall of verbosity that plagues the counselor almost every time he/she seeks to review. In reviewing, perhaps more than in any other technique, the temptation to oververbalize becomes almost impossible to overcome unless continuous awareness is brought to bear on curbing it.

Once more it is suggested that the counselor heed the admonition to say what must be said, then remain silent. Conversely, don't neglect to repeat when the need for it is obvious.

☞ Inquiring

The terms *inquiring* and *questioning* are often used synonymously whenever the intended meaning involves "getting information." As used in reference to counseling techniques, *inquiring* is defined as asking for information, and *questioning* refers to interrogating in order to stimulate thinking.

When, in the course of an interview, the counselor needs information, yet does not require it in writing at the particular moment he/she wants it, inquiring becomes necessary. If the information requires many inquiries, or the inquiring and responses of the client become too time-consuming, the counselor should get the information by using a Personal Data Form (see page 44). As we stated in Chapter 7, when the counselor wants a minimal amount of information about his/her client before beginning counseling or after one interview when additional interviews are planned, the structured form (to be completed by the client) can be used. Or, when more detailed facts or a history are desired, *The California Pre-Counseling Self-Analysis Booklet* is recommended. In the case of getting a history, if the counselor wishes to do this in an interview in order to observe client reactions, this would justify extensive, time-consuming inquiring.

Except for the history, however, efforts should be made to avoid using valuable counseling time by inquiring about matters which might better be handled by having the client complete a structured form or booklet.

However, when only two or three items of information are needed, there are many instances in which inquiring is the most appropriate means of obtaining the data.

It also takes time to supply written information. The client should not be asked to spend several minutes filling out even a short one-page form if the matter may be properly handled by an inquiry or two.

☞ Questioning

As it is used in this section, *questioning* does not refer to seeking information, or to reflecting. Its meaning is limited to "interrogating in order to stimulate thinking."

When the counselor decides that the client needs to "think out loud" regarding whatever it is that concerns him or her, it is appropriate to provoke thinking by posing questions that stir intellectual activity on the client's part.

This technique is particularly apropos when the client is too dependent upon the counselor, knows something but wants the counselor to say it, shirks responsibility for coming to intellectual grips with a problem, needs to think, skirts the issue, tries to circumvent a factual approach to a difficulty, or avoids a confrontation with a dilemma.

This type of questioning is as old as Socrates (469–399 b.c.) who immortalized as a teaching technique the Socratic method, in which the teacher used questioning to elicit responses from the student about things implicitly known by him. Getting the clients to express themselves intellectually when it is appropriate to working on their problems is just as important as the much-publicized value of their expressing their feelings.

☞ Discussing

In this section, we will use *discussing* to mean "declaring factors pro and con."

When discussing, an effort is made to present both sides of something. This may be done by either the counselor or the client or by both as they verbally interact with each other.

Sometimes discussing is closely integrated with evaluating. If the client wishes to go over the strengths and weaknesses his or her evaluation has uncovered, the interaction resulting may become a discussion as the counselor or the client talk over the positive and negative findings of the evaluation.

Discussing becomes appropriate whenever there is more than one side to whatever is being considered, when there are alternatives to identify and reflect upon as possible solutions to a problem, or when the client is confronted with a dilemma. Since the counselor's function here is to see that all sides to the problem, pro and con, are fairly considered, he/she must be objective. He/she often needs to guard against the temptation of favoring or exploiting certain factors as he/she verbalizes about them.

Clients may make the mistake of "pushing under the rug" those factors they discover about self or environment which they do not accept. When his/her self-concept is threatened, the client often resorts to a variety of subterfuges, occasionally distorting findings to salvage his/her self-esteem, or engaging in recrimination of others as a means of ego-strengthening. It is at such times that discussing may be helpful in assisting the client to become aware that everything is not black or white, but much may well be gray.

The discussing technique is not a pure, distinct, totally separate technique. It may include informing, interpreting, clarifying, inquiring, questioning, and suggesting. Discussing is actualized through an assortment of other techniques brought to bear upon a situation in which positive and negative factors are being examined.

☞ Motivating

Motivating means stimulating action. Whenever the counselor says or does anything that incites the client to do something, this is motivating.

Just as in the cases of evaluating and discussing, there is not any motivating technique per se. Motivating is done through one or more of the following techniques: informing, interpreting, clarifying, questioning, discussing, suggesting, nonverbal responses, brief replies, reflecting, empathizing, supporting, and reassuring.

Often, motivating is a by-product of a technique being used for another purpose. The counselor may be presenting the meaning of something, with the goal being the client's understanding of a fact. If, in addition to acquiring the desired knowledge, the client proceeds to act upon it, then he/she has been motivated. If, for example, the counselor interprets with the objective of causing the client to act, then the interpreting serves the direct end of motivating. In fact, the motivating may occur even if the understanding – resulting from the interpreting – is shallow or missed entirely by the client.

☞ Suggesting

Suggesting has often been subjected to the sharp criticism directed toward "advising." If suggesting is used as a subtle means of telling a client what decision he/she should make, if it is psychological manipulating, if it is coercion disguised as permissiveness, then it deserves to be put in the category of "advising," which is, of course, a nasty word in the lexicon of counseling jargon.

But as it is used here, "suggesting" means proposing courses of action. So long as the counselor confines his/her suggestions to presenting alternative ways of doing something, or different activities for choice consideration, he/she remains on sound ground. The trick, however, is to restrict suggesting to these confining limits. There is a very thin margin between offering alternatives without any bias or favoritism, and moving into direct or indirect proposals that "such and such" an action is the best choice the client could make.

Counselors will help themselves to circumvent the possible dangers in suggesting by concentrating on making proposals relating to procedures. It is permissible to propose that some methods are superior to others. However, counselors should tread gently regarding all propositions that come within the area of solutions to problems. This does not mean that alternative solutions to problems should be left unsaid, but that they should be offered sparingly, without emphasis or influence being exerted toward any particular solution.

Since counselors are not machines, it probably will always remain difficult for them to accept passively a client's making poor decisions. Their human reaction is to pounce upon a bad choice by suggesting a better one. But the counselor must refrain from "playing God." It is the client's right to decide unwisely, if he/she so chooses. The decisions must be his/hers. In fact, if he/she is ever to acquire skill in problem solving, he/she must be given the opportunity to select his/her own solutions.

Having taken due precaution to adhere to this admonition, the counselor should be equally diligent to accept his/her responsibility to exercise a commonsense approach to letting the client know that certain actions are fraught with danger, or that other actions are not prudent and that some actions are more worthy of consideration than others. "To do or not to do" is not always the question if the doing is absurd, hazardous, fruitless, valueless, or injurious to the welfare of the client.

Accordingly, it is well within the province of the counselor to propose courses of action which have merit, being careful to permit the client to make his/her own choice of the available alternatives.

As is the case with several other techniques, suggesting is not a separate technique. It is done by informing and questioning.

☞ Nonverbal Responses

The major nonverbal response is listening. Other important ones are waiting, interested facial expression, relaxed bodily appearance, nodding head, and smiling.

The virtues of listening have been extolled by many authorities, but, without meaning to belittle listening or to imply that it is not sound in many instances, we should recognize that sometimes listening should be supplemented by verbal responses.

Particularly in working with brilliant individuals who want an intellectual reaction, it becomes inane for a counselor to gaze into the face of his/her client and say nothing when the client needs a verbalized reaction.

To sit and listen for thirty minutes while an overly verbose client rambles in a disorganized fashion is a luxury few counselors can afford in their busy schedules. To listen while the client just wants to visit or to use up time rather than going back to Mrs. Wilson's geography class, to listen to the same thing repeated again and again, to listen while irrelevant, extraneous, unrelated, or unneeded verbalizing continues interminably are all instances of the abuse of listening.

When the counselor listens, it should be *active listening* rather than *passive listening*. It is an insult to a client to sit and gaze out the window, to yawn in his face, to fuss with papers on the desk, or to give the impression of being disinterested, preoccupied, or too busy. Each client has the right to the counselor's undivided attention. Except when it is simply unavoidable, the client should not be interrupted by telephone, secretary, or another counselor.

Waiting, as used herein, refers to the counselor remaining silent as he waits for the client to speak. The counselor remains in readiness for action. Actually, waiting is not a response, but it is included here as one in order to emphasize the need for delaying any verbal action until the appropriate moment.

A common mistake of the inexperienced counselor is not waiting until the client is ready to talk. Even to some experienced counselors, silence becomes oppressive, embarrassing, or boring; consequently, they hasten to say something when silence should be observed. This does not mean that a busy counselor is obligated to wait indefinitely while a client sits tongue-tied, too shy to speak or too afraid to say anything. But a reasonable period of silence (as dictated by the circumstances) is permissible and acceptable.

An interested facial expression is the least a counselor should offer a client. The "stoney-face" or cigar-store Indian expression, the disinterested look, the harassed appearance, or the patronizing manner is an insult to an alert, sensitive, intelligent client; it is an affront to even the most insensitive or dull client, who has the right to expect a human reaction. The counselor should remember that the client comes to him as a human being, not as a machine.

A relaxed bodily appearance on the part of the counselor does much to set the stage for the informal, at-ease, comfortable atmosphere that should always prevail in counselor-client relationships. As a counselor educator, one of the authors had a counseling intern who epitomized the opposite approach. This intern sat in an exaggeratedly erect position, giving the impression that he/she was conforming to an overly enthusiastic physical-culture faddist's concept of correct posture. This bodily configuration was almost frightening to the young high school students who were his/her clients. All he/she needed to do was recline in his/her chair, put his/her feet on the desk, and light a pipe, all of which could contribute to creating the relaxed image so desperately needed in his/her office.

When a client says something which does not call for a verbal response, this does not mean that the counselor should not react in any way. In such situations, nodding the head occasionally is a courtesy extended by gentlemen and ladies in social situations. It would seem elementary to propose that the counselor should be equally observant of social niceties. That we have to call attention to this matter is indicative of the lamentable fact that some counselors resemble more the "cigar-store Indian" than the "old school gentleman."

It is not necessary for the counselor to keep a fixed, artificial smile on his/her countenance throughout an interview. In fact, there are times when a smile would be most inappropriate. However, the other extreme of presenting a continuous "stone-face" is out of line. Most of the time a pleasant look is sufficient, but frequent smiling – even grinning – is a traditional symbol for acceptance, liking, enjoyable socializing, and rapport. Except in matters of grief, or client reactions of hostility or other similar situations, the smile often is an effective harmonizer, a creator of warmth in the counselor-client relationship.

This does not mean that the counselor should affix a smirk upon his/her face or contrive an artificial smile that is the essence of insincerity. Clients are quick to detect such phoniness, resenting it and its contriver.

The counseling intern would do well to observe his/her facial and bodily appearance in a mirror or through the use of videotape throughout the interview. This will clue him/her on when his/her appearance is not as it should be. The counselor should be alert to avoid appearing bored, irritated, hostile, apathetic, uninterested, insensitive, sleepy, disenchanted, critical, patronizing, frightened, unconcerned, or confused.

☞ *Brief Replies*

Whenever the counselor makes a short verbal response, it may be termed a "brief reply." It is not necessary herein to inventory all of the possible brief replies available to the counselor. Instead, those responses frequently used are listed below:

Certainly	I doubt it
Of course	Unlikely
That's right	Not really
Yes	I see
Perhaps	I understand
It's possible	I know
Probably so	Oh
If you wish	What do you think?
No	How?
Probably not	Why?

The brief reply is actualized through the techniques of informing, inquiring, and questioning.

For the overly verbose counselor, the practice of forcing himself/ herself occasionally to overuse brief replies should be helpful in exercising a degree of control in keeping his/her verbalizing within prescribed limits.

There is, of course, the possibility that the brief reply will be too brief, give the impression of curtness, or foster an illusion that the counselor is too busy to say what should be said. These negative images can be counteracted by the use of positive nonverbal responses, such as interested facial expression, relaxed bodily appearance, and smiling.

If the counselor wishes to achieve frequent verbal reactions on the part of the client, his/her use of brief replies can often bring this about.

The client can hardly be expected to say much if he/she must listen too long or too often to the counselor's lengthy verbalizing.

There also will be occasions when brief replies may serve to stimulate the client to do his/her own thinking rather than relying on the counselor to think for him/her.

The brief reply sometimes is an effective antidote to a counselor's tendency to be redundant. However, even here, unnecessary repetition may insidiously insert itself into a response where one brief reply is usually sufficient.

☞ *Empathizing*

As was pointed out in the previous section, reflecting ought to serve the purpose of helping the client to identify, accept, and deal with his/her emotions. Empathizing also deals with reacting to the client's emotions. It means expressing an appreciation of another's feelings (which depends on being fully aware of them).

In empathizing the counselor engages in informing, interpreting, and clarifying.

It may be helpful to a person suffering grief to receive a reaction from someone who shows that he/she is aware what grief is, not as a theoretical consideration, but from experience.

Letting the client know that he/she, the counselor, has been through the same or a similar experience gives assurance to the client that here is a person who may be able to help him/her, or at the very least should be sympathetic regarding whatever is causing him/her concern.

The quality of empathy is behind the reason why some major-league baseball players accept a new manager who has been a successful major leaguer, but has never managed, yet reject a successful minor-league manager who played in the minor leagues but never made it as a major-league ball player. There often is a built-in rapport in situations where individuals have had similar experience, particularly when those experiences include achievements, problems, dilemmas, conflicts, etc.

Take the case of the white expert going into a black ghetto to proclaim, "I know your problems; I know how you feel. I'm here to improve things for you." Is it any wonder that the residents of the ghetto generally react to this as unmitigated hogwash? They usually believe that it takes one of them, a participating member of their social stratum, to be able to appreciate their situation or deal with their problems.

In some instances an imaginative, widely experienced counselor actually may be able to state truthfully that he/she is sensitive to a client's emotional reaction, even though the experience (from which the feeling is a by-product) is foreign to the counselor. The principle of "transfer of training" applies here. For example, a counselor can empathize about tragedy which has never touched his/her life, such as a death in the client's family, so long as he/she has experienced a tragedy of similar magnitude, such as the death of his/her best friend. The counselor who failed to make his/her college football squad should be able to empathize with the student who failed biology. The counselor with an inadequate income should be able to empathize with a minority-group member who has been deprived of financial increments because of prejudice.

☞ Supporting

Supporting means offering encouragement, hope, or comfort.

When a client is discouraged, the counselor should consider making comments with the objective of helping the client to become more cheerful. Words should tend to gladden and exhilarate. Inspiring remarks, particularly to a client exhibiting fear, often can contribute to stimulating courage.

If a client displays hopelessness, a what's-the-use attitude, the counselor should consider instilling within the client a desire to do, with the expectation of obtaining what is desired. The old saying that the "anticipation is greater than the realization" ought to be altered herein to "anticipation may be a prime requisite to realization."

During those times when the client shows a faltering of his/her resolution, expresses sorrow, or shows weariness, the counselor may give needed aid by imparting strength or simply by consoling.

Supporting involves a utilization of the techniques of informing, interpreting, clarifying, and questioning.

☞ *Reassuring*

Reassuring is a very close relative to supporting. There will be times when the counselor will be reassuring when he/she is supporting, and vice versa. The justification in using two terms to identify what seems in many instances to be one technique rests in the particular emphasis inherent in reassuring: restoring confidence.

Whenever the client shows a faltering in his/her faith in himself/herself, a lessening of his/her conviction that he/she can do, a false lowering of his/her level of aspiration, a negative distortion of his/her self-concept, or an erosion of his/her belief in his/her capabilities, the counselor should consider making comments designed to aid his/her client in restoring his/her confidence in himself/herself.

Informing, interpreting, clarifying, and questioning are the techniques usually involved in reassuring.

Even champions sometimes have recurring doubts about their capabilities and continuing success. Small wonder that most people are confronted with seemingly continuous erosions of their belief in themselves. As Thoreau said, "Most people live lives of quiet desperation." Consequently, the need to be reassured is present in many clients even though it may not be verbalized.

The counselor occasionally must "walk a tightrope," one which separates his giving a "Rockne pep talk" from his/her giving a reasonable statement of reality which is expressed calmly yet forcefully and quietly. When a client needs restoration of confidence, he/she is not apt to derive much reassurance from a "wishy-washy," too-silent, phlegmatic, or aloof counselor. Warmth, power, vibrancy, enthusiasm, and abundant self-confidence should radiate outward from the counselor to the client.

By way of illustration, the amount of lead in various typical categories of counselor remarks might be described as follows:

1. **Acceptance** remarks add no new idea and little pressure (except perhaps to continue talking).

2. **Tentative analysis** brings in a new idea which logically follows but little pressure is exerted to accept it.

3. **Interpretation** remarks state a new idea with definiteness, which indicates that the client is expected to accept the idea.

While a counselor may not intend his/her remark to lead very much, if it seems to do so to the client, it does. The measure of leading is the relation the counselor remark has to the preceding client remark in the eyes of the client.

Studies indicate that typical examples of a particular type of counselor technique have certain average values of amount of lead. They may vary from a little to a great deal. These values of certain techniques have been worked out and are indicated on a rating scale (see p. 84) as reference points for the rating exercise later on. These reference points are defined as follows:

1. **Silence.** Occasionally, following a client remark, the counselor is silent. There is no new idea here and generally little pressure. It is conceivable, however, that silence could mean as much pressure as exerted by a rejection remark.

2. **Acceptance.** Following a client remark, the counselor may merely indicate that he/she understands and accepts what the client has said by a "yes" or "uh-hm" response. Such remarks usually lead very little. Care must be taken, however, to differentiate an acceptance remark from "yes" in response to a client question.

3. **Clarification** or **Reflection.** Following a remark by the client, the counselor rephrases the important ideas in more concise or clearer terms. A clarification leads slightly more than acceptance in that the counselor has done some selecting of the various ideas or emphases in the client's remarks. There is also a reflection of content and a reflection of feeling.

4. **Summary clarification.** The counselor organizes and summarizes the ideas present in a series of client remarks. Since the whole series of remarks is clarified, this technique leads to little more than simple clarification.

5. **General lead.** The counselor asks the client to select a topic for conversation or to continue talking about a topic. It is of the type, "What do you want to talk about today?" or "Will you tell me more about this?"

6. **Tentative analysis.** The counselor presents an additional aspect or a new approach to the problem being discussed, but in a purely tentative, nonforcing manner. The client feels free to accept or reject the idea. Frequently it is in a question form.

7. **Specific lead** or **Probe.** The counselor asks the client a specific question, "Why do you feel that way about it?" or "Were you disturbed?"

8. **Approval.** In response to a client remark, a counselor may express approval of selected points and increase the likelihood of their influence. Since the client has stated his/her point, he/she feels little pressure.

9. **Interpretation.** The counselor states something which can be inferred from what the client has said or done, but which the client has not specifically discussed. It has a wide range of amount of lead, shading into (and difficult to distinguish from) clarification at one extreme and urging at the other.

10. **Introducing an unrelated topic.** In the eyes of the client, the relatedness of a topic which a counselor introduces may vary a good deal, and hence the amount of lead varies considerably. The more unrelated it seems, the more the remark leads. It may seem to the client both a rejection of what he/she has been discussing and the introduction of a new topic.

11. **Assurance.** In response to a client remark, the counselor makes a response of the type, "Everything is going to be all right." This may lead a great deal if it tends to reject the importance of the client's problem.

12. **Urging.** Those instances in which the counselor puts considerable pressure on a client to accept an idea or course of action. It is characterized by the use of such devices as arguments for action and occasionally even threats. Rejection of an idea would be an extreme form of urging.

13. **Rejection.** The counselor rejects the client's remark, which frequently leaves client feeling as though he/she were rejected: "I don't like your ideas at all" or "I think you're wrong."

Rating Scale for Amount of Lead. In the section which follows, you are asked to arrange the counselor responses along the Leading Scales which range from little or no lead at the extreme left end to a great amount of lead at the right end.

Place the number of each counselor response along these scales at the point which best seems to represent the amount of lead shown. An even distribution will not necessarily occur. Numbers may be clustered at one end or be spread out evenly.

Note that you are not asked to judge the appropriateness of the remark but merely the amount of lead.

The essential job is to estimate the degree of leading of each remark and to place the number of this remark at its best location on the scale. After finishing, reread the responses in the order in which you have them arranged and decide whether each statement actually does lead more (whether a little or a great deal) than the preceding one.

Each separate counselor remark must be entered on the scale. A counselor remark is defined as all the counselor talk between two statements by the client. Exceptions to this may occur when the client interjects a remark during a counselor statement, or a break in a long counselor speech indicates that more than one "remark" actually exists. If there are ten counselor speeches in the unit, there will then be almost always ten checks on the rating scale.

Note that silence, which will be shown as "(Silence)" or "(Pause)" when it occurs alone and seems deliberately continued by the counselor, is rated as a counselor remark. Omit responses in which the counselor supplies information in response to a client request, makes a structuring speech within a unit, or makes a social visiting remark.

☞ *Rating Scale*

Criterion of Lead: Relation of counselor remark to client's last remark in eyes of client.

Low lead when: a) the counselor does not go beyond client's last remark, or b) the counselor uses little pressure or definiteness to make client accept ideas.

High lead when: a) the counselor moves ahead of client's last remark, or b) the counselor uses pressure or definiteness to make client accept new ideas.

1. **Silence:** [Pause] or [Silence]. No new ideas, no pressure.

2. **Acceptance:** "Yes" or "Uh-huh." Counselor understands and accepts what client has said.

3. **Clarification:** Rephrases client's ideas in clearer terms. Selects important ideas.

4. **Summary clarification:** Gives summary of ideas in series of client remarks.

5. **General lead:** Asks client what he wants to talk about. Or asks client to tell more about an idea.

6. **Tentative analysis:** Counselor presents new aspects or approach in tentative way, leaving client free to accept or reject.

7. **Specific Lead [or Probe]:** Counselor asks client specific question.

8. **Approval:** Counselor expresses approval of what client has said.

9. **Interpretation:** Counselor states something client has inferred but which client has not specifically discussed.

10. **Introduction of unrelated topic:** Counselor introduces topic which may seem unrelated in eyes of client. This type may vary greatly in degree of lead.

11. **Assurance:** "Everything is going to be all right." May reject importance of client's problem.

12. **Urging:** Counselor pressures client to accept idea. Counselor may use arguments. May reject client's ideas with definiteness.

13. **Rejection:** Counselor rejects client's remark.

1.

Client: It kind of worries me about this first quarter. I don't know whether I can make grades enough to keep from getting put on probation and getting kicked out or not. [Pause] I'm carrying thirteen hours and I study about three or four hours a day. I don't know if that's enough or not.

Counselor:

11. [Silence]

12. Where do you do your studying?

13. Possibly a little more might help but most important is to work out a study schedule and to develop good work skills.

14. You're concerned about how much you ought to study.

15. Oh, I don't think you should have any trouble at all if you study that much.

16. Staying in school seems very important to you.

17. That might or might not, for the nature of the courses probably should enter into our consideration.

Leading scale:

Low	High
Lead	Lead

2.

Client: Well, it's like this. Due to acne on my face, that sort of gives me an inferiority complex. Well, it'd been more noticeable a couple of years ago than it is now. That kind of makes me feel inferior.

Counselor:

21. [Silence]

22. You had better go to a doctor if you don't want to have permanent scars on your face.

23. How do you mean?

24. Uh-huh.

25. You are concerned about what other people think about you. The acne on your face is better now but you still feel inferior.

26. Do you feel that your appearance hinders you in your social relations?

Leading scale:

Low   High

Lead ....Lead

3.

Client: Yeah, the handicap was really from high school. I just don't remember enough of that algebra and it wasn't my fault, 'cause when I took algebra, I did get good grades in it. I think I'll get along in geometry as soon as I get started in it, but it's tough too. Here I am. I want to go into engineering and if the math gets any harder than it is now, I don't know what I'll do.

Counselor:

31. [Silence]

32. What courses are you taking now?

33. The fact that math is so hard for you makes you wonder about engineering.

34. You are finding it harder to settle down to work here in college.

35. Oh, you should be able to do all right in math now.

36. Do you think the trouble might be lack of background in the fundamentals of math?

37. The best thing for you to do is to take the math diagnostic test to find out how good you are and what's wrong.

Leading scale:

Low   High
Lead ....Lead

4.

Client: Well, I've just about decided I want to go into engineering. I've been thinking about it a long time. My father is in construction work, you know, and I liked drawing in high school.
Counselor:

41. [Silence]

42. Uh huh.

43. What you ought to do is go to the junior dean of the engineering college and find out what the necessary qualifications are for getting into engineering.

44. And do your math grades show that you would probably do well?

45. I think you would be making a big mistake to go into engineering. The test scores bear out my opinion that you ought to go into commerce.

46. It sounds good to me.

Leading scale:

Low   High
Lead ....Lead

5.

Client: But the main reason – I'll tell you frankly – I'm taking this course is because I'll learn to study better to get my point average back where it should be and where it ought to be.

Counselor:

51. [Silence]

52. Do you have any ideas about what seems to be causing you your difficulty?

53. Yes, I see.

54. Making your grades for a fraternity initiation is probably your main reason for this.

55. Well, that's worth doing.

56. You feel your grades don't reflect your real ability.

57. The main thing is to learn better study methods and get better grades.

Leading scale:

Low   High
Lead ....Lead

Ranking Instructions. For each counselor remark, determine the rating scale value you gave by counting the number of points (dots on scale) from the left. Write this number beside each counselor remark.

In the blanks below, fill in the rating scale values for each group of remarks. Compute the average value for each type. Then list the types by rank from the lowest rating value to highest. (Only 10 of the 13 types of lead were utilized in the exercise).

1	2	3	4	5
14._____	22._____	13._____	36._____	11._____
16._____	37._____	17._____	44._____	21._____
25._____	43._____	26._____		31._____
33._____	45._____	34._____		41._____
56._____		54._____		51._____
		57._____		
Ave._____	Ave._____	Ave._____	Ave._____	Ave._____

6	7	8	9	10
46._____	12._____	24._____	15._____	23._____
55._____	32._____	42._____	35._____	52._____
		53._____		
Ave._____	Ave._____	Ave._____	Ave._____	Ave._____

Rank order of types (from lowest to highest).

1._____   2._____   3._____   4._____   5._____
6._____   7._____   8._____   9._____   10._____

☞ Amount of "Lead" in Counselor Remarks

Obviously, the seventeen techniques of counseling we have just examined can vary considerably in the amount of stimulus they give to the client to develop his/her thinking during the course of an interview. By looking at the way a typical interview progresses, with the truly great variety of counselor remarks that can be made in response to what the client says, we find that we can approximately judge how much the counselor is leading the client's thinking with each of his remarks. The exercise that follows here should be helpful in understanding the functions of the different types of counselor remarks, and in analyzing how much stimulus or "lead" the counselor is giving to his/her client's thinking.

The degree to which a remark leads usually depends on the following two characteristics:

1.   How far the content of the counselor's remark seems to be ahead of the content of the client's last remark.

2.   The degree of pressure of definiteness in the counselor's remark used to bring about client acceptance of new ideas.

According to Cash (1983),

> The life span human developmental stages and tasks perspective offers a yardstick to use as a descriptive measurement for defining and understanding human problems. In addition, it offers implications for methodology and focusing of interventions. Although elementary and secondary school guidance services are provided only through adolescence, contemporary movements in adult counseling and human services are being made available to assist in meeting the entire life span developmental needs. Bochnek (1976) offers basic tenets relevant to using a developmental perspective in the transformation of guidance services for the future:
>
> 1.   Developmental theory contends that the pressure to change is inherent in all human experience. Thus, guidance services must re-examine and redesign their strategies for intervention.

2. The thrust of developmental change is directional, and often predictable.

3. Growth releases new potential and resources not previously available to the person.

4. Each life period or stage change evokes unique needs, challenges, and resources.

5. Development has a necessary sequencing in the growth experience.

    In review of the above, the developmental perspective offers an alternate approach to the reactive-remedial-therapy model of counseling. It supports the use of client resources to anticipate and prepare to resolve needs (potential problems) and it commits guidance services to a growth, rather than a psychodynamic or personality abnormality model as a primary service.

Part IV
THE SCIENCE OF COUNSELING

Chapter 14

THE INDIVIDUAL

W hat the counselor needs to know about any individual revolves around his/her understanding of the behavior of individuals; in other words, he/she requires a basic and thorough knowledge of psychology.

It goes without saying that this text, or for that matter any one book, does not cover the subject matter of a science. The necessary knowledge of psychology must be acquired through the pursuit of the study of this discipline. In this chapter, the focus of attention is upon especially pertinent items of behavioral knowledge prerequisite to the performance of the art of counseling.

While the name of Part IV is *The Science of Counseling*, we should point out that we have included here only certain significant items within the mass of data which comprise the science of counseling. The knowledge a counselor should acquire and continue to supplement on a lifetime basis needs to be assimilated, digested and applied extensively and intensively in a profound counselor education program. The foundation of this knowledge, which constitutes the science of counseling, must be obtained from the study of several disciplines. The nature of such education is considered in Part V: The Preparation of the Counselor.

The importance of the counselor's understanding cannot be overemphasized. But, the reader should not infer that understanding the individual is all there is to the science of counseling. The importance of environment must be comprehended and applied.

> The subject matter of guidance services is the individual and his/her environment (including the present and possible future environment). The essence of this concept is the individual, but environment must be included. The individual is closely woven into a network

of personal and social interaction between himself/ herself and the environment in which he/she finds himself/herself an integral part. (5, p. 2)

Weitz (14) proposes that human behavior represents a continuous stream of interactions between an individual and his/her environment. There is little doubt that the individual and his/her present and possible future environment are equal partners in terms of value of each as the subject matter of counseling.

The real purpose in a counselor knowing his/her client is to enable the counselor to assist the client in understanding himself/herself. As the Oracle at Delphi said so succinctly, "Know thyself."

Comprehending the behavior of many individuals is based on the study of psychology coupled with continuous experience in working with individuals; these are the prerequisites to understanding the behavior of each individual client. It should be carefully noted that the acquiring of psychological data is not a closed process, but rather a continuous lifelong process. The master counselor should be a scientist as well as an artist. This means perpetual learning.

To assist the counselor in helping the client to enrich his/her self-understanding, there are many tests and instruments available for use. *Chapter 19, Tools of Counseling*, deals with these.

The counseling act itself is, of course, a learning situation in which the counselor obtains data that helps him/her to understand his/her client, and the client is engaged in learning about himself/herself and his/her present and possible future environment.

One significant reason that the counselor's work is so difficult is the complexity of the individual. "One of society's most baffling concerns, it is said, is better understanding of our greatest resource, man himself." (2, p. 328) Add to this the enormous diversity of problems that the present and possible future environments create for his/her many clients and it becomes apparent why a counselor must be "more than a psychologist," and why there is a multidisciplinary approach in counselor education. It would be well for the counselor to read books which aid in understanding this concept: *Future Shock* by Alvin Toffler (13), *Impact and Change: A Study of Counseling Relationships* by Bill Kell and William Mueller (8), *The Greening of America* by Charles A. Reich (12), and *Megatrends* by John Naisbitt (9).

Yes, the counselor needs to know psychology; yes, the counselor needs to know present and possible future environments. The counselor uses psychological and environmental knowledge as the engineer uses mathematics and physics. Just as the engineer is not a mathematician or a physicist per se, the counselor is not a psychologist or an "environmentalist" per se, or even if in either instance, he/she is, then he/she would still need additional study and experience to qualify himself/herself in the missing element.

As will be elaborated in *Part V: The Preparation of the Counselor*, the knowledge of individuals that is needed by the counselor should encompass such concepts as motivation, individual differences, personality, maturation, learning, and normality-abnormality. In a counseling course dealing with the individual (after proper background had been acquired by the student in appropriate psychology classes), the purpose should be to assist the student in relating and applying psychological principles to clients.

Because of the maze of essentials needed for understanding humans, it is wise to heed Chesterfield's admonition: "You must look into people as well as at them." An in-depth analysis of the individual sometimes is mandatory to aiding the client to achieve a realistic self-analysis on his/her way to self-understanding.

Experience in counseling often is the major contributor to understanding individuals. In this way the counselor may check out such propositions as Cicero's: "I add this also, that natural ability without education has oftener raised man to glory and virtue, than education without natural ability."

It becomes increasingly more apparent as the counseling years pass that an understanding of philosophy and its application to aiding clients ranks high in importance. The enrichment of Dr. William James the psychologist by being a philosopher, and vice versa, is a case in point.

Would it not be of value to a counselor, who is attempting to aid an overly ambitious, too-aggressive, socially destructive type of person, to have sufficient philosophical study and reflection in his/her background to enable him/her to interpret to his/her client Gray's lines:

The boast of heraldry, the pomp to power,
And all that beauty, all that wealth ere gave,
Await alike the inevitable hour,
The paths of glory lead but to the grave.

Some psychologists and educators still cling to the theory that an individual can do most anything or become just about whatever he/she chooses to be, regardless of hereditary limitations, so long as he/she is subjected to the right environment in terms of maximal growth and development.

Not withstanding the limitations imposed by realities, the counselor needs to accept the fact that man often is not a rational being, but rather an emotional being – very human, which translates as very susceptible to error, to behaving more like an animal than a machine.

A useful but not well-known aid to the counselor who is striving to sharpen his/her effectiveness in the individual inventory is the *Counselor's Handbook* (3), which deals with interviewing guides in individual appraisal and serves as a resource to the counselor as he/she works with the individual personality.

In view of the multiplicity of texts dealing with personality, the paucity of data relating to adults has been discouraging. For the counselor planning to work primarily with college students and adults, "The Personality of the College Student," (7) and *The Counseling Center in Higher Education* (4), should prove helpful.

In an age in which computer science has made a profound impact in many industries, there are several exciting potential uses in counseling. Pierce (11) proposes that data processing systems can help to cut down on the clerical time required of guidance personnel in the performance of their functions, and provide for better evaluation of individual abilities and educational goals.

The environment of the counselor's office often is conducive to the client resolving to take certain steps to employ better methods, to do what must be done, etc. But, as the client gets into his/her daily routine in his/her student environment or work environment, he/she often does not proceed as planned, follow through as he/she decided, or simply do what he/she intended to do.

Defending one's ego is common practice among all of us, so certainly the counselor must expect to be confronted with defense mechanisms and devious responses as his/her clients attempt to maintain their self-esteem. Lawyers and physicians have been better prepared than most other professionals to cope with their clients' and patients' deviations from the truth and failures to do what they say they will do.

But since the counselor, probably more than any other professional, adheres to the policy of not telling his/her client "what to do" in decision-making, of not prescribing action (except in terms of procedures), and not "advising," the counselor must expect clients, who have been conditioned to expect "advice" from professionals, to react with resentment, confusion, fear, or hostility when the burden of choice is not lifted from their shoulders.

Counselors tend to forget the naivete of many clients. Sophistication should not be assumed – it ought to be established before the counselor proceeds as if he/she were working with a sophisticated client.

High school counselors, particularly, are often guilty of using a vocabulary that many of their clients cannot begin to comprehend. It is not necessary for the counselor to attempt to adopt the current jargon being used by teenagers, but if communication is to be established and maintained, professional nomenclature must be defined or the language of the layperson used.

Adolescents especially dislike being "talked down to," patronized or reminded of "the wetness behind their ears." Some of them despise the word "children" as a label for themselves. Teachers and coaches who refer to their high school or college students or players as "my kids" should not be surprised to detect resentment resulting from the use of such a label.

Since many counselors are members of the middle class and possess a lamentable lack of contact with life away from the cloister of schools, an understanding of the individuals from the ghetto, the barrio, the bilingual home, the minority group, etc., is a prerequisite to helping them.

When the cabinetmaker completes a beautifully constructed bit of woodwork, he/she has tangible evidence of the superiority of what he/she has done. The physician who diagnoses an illness, then prescribes therapy which effects the patient's return to good health, can perceive his/her success. But the counselor rarely knows whether or not his/ her work is appreciated, effective, or significant. He/she must sustain himself/herself with a unique form of self-confidence. He/she should remember that most of his/her clients are not going to return at all, let alone with concrete evidence that the counselor's help was successful.

☞ References

1. Cash, Robert. "Upstream Counseling." McDaniel Foundation, Palo Alto, California, 1983

2. Cottingham, Harold F. "The Challenge of Authentic Behavior." *Personnel and Guidance Journal.* December, 1966, pp. 328–334.

3. *Counselor's Handbook.* U.S. Department of Labor. U.S. Government Printing Office, Washington, D.C., 1967.

4. Gallagher, P. and Demos, G. *The Counseling Center in Higher Education.* Prager, Springfield, Illinois, 1983.

5. Grant, Bruce and Oldenburg, Richard. *A Philosophy of Guidance Services.* Lucas Brothers, Columbia, Missouri, 1964.

6. Hoppock, Robert. *Occupational Information.* McGraw-Hill Book Company, New York, 1963.

7. Impellizzeri, Irene. "The Personality of the College Student." From Siegel, Max. *The Counseling of College Students.* The Free Press, New York, 1968.

8. Kell, Bill and Mueller, William. *Impact and Change: A Study of Counseling Relationships.* Appleton Press, New York.

9. Naisbitt, John. *Megatrends.* Warner Books, New York, 1982.

10. Patterson, C. H. "Phenomenological Psychology." *Personnel and Guidance Journal,* June 1965, pp. 997–1005.

11. Pierce, G. E. *Data Processing for Guidance and Counseling Handbook.* Automated Education Center, Detroit, 1967.

12. Reich, Charles A. *The Greening of America.* Random House, New York, 1970.

13. Toffler, Alvin. *Future Shock.* Random House, New York, 1970.

14. Weitz, Henry. *Behavior Change Through Guidance.* John Wiley & Sons, New York, 1964.

☞ *Suggested Additional Readings*

Blanck, Rubin and Blanck, Gertrude. *Marriage and Personal Development.* Columbia University Press, New York, 1968.

Coopersmith, Stanley. *The Antecedents of Self-Esteem.* W. H. Freeman and Co., San Francisco, 1967.

Garcia, Eugene, & Nunez, Jose, Bilingualism and Cognition, APA, 2011.

Riesman, D. *The Lonely Crowd: A Study of the Changing American Character.* Yale University Press, New Haven, Connecticut, 1956.

Rogers, Carl R. *Freedom to Learn.* Charles E. Merrill, Columbus, Ohio, 1969.

Tyler, Leona. *The Work of the Counselor,* 3rd ed. The Century Psychology Series. Appleton-Century Crofts, New York, 1969.

Wrenn, C. Gilbert. *The Counselor in Changing World.* American Personnel and Guidance Association, Washington, D.C., 1962.

Chapter 15

THE PRESENT AND POSSIBLE
FUTURE ENVIRONMENT

U nfortunately, there is not a science of environment. In understanding the individual, the scholar has access to the science of psychology and the auxiliary disciplines of anthropology, biology, and sociology. However, by pursuing the multidisciplinary approach to basic knowledge the counselor can acquire an understanding of environment. Those sciences making the most significant contributions to environmental knowledge include anthropology, sociology, economics, geography, commerce, chemistry, physics, geology, and political science.

The close integration of the individual and environment is apparent in the usefulness of anthropology and sociology as sciences which contribute to the understanding of both the individual and his environment. While anthropology primarily deals with the individual, since it is the science of mankind, it also focuses on the relation of man to environmental factors. Sociology is the science of the origin and evolution of society, the forms, institutions, and functions of human groups. Anthropology and sociology are significant examples of the near impossibility of separating the individual and environment. In order to comprehend adequately either the individual or the environment, it becomes necessary to study the other.

In using the term "environment" it is important to remember that each individual may live in several environments – for example, home, school, work, church, and recreation. Hereafter, whenever the word "environment" is used in the singular form, it should be thought of in its multiple aspects. The impact of one environment upon the others may range anywhere from negligible to severe. It certainly should be (but in too many instances isn't) a truism to state that if a counselor is to help a client in the resolution of some problems, the counselor often needs to understand the environment in which the client lives.

This does not mean that the counselor should rush right out to study each client's environment. It does mean, however, that prior to beginning a counseling career, the counselor's education and experience should have yielded an adequate degree of sophistication regarding family life, schools, the world of work, churches, and recreational activities; each of these should be understood at the various socioeconomic levels existing in society.

Some counselors simply have not lived long enough or engaged in sufficiently diverse experiences to fully qualify themselves to cope with the problems of individuals and their environments. Even if depth education is not adequate to enable the counselor to acquire the worldly knowledge he/she needs in the practice of his profession, there still must be considerable experience in living. The counselor certainly ought to be sophisticated in living as well as in education.

For the counselor trainee who has a dearth of worldly experience, the counselor educator has a responsibility to attempt to alleviate this deficiency by encouraging the student to expand his/her living horizon and by providing a lengthy and varied internship.

Another complicating factor in the understanding of environment is the fact that not only is there the present environment but also the possible future environment to consider. So much of the planning and so many of the choices of students revolve around the future – schools beyond high school, career, marriage, etc.

What is decided today often must be related to the effect it will have on the tomorrows to follow. Success or failure in the present environment usually conditions what will happen in the possible future environment.

Most of the data on environment in the counseling literature deals with the world of work and schools. A classic in work and education is *The Occupational Structure and Education.* (14) There is a real paucity of information relative to the environmental aspect of the personal-social area of counseling; much research needs to be done here. Meanwhile, the counselor must draw mainly upon the sciences of sociology and anthropology for major assistance in pursuing knowledge pertinent to the environmental factors involved in personal-social counseling.

An excellent source on environmental information applicable to all three counseling areas – educational, career, and personal-social – is *The Information Service in Guidance: Occupational, Educational, Social. (11)*

A very helpful source of data pertinent to environmental factors is *The Disadvantaged and Potential Dropout*, which also includes a bibliography of over 2,000 citations. (7)

> The academic mortality in high schools continues to plague society with the problem of dropouts. Colleges which (in theory) deal with the 'cream of the crop' in reference to potentialities continue to be harassed by an attrition rate that runs close to 50 per cent. This is a staggering indictment of our society. (8, pp. 7–8)

Knowing the possible dangers inherent in college as a future environment is necessary for any realistic thinking on the subject of educational planning.

In the counselor education curriculum there certainly should be provision for courses in socioeconomic information which would include and relate the findings of several disciplines to the individual's present and possible future environment.

Of the many counseling sources of environmental data in the world of work, the following are recommended for careful study:

1. *Occupational Information: The Dynamics of Its Nature and Use* (1)

2. *Vocational Guidance Readings* (4)

3. *The Macmillan Job Guide to American Corporations* (10)

4. *Occupational Information* (9)

5. *Occupational Information: Its Development and Application* (12)

Man in a World at Work (3) is a comprehensive interdisciplinary analysis of the work experience.

Significant changes from 1960 to 1970 to 1975 in occupational and industrial employment patterns are predicted. (6, p. 10)

Among the most important contributions a counselor can make to his clients is the assistance he renders in acquainting and alerting them to life as it is.

It is helpful to high school counselors, as well as to their clients, to keep in mind that "it is estimated that about 40 per cent of the workers in the 1970's will still be in semiskilled, unskilled, and service occupations." (1)

All counselors should reflect upon the impact of this: "Half of the jobs you'll see ten years from now do not exist today." (15, p. 16)

Unless people are alerted to environmental realities, trends, and probabilities so that they can strive to cope with and improve their environment, Emerson's dire prediction may come true: "Humanity will eventually die of civilization."

Toynbee's observation that "of 21 notable civilizations, 19 perished not from conquest from without, but from decay from within" is dramatically supported in the following prognosis of shatteringly drastic happenings to the possible future environment of a great city:

> Man's excesses of the 20th century are the biggest threat to the 21st century.
>
> For 21st century Chicago the price could be the creation of a city in which the sun never shines because it cannot penetrate the tons of airborne pollutants and a city where rainfall strikes terror because it drenches everything with destructive and deadly acids.
>
> For 21st century Chicago the price could be the rationing of water that, to be potable, must be treated again in the home before it can be used and a city in which every man, woman, and child lives and works in sealed structures where all air is washed. (1)

> The handwriting is on the wall. And the message is clear. Either man controls his exploding population, his crowding into cities, and his industrial activities, or he faces disaster through his pollution and manipulation of our planetary environment. (2)

The insulated, secluded environments of the student, whether he be in elementary school or graduate school, is markedly different from those in which he must live in the future. Even the present, with its variety of environments, often becomes overwhelming to the too protected, the too naive.

While the family is a sociological unit with distinguishing characteristics which identify it as being different from the church, the school, etc., each family differs from other families. The only-child family, the matriarch family, the broken-home family, and the bilingual family are examples of the categorical differences in types of family environments.

Since most counselors are middle class, it is small wonder that they have so much trouble empathizing with youngsters from the ghetto, or the barrio, or the neighborhood of the extremely wealthy.

Clients need to be made aware of the realities of life outside their own family, neighborhood, church, and school. Realistic planning, which is the basis of making wise choices, into the future can hardly be done unless the client achieves sophistication in terms of the possible environments he is considering for the future.

The magic word is "investigation." Clients need to do their own research into any environments in which they are contemplating living. Their major research procedures should be reading, interviewing, and observing, with as much time and energy as possible devoted to the latter two.

For the girl who thinks being a nurse will be glamorous, observations of nurses at work coupled with interviewing them should provide evidence to support or refute the assumption regarding nursing. The same procedures should be applied to studying other types of work so that comparisons can be made.

When a client makes a judgment that any type of work, or for that matter any activity, is good, he/she should question himself/herself, "good in relation to what?" This question cannot be answered without sufficient knowledge of that activity and related ones. Since activities do not occur in vacuums, it is fundamental that knowledge of the environment in which the activity takes place is needed to understand the process. It is amazing and alarming to note the numbers of people who try to make decisions without an understanding of the environment in which the actions resulting from their decision will be carried out.

How does an individual justify to himself/herself rejecting a possible career in agriculture when he/she has never been outside of metropolitan New York? How can anyone claim immunity from the hazards of a career in management when he/she has never read about management, never conversed with a manager, and never observed anyone in management work?

"Should I do this or should I do that" hinges upon the two basics: the client needs to know himself and the processes he is considering; and understanding the processes inevitably includes knowing the setting in which they occur, in other words, knowing the environment.

It is not necessary for the counselor to attempt to assume the burden of knowing everything; he/she, of course, couldn't even if he were as old as Methuselah, a Biblical patriarch who reputedly lived 969 years. However, it is the responsibility of the counselor (prior to beginning the practice of counseling) to be environmentally sophisticated. This certainly presupposes that, while he/she doesn't know many things about many environments, he/she does have in-depth knowledge of living, and he/she knows where to refer clients in their pursuit of environmental knowledge.

As has been said of a lawyer concerning his law library, he/she cannot be expected to remember everything recorded in the many texts, but he should know how and where to look when he/she is seeking data in the preparation of his cases. Such is true of the counselor even in those categories in which he is an expert, such as graduate schools, vocational schools, etc. It is not necessary for him/her to recall verbatim passages from graduate school catalogs; however, it is essential that he/she know how to use these catalogs, which schools a client should consider investigating, faculty members who can serve as referral sources regarding certain schools, etc.

The knowledge explosion places a terrific burden upon any professional worker. The counselor, especially, faces the awesome responsibility of needing to keep continuously abreast of environmental changes. Accordingly, the counselor has no choice but to be a lifelong scholar. If he/she thinks that when he/she completes his/her graduate studies, his/her education is complete, he/she should immediately enroll in additional graduate courses, enter the world of work outside of college and remain there until he/she learns how much more he/she needs to learn.

It is not enough either for the counselor to sit in his/her office reading about the outside world. In addition, he/she needs to go into this outside environment to do his/her own observing and interviewing as he/she keeps abreast of the changing milieu.

☞ References

1. Baer, Max F., and Edward C. Roeber. *Occupational Information: The Dynamics of Its Nature and Use.* Chicago: Science Research Associates, Inc., 1964.

2. Bengelsdorf, Irving S. "Environmental Change Caused by Our Misuse of Technology." *Los Angeles Times,* February 2, 1969, Section G, p. 1.

3. Borow, Henry. *Man in a World at Work.* Boston: Houghton Mifflin Co., 1964.

4. Demos, George D., and Bruce Grant. *Vocational Guidance Readings.* Springfield, Illinois: Charles C. Thomas, 1965.

5. *89 Million Jobs by 1975?* A Reprint from the *Occupational Outlook Quarterly,* May, 1967. U.S. Department of Labor, Bureau of Labor Statistics. Washington, D.C.: U.S. Government Printing Office, 1967.

6. *Employment Projections, by Industry and Occupation, 1960–1975.* Special Labor Force Report, No. 28. U.S. Department of Labor,

Bureau of Labor Statistics, Washington, D.C., U.S. Government Printing Office, 1963.

7. Gowan, John, and George D. Demos. *The Disadvantaged and Potential Dropout.* Springfield, Illinois: Charles C. Thomas, 1966.

8. Grant, Bruce, and George D. Demos. "Pertinent Factors for the Consideration of Students, Educators, and Practitioners." From *Vocational Guidance Readings,* edited by George D. Demos and Bruce Grant. Springfield, Illinois: Charles C. Thomas, 1965.

9. Hoppock, Robert. *Occupational Information.* New York: McGraw-Hill Book Company, 1963.

10. McKay, Ernest A. *The Macmillan Job Guide to American Corporations.* New York: The Macmillan Company, 1967.

11. Norris, Willa, Franklin R. Zeran, and Raymond N. Hatch. *The Information Service in Guidance: Occupational, Educational, Social.* Chicago: Rand McNally, 1968.

12. Shartle, Carroll L. *Occupational Information: Its Development and Application.* Englewood Cliffs, New Jersey: Prentice-Hall, 1959.

☞ *Suggested Additional Readings*

Blimline, Carol A., ed. *Innovations in Counseling Services.* Falls Church, Virginia: International Association of Counseling Services, not dated.

Borland, David T. "Organization Development: A Professional Imperative." In *Student Development in Higher Education,* edited by Dan G. Creamer, pp. 205–227. Cincinnati: American College Personnel Association, 1980.

Burtnett, Francis E., Brooke B. Collison, and Allen E. Segrist. "The Comprehensive Involvement of the School Counselor in Career Education." In *The School Counselor's Involvement in Career Education,* edited by Francis E. Burtnett, pp. 131–135. Falls Church, Virginia: American Personnel and Guidance Association, 1980.

Caplow, T. *The Sociology of Work.* Minneapolis: University of Minnesota Press, 1954.

Cerlotta, Beverly. "The Systems Approach: A Technique for Establishing Counseling and Guidance Programs." *Personnel and Guidance Journal* 57, no. 8 (1979), pp. 412–414.

Creamer, Don G., ed. *Student Development in Higher Education.* Cincinnati: ACPA Media, University of Cincinnati, 1980.

Giroux, Roy F., Donald A. Biggs, Alan M. Hoffman, and John J. Pietrofesa, eds. *College Student Development Revisited: Programs, Issues, and Practices.* Falls Church, Virginia: American Personnel and Guidance Association, 1979.

Hill, George E. *Management and Improvement of Guidance.* 2nd ed. Englewood Cliffs, N.J.: Prentice-Hall, 1974.

Hosford, Ray E., and T. Antionette Ryan. "Systems Design in the Development of Counseling and Guidance Programs." *Personnel and Guidance Journal* 49, no. 3 (1970), pp. 221–230.

Huse, Edgar F. *Organization Development and Change.* New York: West Publishing Company, 1975.

Jacobson, Thomas J., and Anita M. Mitchell. "How to Develop a District Master Plan for Career Guidance and Counseling." *Vocational Guidance Quarterly* 25, no. 3 (1977), pp. 195–202.

Krumboltz, John D. "An Accountability Model for Counselors." *Personnel and Guidance Journal* 52, no. 10 (1974), pp. 639–646.

Krumboltz, John D., and Carl E. Thoresen. *Behavioral Counseling.* New York: Holt, Rinehart and Winston, 1969.

Kurpius, DeWayne. "An Introduction to Consultation II." *Personnel and Guidance Journal* 56, no. 7 (1978), p. 394.

Lewis, Judith A., and Michael D. Lewis. *Community Counseling: A Human Services Approach.* New York: John Wiley and Sons, 1977.

Miller, Theodore K., and Judith S. Prince. *The Future of Student Affairs.* San Francisco: Jossey-Bass, 1976.

Riesman, D. *The Lonely Crowd: A Study of the Changing American Character.* New Haven, Connecticut: Yale University Press, 1956.

Rosenfeld, Anne H. *New Views on Older Lives.* Washington, D.C.: U.S. Government Printing Office, 1978.

Shaw, Merville C. *School Guidance Systems.* Boston: Houghton Mifflin Co., 1973.

Shertzer, Bruce, and Shelley C. Stone. *Fundamentals of Guidance.* 4th ed. Boston: Houghton Mifflin Co., 1981.

Super, Donald E. *A Psychology of Careers.* New York: Harper & Brothers, 1957.

Thompson, Bruce & Sobotnik, Rena, Methologies for Conducting Research on Driftedness, 2010, 266 p.

Toffler, Alvin. *Future Shock.* New York: Random House, 1970.

Walz, Garry R., and Libby Benjamin, eds. *New Imperatives for Guidance.* Ann Arbor, Michigan: ERIC Counseling and Personnel Services Clearinghouse, 1978.

Wrenn, Gilbert. *The Counselor in a Changing World.* Washington, D.C.: American Personnel and Guidance Association, 1962.

Zax, Melvin, and Gerald A. Specter. *An Introduction to Community Psychology.* New York: John Wiley and Sons, 1974.

Chapter 16

EDUCATIONAL COUNSELING

Whenever a counselor engages in counseling that is concerned with curriculum, cocurricular activities, studying, school regulations, school plant, grounds, and transportation, program planning, and preparation for a vocation or career, he/she usually is doing educational counseling.

The word "usually" is inserted as an exercise in caution, for sometimes any of the foregoing categories may involve personal-social as well as educational counseling. Also – and unfortunately – within educational counseling there often occurs the abuses of advice giving, decision making by the counselor for the client, and disciplining.

For obvious reasons, most educational counseling happens in schools. From elementary to graduate school there exists considerable variance in the educational counseling offered.

In the elementary school what little educational counseling there is usually involves the counselor and parent, rather than the counselor and pupil. Program planning is virtually nonexistent, for each pupil generally takes all of the subjects offered so that the necessity of choosing among alternative electives seldom occurs. However, the upper elementary grades (7 and 8) or junior high school (7 to 9 or 7 to 8) usually involve some choice making because of the introduction of electives.

High schools (9 to 12) or senior high schools (10 to 12) usually offer major courses or majors plus a choice of electives so that students have to make educational choices.

Junior colleges, colleges, and universities require students who seek a degree to choose a major and make decisions on required subjects and electives.

One of the differences in educational counseling between junior colleges and four-year colleges or universities is the usual practice of junior college counselors doing practically all of the academic counseling (program planning), while in colleges and universities this is done within the academic department of the student's major. College or university counselors sometimes do academic counseling for students who do not have a major.

At the college level it is better that program planning be done by the academic departments. Even the programs of undeclared majors should be handled by an academic department. Preferably, there should be a liberal education major leading to a degree in which all students would major if they did not select a particular subject (e.g., economics) in which to major.

Academic counseling could well be moved into the academic departments in high schools were it not for the lamentable fact that most high school teachers do not have, nor can principals give them, the educational time to add this activity to their already imposing list of responsibilities.

One of the regrettable aspects of program planning by academic personnel is that too much of it is advicegiving, with little if any real counseling taking place. It could hardly be otherwise, for most academic personnel have no counseling education whatsoever.

Even though program planning is handled by academic departments, the counselor finds many opportunities to help the student through educational counseling. This is particularly true in career counseling whenever the matter of career preparation enters the picture, which it inevitably must in the evolution of a career plan.

Plummer (13) reports Endicott's list of factors that employers believe contribute to unsatisfactory occupational performance. Note in this list that numbers 3 and 4 are excellent examples of by-products which should not appear if an individual's liberal education has been effective. It might further be argued that an adequate liberal education at the collegiate level should prevent the college graduate from having any of the following eight liabilities:

1. Overemphasis on wanting a management position

2. Lack of realism as to what is expected in business

3. Lack of ability to write clearly and concisely

4. Inability to speak effectively

5. Lack of specific goals; not knowing what one wants to do

6. Failure to recognize the value of experience and on-the-job training

7. Immaturity and poor social adjustment

8. Unrealistic appraisal of one's own abilities (13, pp. 40–41)

Fullmer believes that "educational guidance is helping a youngster work through a plan designed to develop his talents and abilities by utilizing the resources of the school." (5, p. 101) It would be difficult to separate this task from being integrated with career counseling.

"In Grant's study of the freshmen of the Antelope Valley Joint Union High School, Lancaster, California, 275 students reported 13,487 problems. These problems were classified into eighteen problem areas." (7) It is interesting to note **that** of the eighteen problem areas, curriculum was ranked fourth in frequency; school plant, sixth; studying, fourteenth; regulations, fifteenth; co-curricular, sixteenth; and college seventeenth. The two problems reported most frequently were "concerned about getting good grades" and "lack of transportation to attend sports and social activities."

To function effectively in educational counseling the counselor outside the schools needs to keep abreast of the school market, just as the career counselor must keep in tune with the labor market. Knowing when to refer to school counselors is important, but the counselor in an agency or in private practice should be able to give some assistance in career preparation without having to make a referral every time the matter occurs.

The counselor in a school certainly should know the curricular and cocurricular offerings available in his/her school, the school regulations, and school plant, grounds, and transportation. In junior and senior high schools he/she should understand the offerings of each department to such an extent that he/she can assist the students in selecting majors in relation to goals and in making choices on alternatives in required courses and among electives. In colleges and universities he/she should be able to help the student on questions involving career preparation and refer to the appropriate academic department those items pertinent to program planning, qualifying for credentials or licensing, and meeting degree requirements. Where the junior colleges fit into the above depends primarily on whether they consider themselves an extension of secondary education or a part of higher education. Special schools (e.g., business college, barber college, trade school, etc.) may adapt themselves to the above in whatever manner best fits their philosophy and the availability of their personnel; for example, a given school may not even employ a counselor.

Elementary, high school, junior college, special school, college and university counselors should all understand study methodology and be able to assist students in acquiring and enhancing their study skills. There are several helpful texts dealing with study methodology. Some of them, however, are so verbose that they discourage student reading and the application of findings. To circumvent this difficulty by providing a very brief presentation of several workable concepts and the necessary background for needed skills, the authors prepared *How to Study Successfully.* (4)

In the preparation for a vocation or career, the integration of educational and career counseling occurs whenever the client is seeking assistance in the educational aspects of career planning.

The more students who continue in school and who seek help in school selection beyond high school, the more the counselor needs to know about other schools: " ...there has been a large increase in the proportion of high school graduates who go in pursuit of higher education." (11, p. 10)

Berrick's text (1) is worthy of examination for the counselor who will be involved in academic and preprofessional counseling.

There is a recurring societal emphasis on the value of more and more education. The *Career Guide for Demand Occupations* (3) stresses the necessity of education. It logically follows that counselors have an obligation to keep abreast of the amount of education companies are requiring of their employees, not only when the individual begins his/

her career in a company, but throughout his/her career. Some companies encourage all their potential management people to return to college to obtain an MBA (Master of Business Administration).

Even the young employee (in his twenties) who begins his/her career with a master's degree should be aware of the need for continuous informal (out of school) study. "Top-flight executives require two to three hours of reading per day in most fields to keep up with new knowledge developments." (2, p. 13)

Isaacson (10) stresses preparation and entrance to the world of work at all occupational levels and offers school and college information.

While the counselor cannot be expected to function as an encyclopedic source of school and college information, he/she should be sophisticated in this area.

In this era, when so much attention is focused on the need for educational assistance to the disadvantaged, together with society's growing awareness of the deterioration or societal residual of the dropout, *The Disadvan*taged *and Potential Dropout* (6) contributes to the knowledge of these twin social disasters. The text consists of fifty articles which provide data on definitions, statistics, diagnosis, theory, curriculum, change, guidance efforts, and educational and vocational rehabilitation of disadvantaged youth and dropouts. It also includes an extensive bibliography.

Norris, Zeran, and Hatch (12) offer an excellent approach in showing the need for the counselor's acquisition of knowledge to support his/her work in the three major areas of counseling – career (which is labeled occupational), educational, and personal social (which is labeled social). This integrative approach should serve to alert the counselor to just how closely related educational, career, and personal social counseling can be.

For those counselors in colleges, special schools (beyond high school), adult education, private practice, and in agencies who work primarily with adults, Thoroman (14) deals with the educational and vocational counseling of adults, giving special attention to disabled individuals and older citizens.

Hollis and Hollis (9) present a new and dynamic theory of how counselors should go about giving many kinds of information to their clients. While the "how" may in itself be intriguing for the purposes of this chapter, the counselor should note what kinds of information are suggested for dissemination.

Junior high and senior high school counselors in particular have a responsibility for assisting incoming and transfer students in becoming oriented to the new school. Providing information regarding the school plant, grounds, transportation, school regulations, curriculum, and cocurricular activities to these students is most helpful and reassuring to many of the prospective students.

Senior high school counselors going into the junior high schools and junior high school counselors going into the elementary schools to disseminate data regarding the above categories are practices that improve the adjustive process of the students as they move upward in the educational hierarchy from one level to a more advanced and mature environment.

"Part II: Educational Guidance" in *Guidance for Youth* (8, pp. 17–57) contains information to which the high school counselor can refer his counselees for help in acquiring understanding of the "Value of High School Education," (pp. 17–18) "Citizenship," (pp. 19–20) "Opportunities at Your High School," (pp. 21–23) "How to Learn," (pp. 25–46) and the "Five Year Educational Program." (pp. 49–57)

The school's handbook can be a most satisfactory orientation aid for incoming students, particularly if it is prepared by the current students who also confer with the prospective students of the feeder schools.

The high school counselor ought to be thoroughly familiar with all the categories specified in this chapter. In fact, a new counselor should report to work far enough ahead of the arrival of the students that he/she has sufficient time "to learn the school."

☞ References

1. Berrick, Myron E. *General, Academic, and Pre-Professional Counseling.* From *The Counseling of College Students,* edited by Max Siegel. New York: The Free Press, 1968.

2. Bush, Thomas W. "Executive Need for More Schooling Stressed." *Los Angeles Times,* October 26, 1967, Part III, pp. 13, 15.

3. *Career Guide for Demand Occupations.* U.S. Labor Department, Bureau of Labor Statistics, Washington, D.C.: U.S. Government Printing Office, 1965.

4. Demos, George D., and Bruce Grant. *How to Study Successfully.* Columbia, Missouri: Lucas Brothers, 1965.

5. Fullmer, Daniel W. *Counseling: Content and Process.* Chicago: Science Research Associates, Inc., 1965.

6. Gowan, John, and George D. Demos. *The Disadvantaged and Potential Dropout.* Springfield, Illinois: Charles C. Thomas, 1966.

7. Grant, Bruce. "Survey of Studies on Problems of Adolescents." *California Journal of Secondary Education,* May 1953, pp. 293–297.

8. Grant, Bruce, George D. Demos, and Willard Edwards. *Guidance for Youth.* Springfield, Illinois: Charles C. Thomas, 1965.

9. Hollis, Joseph W., and Lucile U. Hollis. *Personalizing Information Processes: Educational, Occupational, and Personal-Social.* New York: The Macmillan Company, 1969.

10. Isaacson, Lee E. *Career Information in Counseling and Teaching.* Boston: Allyn and Bacon, 1966.

11. Johnston, Denis F. *Education of Adult Workers in 1975.* Special Labor Force Report No. 95. United States Department of Labor, Bureau of Labor Statistics. Washington, D.C.: U.S. Government Printing Office, 1968.

12. Norris, Willa, Franklin R. Zeran, and Raymond N. Hatch. *The Information Service in Guidance: Occupational, Educational, Social.* Chicago: Rand McNally, 1968.

13. Plummer, Robert H., and Clyde E. Blocker. *College, Careers, and You.* Chicago: Science Research Associates, Inc., 1963.

14. Thoroman, E. C. *The Vocational Counseling of Adults and Young Adults.* Boston: Houghton Mifflin Co., 1968.

☞ *Suggested Additional Readings*

Bovard, James A, et al., High Stakes Testing in Education, A.P.A., 2011.

Gowan, John C., George D. Demos, and E. Paul Torrance. *Creativity: Its Educational Implications.* New York: John Wiley and Sons, 1967.

Lester, Richard A. *Manpower Planning in a Free Society.* Princeton, New Jersey: Princeton University Press, 1966.

Thomas, Lawrence. *The Occupational Structure and Education.* Englewood Cliffs, New Jersey: Prentice-Hall, 1956.

Chapter 17

CAREER COUNSELING

The counselor who is engaged in providing assistance to individuals involved in vocational selection, changing vocations, and career planning is doing career counseling.

While agreeing that the matter is primarily, if not solely, of concern only to semanticists, the authors use the term "career counseling" instead of "vocational counseling." The rationale here is that the word "career" refers to the lifelong pursuit of work; it may include one vocation or many. A vocation is what a worker does; it is a combination of activities that identifies a type of work as being different from other types (e.g., lawyer, truck driver, waitress, etc.). By broadening the concept from vocational to career counseling, the counselor facilitates long-time planning, rather than limiting professional help to entry work or to only an interval in a worker's life. This does not preclude vocational choice or change, but it encourages the long view, even in vocational choice or change.

The word "occupation," as used by most authorities, is synonymous with "vocation." Still another term, "job," enters into the nomenclature to invite possible confusion of meanings. A job is a specific assignment of work within a company. Hence, an accountant (the name of the vocation) may be employed by Company A as an accountant, but in a special niche, or "job," according to the company's own concept of what it expects an accountant to do.

One of the mistakes college students often make in choosing a career, for example as a mechanical engineer, is failing to determine what mechanical engineers are required to do in different companies. Often the variation of job requirements in mechanical engineering are so significant that a sophisticated student will realize that the job title of mechanical engineer is only a vague identifying label of work responsibilities to be performed within a variety of companies.

Clients need to be cognizant of the right and practice of companies to assign job titles as they please. If a company wishes to designate an employee as a vice-president, when his occupational functions are the work of a salesman, it, of course, will do so. The prestige of job titles is a vital factor in employee relationships, both within the company and in employee-customer relationships, regardless of the fact that there may be great disparity between certain job titles and what the employees do.

> ... an occupation is only a name for a group of jobs which have something in common. The specific jobs within one occupation may differ in many ways. They may involve different supervisors, different employers, different physical surroundings, different associates. Because of these differences a person may be satisfied in one job and dissatisfied in another job in the same occupation if one of the jobs meets more of his needs than the other. (25, p. 158)

Counseling originated in vocational guidance. Frank Parsons, who has been referred to as "the father of guidance," presented his interpretation of vocational selection by introducing in 1909 a book expressing his concepts. His book was recently reprinted, (32) and every career counselor should regard it as must reading. Though some authorities may be reluctant to agree that the statement below (from Parson's text) still remains the essence of career counseling, certainly there is little evidence that any of the dissenters have developed anything that is better.

> In the wise choice of a vocation there are three broad factors: (1) A clear understanding of yourself, your aptitudes, abilities, interests, ambitions, resources, limitations, and their causes; (2) a knowledge of the requirements and conditions of success, advantages and disadvantages, compensation opportunities, and prospects in different lines of work; (3) true reasoning on the relations of these two groups of facts. (32, p. 5)

Throughout its history, counseling has had theorists and practitioners who favored placing more emphasis on personal-social than on vocational counseling, or on educational rather than vocational counseling. There is, of course, a need for attention to all three of these areas. And it is good that there are counselors who desire to specialize in one of the three and others who prefer to function as generalists, moving easily from one area to another. Even the specialist should be competent in the areas other than his specialization. For reasons of practicality, most secondary school counselors should be generalists. Usually, it is only at the college level, in agencies, or in private practice that the luxury of the specialist can exist.

Of the three kinds of counseling – educational, career, and personal-social – it has been the authors' observation that more counselors are uninformed, naive, and poorly prepared in career counseling than in either of the others. As a classic case in point: a colleague of the authors told of being assigned as the vocational counselor in a college counseling center, simply because he was the only member of approximately ten counselors who (though not a specialist) admitted to knowing anything about vocational counseling. This was not a little 100-pupil high school; it was a **college** with an enrollment of more than 10,000, with 80 percent of the counselors holding the doctorate, yet all but one professing ignorance in vocational counseling.

In **Part V: The Preparation of the Counselor,** the author's recommendations for counselor education would prevent counselors from leaving their counselor education programs without the proper background, the science, required for career counseling.

There is a wide chasm separating scientific career counseling from the counselor who conceives of career counseling as the act of giving the client a vocational interest test and then interpreting the results. Recognizing this gap, the authors were compelled to devise new tools and approaches for aiding their clients. Some of these innovations are available in *Career Study Guide* (19), and *Designing Your Career* (9).

Clients and career counselors alike can profit from a perusal of *Designing Your Career, Part I* (10), which uses an informal approach in dealing briefly with the following topics:

1. Value to Individual of Finding Proper Career

2. Counseling Can Help Whenever Job Decision Necessary

3. Job Choices Open to Young – How to Prepare for Career

4. Error of Forcing Youngster to Prepare for "Glamour" Career for Which He Is Not Qualified

Designing Your Career, Part II, (11) deals succinctly with four other pertinent topics:

1. Understanding World of Work

2. What Is Vocational Guidance?

3. Value to Country of Having People Do What They Can Best Do

4. How Older Persons Should Go About Changing Job

While some counselors are knowledgeable about the role of vocations in choosing an occupation, few are aware of the industrial and company concepts in career planning, let alone having their clients investigate industries and companies as well as vocations. For counselors who desire to achieve this degree of sophistication, the *California Career Study Guide* (19) and *Designing Your Career* (9) will be most helpful; in addition, they will serve as valuable tools for clients to use in career planning.

> In career counseling the only way to help the client as he/she should be helped is to assist him/her in scientific career planning. This is the function of the *California Career Study Guide* and *Designing Your Career.*
>
> If a counselor wishes to do career counseling in depth, it is his/her responsibility to acquaint his/

her clients with the need for a diversification of self-environmental information.

Superficiality is the antithesis of career planning as it must be conducted if it is to afford a basis conducive to wise choices.

In his study of self the client should learn about his/her vocational values, vocational interests, psychological needs, personality traits, life goals, value system, and health.

In his/her study of the world of work the client should learn about industries (such as the industrial categories of: insurance, merchandising, transportation, etc.), companies (such as New York Life Insurance Company, Marshall Field & Company, TransWorld Airlines, etc.), and occupations (such as actuary, buyer, airline stewardess, etc.). (8)

An approach to the science of career planning is outlined in *Career Counseling in Depth.* (8)

While a career counselor cannot be expected to know every occupation, let alone every company and industry, he/she certainly should understand the industrial, company, and vocational concepts and know something about industrial, company, and vocational categories. He/she should also have in-depth knowledge concerning some industries, companies, and occupations.

Knowing, for example, about the quality of companies and the regard in which they are held is important.

The Presidents' Panel of *Dun's Review and Modern Industry* voted on the best managed companies in the United States. The top ten, together with the reasons for selection, are listed below.

Companies	Reasons for Selection
Du Pont	Fiscal Acumen
General Motors	Organization

IBM	Growth Power
AT&T	Vitality
Minnesota Mining and Manufacturing	New Products
General Electric	Management
Eastman Kodak	The Quality Image
Procter & Gamble	Marketing and Merchandising
Sears Roebuck	Performance and Planning
Jersey Standard	Corporate Longevity (37)

The counselor should know the language of the world of work. The fact that so many counselors are naive in this is the basis for many authorities having recommended throughout the years that a counselor supplement his/her education with work experience outside schools. This matter will be considered in **Part V: The Preparation of the Counselor.** However, at this point it is pertinent to observe that any counselor who attempts to do career counseling should be much better prepared for this function than the vast majority of counselors practicing today – in or out of schools – and this statement certainly includes college counselors who should be the best educated of all counselors.

Education for career counseling is not the final answer, for even if graduate schools construct counselor education programs that permit the emergence of well-trained career counselors, it still will be necessary for the practicing career counselor to continue to study the world of work on a lifelong basis. How else can he/she hope to remain knowledgeable about a world of work in which the amount of change and growth is staggeringly massive? "Half the jobs you'll see ten years from now do not exist today." (39, p. 16)

Continuous study must include reading, supplemented by visits into the world of work to observe industries, companies and workers, plus interviewing workers.

The career counselor should allocate a certain portion of his weekly schedule to getting out of his/her office into the world of work to pursue – as a scientist – a perpetual program of investigation. Only in this manner will the profession of counseling be able to designate some of its members as specialists in career counseling.

It is important for the career counselor to keep abreast of trends in the word of work, including employment predictions and projections, the introduction of new vocations and the obsolescence of old ones, the growth or deterioration of industries and companies, factors contributing to employee progress or regression, new products and product obsolescence, wage levels, etc. The federal and state governments do an excellent job in supplying the citizenry with information on all these subjects.

Below is some data that are typical of the type of information about which the career counselor should be familiar.

> By 1975, the adult work force (25 years old and over) will include as many college graduates as those with 8 years of schooling or less. Less than a decade ago (in 1959), college graduates as a group in the work force were but one-third the size of the older component. At present, workers who are starting their careers have completed more years of schooling, on balance, than those who are retiring. Thus, with the passage of time, the upward trends in the educational achievement of the population cause a continuing improvement in the educational levels of the work force. (26, p. 10)

This points out once again the close relationship of career counseling and educational counseling. It also demands that considerable thought be given to the individual and societal problems which may accrue as by-products of a work force that becomes increasingly better educated. There is room for only so many workers in the professions, technological occupations, and management. If the work market becomes inundated with college graduates, particularly the products of liberal education, there may well be multiple difficulties resulting therefrom.

Wolfbein (41) offers a synthesis of future job opportunities based on current trends in population growth and movement, industrial manpower needs, job availability, and salary levels.

Here is part of a report on one specific trend:

Moonlighting habits of the American worker have not increased or even changed much in recent years. The most recent survey of dual jobholding shows 3.6 million workers, just under 5 per cent of all employed persons, held two jobs or more in May, 1966.

The typical multiple jobholder is a comparatively young married man with children who feels a financial squeeze. He has a full-time primary job and moonlights about 13 hours a week at a different line of work. Teachers, policemen, firemen, postal workers, and farmers are most likely to moonlight. Many of them work for themselves on their extra jobs (operating farms or small businesses) while many others are sales or service workers. (22, p. 17)

Obviously, most people do not moonlight because they are infatuated with work. The need for more money is, of course, the compelling motivation. Those youths who are inclined to belittle the profit-making role that permeates companies or to rationalize that the nonfinancial benefits of certain types of work outweigh the small salary factor might well face the reality that moonlighting may become their way of life, in spite of the fact that making money for its own sake goes against their "intellectual grain."

Another trend: "Over 24 million women now hold jobs, one out of every three women in the country. Three out of every five of these women are married, and one of every three has children under 18 years of age." (24, p. 2)

The philosophical implications involved in a young married woman trying to plan a career and reconcile it to a traditional role in marriage is of the utmost importance to both the individual and society. It has been the authors' observation that many college women feel guilty if they do not construct their college education as preparation for working; even many of those women who have no intention of having a career find it difficult to accept the values of a liberal education. This dilemma of college women often is one of the counselor's most frustrating and crucial problems.

With many students following the route of liberal education, hoping to get into management, the career counselor needs to have more than a casual understanding of management.

Goal: Barnard's **The Functions of the Executive** (2) has been referred to as the most thought-provoking book on organization and management ever written by a practicing executive. This book is in its eighteenth printing.

I. It is true that many people aspire to management and only a few achieve it.

> In general, opportunities for advancement tend to be overemphasized in choosing an occupation. Our American culture places such a high value on financial success and we talk so much in school about our land of opportunity that we tend to leave students with the expectation that all, or nearly all, of them will advance to positions of prestige, influence, and affluence. Actually, most of them will remain at, or near, the level at which they get their first jobs. (25, p. 158)

In spite of this realistic warning, recognition should be accorded to the following: "The shortage of business managers in the United States is now estimated at 200,000. In ten years the shortage will have reached 600,000 and in 20 years it will exceed one million. (4, pp. 13, 15)

The issue of the most appropriate educational avenue for potential management personnel to follow has never been satisfactorily resolved. However, recent thinking is leaning in the direction of favoring the liberal education approach, particularly in terms of top management: " ...top-flight executives, in order to successfully run their companies, must leave fields of specialization to others and become overall managers with intimate knowledge of all phases of the company's operations." (4, p. 13)

Knowing the levels of management is essential in career counseling.

Executive positions exist on many different levels. But they may be divided into three broad categories: top management, middle management, and first line management.

Top management usually consists of officials who have a say in forming top-level company policy, such as the president, the company officers, and the members of the board of directors.

Middle management includes executives who are responsible for seeing that this policy is carried out. In many companies the department and division heads belong to the middle group.

First line management includes all those who directly supervise the rank-and-file workers. First line management is responsible for putting into practice the procedures established by middle management. (17, p. 1)

Theories of Career Development (31) is informative in explaining and appraising most of the major theories of career choice and related research. In this text an attempt is made to synthesize some general theoretical statements and to identify the ingredients common to most of the theories, as well as to consider their implications for career counseling.

Peters' and Hansen's text (33) contains sixty selections pertinent to career development from the school years through adulthood.

Goal: In a fine collection of twenty-four writings, most of which are original, Borow (3) offers a comprehensive interdisciplinary analysis of the work experience.

I. *Work and the Nature of Man* (23) presents information on the goals of work for the individual and the organization. These goals are related to man's biological, psychological, and existential needs, with new concepts for understanding the behavior of people on their jobs and toward their company. Neff (28) presents data on how people become workers, how the ability to work becomes impaired, and how work maladjustment can be assessed.

Goal: The status ranking accorded certain occupations is a potent factor in influencing occupational choices. Parental and societal pressures are so often brought to bear against youngsters of college graduates and affluent citizens who cannot accept anything less than a prestigious choice for their offspring.

☞ *Occupations Listed in Order of Frequency of Identification as Being of High Status (27)*

Occupation	College Students (n = 274)
Physician	251
Lawyer	248
Psychiatrist	209
Dentist	189
Engineer	180
President Mfg. Co.	176
Architect	149
Banker	141
Minister	137
Physicist	128
School Supt.	114
Chemist	114
Psychologist	112
Author-Journalist	83
Veterinarian	50
Mathematician	48
Pharmacist	44
Osteopath	40
Senior C.P.A.	38
Public Administrator	37
C.P.A. Owner	30

The realization that work is not simply a means of earning a living, but that it is also a way of life, a social role, is stressed by Super. (36)

The philosophical considerations that impinge upon career planning are in such areas of decision as the role of career in life, the vocational career vs. the company career, the industrial career or not, the life goals, and value system. These matters are included for study in the **California Career Study Guide.** *(19)*

Vocational Guidance Readings (12) is a collection of writings offering data of considerable significance to students and practitioners of career counseling. There are fifty-five contributing authors who cover a range of fifteen aspects of vocational guidance.

Of particular value to counselors in private practice, agencies, and colleges is Thoroman's treatment (38) of the vocational and educational counseling of adults. Those counselors involved in assisting adults in making career changes necessitated by injuries or illness should find the author's attention to these problems valuable. Also, reference is made to older workers. Much more attention needs to be devoted to the place of the senior citizen in the world of work.

Looking at the other end of the age continuum it is important to remember, as Dugan (18) states, the challenge of the massive number of youths who will seek assistance with vocational planning and related concerns in the next decade.

Guidance for Youth (20) is a succinct book covering the areas of vocational and educational guidance, intended primarily for high school students, but with several chapters useful to college students. It serves as "An Aid to Teachers, Counselors, Parents, Physicians, and Other Professionals Dedicated to Helping Youth." In Neff's **Work and Human Behavior,** in the section entitled "Five Year Educational Program," (28, pp. 49–57) there is an interesting integration of educational and vocational planning.

For individuals seeking work in an occupation which usually requires no more than two years of training beyond high school, Whitfield and Hoover (40) have prepared information on 145 of such occupations.

A good presentation of occupational information, along with educational and personal-social information, appears in an excellent text by Norris, Zeran, and Hatch. (29) This integration of data pertinent to all three areas of counseling is most helpful in focusing the career counselor's attention on the close correlation among the educational, career, and personal-social categories.

The classic literary sources of world-of-work data are the four volumes of the *Dictionary of Occupational Titles, Vol. I* (13), *Occupational Classifications and Industry Index, Vol. II (14), A Supplement to the Dictionary of Occupational Titles: Selected Characteristics of Occupations (Physical Demands, Working Conditions, Training Time)* (15), and *Supplement 2 to the Dictionary of Occupational Titles: Selected Characteristics of Occupations by Worker Traits and Physical Strength (16),* and the *Occupational Outlook Handbook.* (30)

Goal: There are several excellent sources of career information as represented in the following list of publishers of career information.

1.   Bellman Publishing Company

2.   B'nai B'rith Vocational Service

3.   Bureau of Employment Security

4.   Bureau of Labor Statistics

5.   Careers

6.   Chronicle Guidance Publications, Inc.

7.   New York Life Insurance Company

8.   Occupational Index, Inc.

9.   Occu-Press

10. Personnel Services, Inc.

11. Research Publishing Company

12. Science Research Associates

13. State Department of Employment Service

14. Superintendent of Documents

15. The Guidance Center

16. U.S. Civil Service Commission

17. U.S. Department of Health, Education and Welfare, Office of Education, Guidance, and Student Personnel Section

18. Vocational Guidance Manuals

Professional associations, governmental agencies, many companies and civic organizations often make available publications which provide career information. Examples of professional associations which offer career data are listed below.

1. American Dental Association

2. American Dietetic Association

3. American Home Economics Association

4. American Library Association

5. American Medical Association

6. American Nurses Association

7. American Occupational Therapy Association

8. American Optometric Association

In career counseling it is vital for clients to extend and intensify their self-understanding as they proceed with enriching their knowledge of the world of work. Clients should carefully compare their characteristics to the requirements of the types of work they are considering.

Part II of the **Counselor's Handbook** (7) deals with "Counselor Appraisal Patterns Related to Fields of Work." The concepts of temperaments, interests, and educational development are included.

The **Dictionary of Occupational Titles, Occupational Classification and Industry Index, Vol. II** (15) is a most valuable tool in enabling clients to compare their characteristics with those required by the types of work they are considering.

Contrary to popular belief, a lack of interest or not enough ability usually is not the most crucial factor in causing people to fail in their careers. Important as they are, together with other ingredients, the most significant barrier to career success is one or more personality defects or an incompatibility among the individual's characteristics and the qualities demanded by the work.

> The Harvard Bureau of Vocational Guidance found that 77 percent of all people who lost their jobs do so because of such traits as bad manners, lack of tact, or bad disposition. (6, p. 2)

> A number of studies show that workers lose their jobs more often because of unsuitable personal traits than through lack of skill in what they do. (21, p. 33)

> A recent report of a management-consultant firm of a large city revealed that 42 percent or 490 college students failed to make good in their studies or left their jobs before the end of one year. The study covered 1167 college trainees in 247 companies. Not only did those young men fail in their vocation but they lost valuable time, had to find a new way to adjust themselves, and cost the companies which sponsored them a total of $1,347,500. The report pointed out that too much stress had been placed on academic record, high I.Q., and good appearance. It was found that seven personality

traits proved most helpful. These traits were: stability, industriousness, perseverance, loyalty, self-reliance, ability to get along with fellow-workers, and willingness to lead and take responsibility. (1, p. 2)

Greenleaf reports on personality traits affecting occupational choice:

☞ *Traits Desirable in Teachers*

1. Adaptability

2. Attractive personal appearance

3. Breadth of interest

4. Carefulness

5. Considerateness

6. Cooperation

7. Dependability

8. Fluency

9. Forcefulness

10. Good judgment

11. Health

12. Honesty

13. Industry

14. Leadership

15. Magnetism

16. Neatness

17. Open-mindedness

18. Progressiveness

19. Promptness

20. Refinement

21. Scholarship

22. Self-control

23. Thrift

24. Enthusiasm

25. Originality (21, p. 33)

A number of studies show that individuals lose their jobs because of:

1. Carelessness

2. Inability to get along with people

3. Laziness

4. Lack of ambition and initiative

5. Staying off the job

6. Dishonesty

7. And other habits and skills that are not related to acquired skills (21, p. 34)

Items differentiating top and middle management as revealed in a study showing the concepts these executives have of themselves are reported below (34):

Top management see themselves as:	Middle management see themselves as:
capable	discreet
determined	courageous
industrious	practical
resourceful	planful
sharp-witted	deliberate
enterprising	intelligent
sincere	calm
sociable	steady
pleasant	modest
dignified	civilized
sympathetic	patient
Do not see themselves as:	**Do not see themselves as:**
unambitious	reckless
unfriendly	self-seeking
stingy	shallow
irritable	tense
apathetic	egotistical
rattle-brained	disorderly
pessimistic	opinionated
cynical	aggressive
dissatisfied	outspoken
sly	excitable

In Sederberg's article, "Management: Ability PLUS the Will to Excel Called Key to Executive Success," (35) he quoted Dr. Spaght, president of Shell Oil Company, as follows:

> It seems to me that the man who does anything best is the man who has a drive, the will to succeed, the urge to excel. Ability alone isn't enough. The good qualities must be coupled with a will to do something.

Sederberg also reports that:

> The "average" president is a man who:
> Is in his fifties and assumed his present job when he was just under 50.
> Has a bachelor's degree.
> Has worked for only one or two companies.
> Takes a briefcase of work home at night.
> Came up through the ranks via manufacturing or marketing …
> They used to be predominantly lawyers and financial men, but today they are more and more engineers and scientists. (35)

In the quote above, the words "they used to be" should serve as a stringent warning to career counselors that the world of work is not static; it is dynamic. The career counselor must keep abreast of what is and what probably will be. He/she must exemplify the concept of the counselor as a scientist.

☞ *References*

1. *A Career Opportunity for You*. Columbus, Ohio: American Cemetary Association, 1960.
2. Barnard, Chester I. *The Functions of the Executive*. Cambridge, Massachusetts: Harvard University Press, 1968.

3. Borow, Henry. *Man in a World at Work*. Boston: Houghton Mifflin Company, 1964.

4. Bush, Thomas W. "Executive Need for More Schooling Stressed." *Los Angeles Times,* October 26, 1967, Part III, pp. 13, 15.

5. Byrn, Delmont K. *Career Decisions*. Washington: National Vocational Guidance Association, 1969.

6. *Ceramic Engineer, Chronicle Occupational Briefs*. Moravia, New York: Chronicle Guidance Service, (no date).

7. *Counselor's Handbook*. U.S. Department of Labor, Washington, D.C.: U.S. Government Printing Office, 1967.

8. Demos, George D., and Bruce Grant. *Career Counseling in Depth*. Moravia, New York: Chronicle Guidance Publications, Inc., 1968–69.

9. Demos, George D., and Bruce Grant. *Designing Your Career*. Columbia, Missouri: Lucas Brothers, 1965.

10. Demos, George D., and Bruce Grant. *Designing Your Career – Part I*. Moravia, New York: Chronicle Guidance Publications, Inc., 1968–69.

11. Demos, George D., and Bruce Grant. *Designing Your Career – Part II*. Moravia, New York: Chronicle Guidance Publications, Inc., 1968–69.

12. Demos, George D., and Bruce Grant. *Vocational Guidance Readings*. Springfield, Illinois: Charles C. Thomas, 1965.

13. *Dictionary of Occupational Titles: Definition of Titles, Vol. I*. Washington: U.S. Government Printing Office, 1965.

14. *Dictionary of Occupational Titles: Occupational Classification and Industry Index, Vol. II*. Washington: U.S. Government Printing Office, 1965.

15. *A Supplement to the Dictionary of Occupational Titles: Selected Characteristics of Occupations (Physical Demands, Working Conditions, Training Time)*. Washington: U.S. Government Printing Office, 1966.

16. *Supplement 2 to the Dictionary of Occupational Titles: Selected Characteristics of Occupations by Worker Traits and Physical Strength*. Washington: U.S. Government Printing Office, 1968.

17. Dugan, W. F. "Vocational Guidance: A New Accent in American Education." *American Vocational Journal,* 41, 1966, pp. 14–15.

18. *Executives, Occupational Briefs.* Chicago: Science Research Associates, Inc., 1961.

19. Grant, Bruce, and George D. Demos. *California Career Study Guide.* Los Angeles, California: Western Psychological Services, 1964.

20. Grant, Bruce, George D. Demos, and Willard Edwards. *Guidance for Youth.* Springfield, Illinois: Charles C. Thomas, 1965.

21. Greenleaf, Walter J. *Occupations, A Basic Course for Counselors.* Washington: U.S. Government Printing Office, 1951.

22. Hamel, Harvey R. *Moonlighting – An Economic Phenomenon.* Special Labor Force Report No. 90, U.S. Department of Labor, Bureau of Labor Statistics, Washington: U.S. Government Printing Office, 1967.

23. Herzberg, Frederick. *Work and the Nature of Man.* Cleveland, Ohio: The World Publishing Company, 1967.

24. *Home Economist in Business.* Sacramento: Department of Employment, State of California, 1964.

25. Hoppock, Robert. *Occupational Information.* New York: McGraw-Hill Book Company, 1963.

26. Johnston, Denis F. *Education of Adult Workers in 1975.* Special Labor Force Report No. 95, U.S. Department of Labor, Bureau of Labor Statistics, Washington: U.S. Government Printing Office, 1968.

27. Lewis, Donald W. "Pick Your College Placement Bureau Carefully." *Vocational Guidance Quarterly,* December 1967, pp. 116–124.

28. Neff, Walter S. *Work and Human Behavior.* New York: Atherton Press, 1969.

29. Norris, Willa, Franklin R. Zeran, and Raymond N. Hatch. *The Information Service in Guidance: Occupational, Educational, Social.* Chicago: Rand McNally, 1968.

30. *Occupational Outlook Handbook.* Bureau of Labor Statistics, Washington: U.S. Department of Labor, 1968–69.

31. Osipow, Samuel H. *Theories of Career Development.* New York: Appleton-Century Crofts, 1968.

32. Parsons, Frank. *Choosing a Vocation.* Agathon Press, Inc., 1967.

33. Peters, Herman J., and James C. Hansen. *Vocational Guidance and Career Development: Selected Readings.* New York: The Macmillan Company, 1966.

34. Porter, Lyman W., and Edwin E. Ghiselli. "Self-Perception of Top and Middle Management Personnel." *Personnel Psychology,* Winter 1957, pp. 397–400.

35. Sederberg, Arleo. "Ability PLUS the Will to Excel Called Key to Executive Success." *Los Angeles Times,* March 17, 1965, Part III, p. 8.

36. Super, Donald E. *The Psychology of Careers.* New York: Harper, 1957.

37. "The Ten Best Managed." *Dun's Review and Modern Industry,* February 1963, p. 43.

38. Thoroman, E. C. *The Vocational Counseling of Adults and Young Adults.* Boston: Houghton Mifflin Co., 1968.

39. *You'll Need Math ... in Many Careers besides Mathematics.* Buffalo, New York: The Mathematical Association of America, Inc., 1967.

Chapter 18

PERSONAL-SOCIAL COUNSELING

The category of personal-social as used in counseling usually serves as the catch-all for all types of counseling which do not fit neatly into the educational or career classifications.

From one viewpoint, the word "personal" by itself may be extended to include all counseling, on the grounds that anything about which an individual becomes concerned, or any difficulty he has to resolve, is personal. This, however, is stretching the word unrealistically to encompass so much that it would serve no useful purpose to refer to all counseling as personal counseling, for obviously the word "personal" could be dropped without any loss of meaning.

Some authorities refer to the personal-social category as "social." Norris, Zeran, and Hatch (5) use "social," just as they select "occupational" instead of "vocational" or "career," as indicated by their title. Others prefer to label this category "personal-social." (2)

The authors choose to use the designation of personal-social, defining personal-social counseling as assisting individuals who are involved in making choices and adjustments relating to self and/or others in all aspects not related to educational or career areas.

To clarify what these aspects are, we have broken down the personal-social category into thirteen principal classifications:

1. Emotional

2. Financial

3. Goal Selection

4. Marital

5. Mental

6. Moral

7. Motivation

8. Needs

9. Parental

10. Personality Evaluation

11. Recreational

12. Sexual

13. Socializing

It is also helpful here to review the classifications of the educational career categories:

Educational:

1. How to Study

2. Preparation for Career

3. Program Planning

Career:

1. Career Planning

2. Vocational Changes

3. Vocational Choice

An examination of the kinds of problems experienced by individuals is most informative. The *Mooney Problem Check List* (4) contains 330 problems that extend into each of the areas of counseling.

One of the author's classifications (1) of problems into eighteen problem areas reveal the frequency that personal-social problems were reported by high school freshmen.

Rank	Problem Area	Frequency	Percent	Mean
1	Heterosexual	983	7.3	3.6
2	Emotional	974	7.2	3.5
3	Financial	971	7.2	3.5
4	Curriculum	884	6.6	3.2
5	Getting a Job	864	6.4	3.1
6	School Plant	784	5.8	2.9
7	Moral	776	5.7	2.8
8	Recreational	768	5.7	2.8
9	Mental	750	5.6	2.7
10	Manners	721	5.3	2.6
11	Health	712	5.3	2.6
12	Home	710	5.3	2.6
13	Socializing	681	5.0	2.4
14	Studying	639	4.7	2.3
15	Regulations	615	4.6	2.3
16	Cocurricular	595	4.4	2.2
17	College	564	4.2	2.1
18	Vocational	496	3.7	1.8
	Total	13487	100.0	49.0

Thinking about these problem areas and the statistics reported should make it quite evident to the student that normal individuals have many normal problems. Accordingly, caution should be exercised by students of psychology (who are laying the ground-work for personal-social counseling) to avoid overemphasis on the abnormal.

Certainly there is a place in personal-social counseling for the counselor to attempt to help the atypical individual. At this point, a review of *Chapter 3, Counseling and Psychotherapy,* would be appropriate.

Let us assume, then, that some attention will be given to the personal-social counseling of atypical individuals. The principal point of concern is that counselors have throughout the years devoted far too much time and energy to these individuals, while neglecting to help the vast majority of normal persons with their myriad of problems.

The fact remains that most people fall within the normal category; about two out of every three people can claim this distinction. It would seem to be an elementary premise that this majority is entitled to its fair share of personal-social (as well as educational and career) counseling. This will be difficult for schools to achieve, even if they can afford to hire an adequate number of counselors, so long as counselor educators permit their trainees to focus on working with the abnormal – because it is the most fun, most prestigious, most necessary, and/or most lucrative.

It is time to recognize the normal person's right to be helped. These people also should be served, and it is in personal-social counseling that they usually have been expected to fend for themselves without benefit of counseling.

As will be covered in *Part V: The Preparation of the Counselor,* the science pertinent to educational and career counseling may be studied within the normal curriculum designed for counseling or guidance. This has been done in the past, with such courses appearing in the education department in some colleges and in the psychology department in other schools, depending upon the training or philosophy of the counselor educators of a particular college.

Whatever the arguments may be for placing educational and career counseling courses in the education or psychology departments, there appears to be little question about the propriety of assigning most of the courses pertaining to the science of personal-social counseling to the psychology department. Again, what the counselor needs to know about any individual revolves around his/her understanding of the behavior of individuals; in other words, he/she requires a basic and thorough knowledge of psychology.

Since personal-social problems are obviously concerned with the behavior of the individual, psychology inevitably must be the basic science supporting personal-social counseling.

The behavior of the individual often becomes entwined with groups. Accordingly, some sociological training is needed. Depending upon the nature of the problem, the counselor will be called upon to use his reservoir of knowledge derived from the study of philosophy, economics, business, physical education, and recreation as well as education. So, while psychology might well be given precedence as the number one discipline supporting personal-social counseling, the necessity for an interdisciplinary approach to the science of counseling once again is apparent.

Any course offered within a counseling department, such as individual inventory, personal-social counseling, etc., should have an imposing array of prerequisites which the student must have completed prior to becoming eligible for admission to these courses. A list of courses which the authors recommend for inclusion as these prerequisites is given in **Part V: The Preparation of the Counselor.**

In personal-social counseling the counseling art probably reaches its highest level. It is here that the "bedside manner," charm, smoothness, and magnetism make their greatest impact. The techniques of nonverbal responses, brief replies, reflecting, and empathizing may be employed with great effectiveness in aiding clients with personal-social difficulties.

While recognizing the monumental contributions of the so-called non-directive or client-centered method to the art of counseling, especially to personal-social counseling, the student and practitioner should not lose sight of the reality that many instances arise in personal-social counseling in which the client wants information and interpretation. What Hoyt said about increasing the use of information in educational-vocational counseling sometimes may be applied to personal-social counseling.

> We have for too long had counselors and clients, both of whom are ignorant regarding pertinent characteristics and information regarding environmental opportunities, sitting down together and sharing their ignorance. (3)

It is pertinent to point out that even when a reaction to feelings should take precedence over dealing with the intellectual content of what the client is conveying, there are times when facts are needed regarding the feelings, and no matter how beautiful a relationship has been established between counselor and client, attempting to maintain it through mutual ignorance when knowledge is required is a questionable practice.

Whether the counselor is using client-centered or more directive methodology in his/her personal-social counseling, it is clear that his/her exercise of the art of counseling at its highest level is needed for maximal effectiveness in personal-social counseling.

The counselor should know what he/she is doing and why he/she is doing it when he/she smiles, assumes a relaxed posture, controls his/her facial-expression to portray concern, interest, approval, liking, or sharing. The counselor's own particular personality influences to a significant degree the use of these techniques. The wisdom of the following statement is immediately apparent: "I know what I'm supposed to do, but executing it is another matter."

As with many skills, the knowledge required to execute may be simple but the execution itself may be highly complex.

Then, of course, there are some skills which require extensive knowledge to perform and which are just as complex in the execution. In counseling, perhaps the most difficult skill to achieve is the establishment of a harmonious relationship, a rapport, with a hostile or fearful client. Here again, this puts a premium on the need for the personal-social counselor to be perhaps the most skillful of all types of counselors in this matter of relating well to the client. The old-time general practitioner (physician) or the modern-day internist *usually* must be more effective in the art of medicine than his/her specialized colleagues (e.g., ophthalmologist, surgeon, dermatologist, etc.).

Knowledge of behavior and how to react to its variations in a multiplicity of situations is basic to the attempt to express tender loving care, empathy, and warmth. But while knowledge does play its role in this, the personality of the counselor undoubtedly exercises the paramount influence.

It is most apparent in personal-social counseling that there is no place for the unfeeling type of counselor. While maintaining objectivity in relationships with clients is fundamental to the professional worker, too much objectivity may lead to unperceived but felt barriers between the counselor and his/her client. The avenue of nonverbal communication should be kept open; this is virtually impossible if the counselor is being so objective that he/she withholds too much of himself/herself in the interacting process with his/her client. Overinvolvement is not the answer either. A compromise between excessive objectivity and excessive subjectivity is the best solution for the counselor striving to relate most effectively in a personal-social counseling situation.

☞ References

[1.] Grant, Bruce. "Survey of Studies on Problems of Adolescents." *California Journal of Secondary Education*, May 1953, pp. 293–297.

[2.] Hollis, Joseph W., and Lucile U. Hollis. *Personalizing Information Processes: Educational, Occupational, and Personal-Social*. New York: The Macmillan Company, 1969.

[3.] Hoyt, Kenneth B. "High School Guidance and the Specially Oriented Student Research Program." *Vocational Guidance Quarterly*, Summer 1965, pp. 229–236.

[4.] Mooney, Ross L. *Mooney Problem Check List*. New York: The Psychological Corporation, 1950.

[5.] Norris, Willa, Franklin R. Zeran, and Raymond N. Hatch. *The Information Service in Guidance: Occupational, Educational, Social*. Chicago: Rand McNally, 1968.

[6.] Rogers, Carl. *Client-Centered Therapy*. Boston: Houghton Mifflin Co., 1951.

[7.] Rogers, Carl. *Counseling and Psychotherapy*. Boston: Houghton Mifflin Co., 1942.

☞ Suggested Additional Readings

Gallagher, Phillip J., and George D. Demos. *The Counseling Center in Higher Education*. Springfield, Illinois: Charles C. Thomas, 1970.

Nickelly, Arthur G. *Mental Health for Students.* Springfield, Illinois: Charles C. Thomas, 1966.

Patterson, C. H. "Phenomenological Psychology." *Personnel and Guidance Journal,* June, 1965, pp. 997–1005.

Rogers, Carl R. *Freedom to Learn.* Columbus, Ohio: Charles E. Merrill, 1969.

Steinzor, Bernard. *When Parents Divorce.* New York: Pantheon Books, 1969.

Chapter 19

TOOLS OF COUNSELING

The word "tool" in its usage in counseling has been applied rather loosely, sometimes meaning tests, in other instances including concrete aids except tests, occasionally involving techniques, and often encompassing all of these.

As used here, a tool of counseling is any professional material aid used by the counselor in the process of counseling. The word "professional" is inserted to eliminate the material necessities, e.g., desk, chair, etc. These professional material aids include tests, Counseling Record, Personal Data Form, Cumulative Record, any form for obtaining a case history, and any paper instrument. (See Chapter 7 for a discussion and examples of the various records and forms.)

It may be said that counseling is implemented through its tools; this is particularly true in terms of the science of counseling.

In this chapter the emphasis is on tests, for they serve as the major tool of the counselor. The word "test" has also been frequently obscured by making it encompass every measurement device. One interpretation of "test" would limit its usage to only those devices employed to measure an individual's knowledge or skill in comparison with others, and using responses which can be labeled right or wrong.

Another viewpoint would allow the foregoing definition to be expanded to include any device which yields a comparison with others in terms of average, below average, and above average. The authors have adopted this interpretation as most fitting for the word "test." Accordingly, they exclude any measuring or fact-obtaining device from being identified as a test unless it has been standardized.

The most appropriate term for the measuring device which excludes a comparison with others by use of the derived score is the term "instrument." A handy reference for reviewing the meaning of terms used in measurement is *A Glossary of 100 Measurement Terms*. (30)

Nonmeasuring devices which may be utilized by the counselor include anecdotal record, autobiography, counseling record, personal data form, career guide, booklets, pamphlets, case history – structured or unstructured form – and problem checklists.

Each counselor must inevitably lean toward his/her own preferences and be governed by his/her own experience. But the failure of some counselors to utilize any nonmeasuring devices is questionable from any viewpoint and most difficult to justify within the frame of reference of the science of counseling. As a case in point, there are situations and clients which quite obviously indicate the need for obtaining a case history. The authors recommend the utilization of a structured form, such as *The California Pre-Counseling Self-Analysis Protocol Booklet.* (13)

Before suggesting tests worthy of the counselor's consideration, it is necessary to draw attention to the lamentable and rather frightening weakness of tests, here vividly illustrated by Goldman:

> The crudeness of a test as an instrument of measurement may be appreciated by applying a degree of error (e.g., 6) to a bathroom scale. This means that if an individual gets on the scale once and weighs 140 pounds, we could expect that if he gets on the scale 100 more times, 68 out of 100 of those times the weight would register between 134 and 146 pounds, and the remaining 32 times it would be outside this range. We would probably not use a bathroom scale of this sort for very long (without having it repaired). But our most reliable tests have only this degree of precision. (20, p. 283)

Counselors lack the precision tests available to physicians and dentists. At times they are inundated with discouraging data about the futility of some of their supposedly best tests. As a case in point, the scholastic aptitude test has long been regarded as the most valid and reliable of counseling tests.

Yet, it is with increasing dismay that counselors continue to be confronted with evidence of individuals with high scholastic aptitude flunking out of college and students with poor scores succeeding in college. The answer, of course, lies not in making a blanket condemnation of these tests, or generalizing that all tests must be worthless, but rather in recognizing that there are factors other than scholastic aptitude determining whether or not a person will succeed scholastically.

Maturity, motivation, values, goals, good study skills, appropriate personality strengths (e.g., responsibility, industriousness, self-reliance, dedication, competitiveness, perseverance, etc.), interest, and health, the lack of any one which, or in any combination of two or more, could be more significant than mediocre scholastic aptitude in causing academic failure.

However, in spite of these factors, Dr. Goldman's admonition pertinent to the limitation of all tests should not be ignored.

In career counseling, the way for clients to circumvent the weaknesses of tests is through the investigation (by reading, observing, and interviewing) of the leads derived from the tests. Knowledge gained about the type of work under consideration will exercise the necessary control in prohibiting unwise choices resulting from erroneous test data. The same is true in educational counseling; investigating yields facts to support or refute the clues or implications derived from tests.

In personal-social counseling, the clues picked up from personality-type tests should be examined empirically in the counseling sessions, where the counselor is able to make clinical judgments in support or in refutation of the leads derived from tests.

There are several excellent texts that devote themselves to dealing with testing and instruments. The authors suggest that students of testing would do well to study several of them and select two or three to serve as basic referral sources in test selection, test continuation or discontinuation, and for comparative purposes.

Buros' monumental *Mental Measurements Yearbook* (9) is a classic in the psychometric field. The yearbook lists all tests that were currently in print during the period of its preparation for publication. There are 396 contributing authorities and nearly 800 critical reviews of more than 500 tests, covering 1,714 pages.

Anastasi (4) devotes attention to current uses of psychological tests. Intelligence tests, group testing, achievement tests, measurement of personality, interpretation of test scores, norms and their uses, statistical concepts, age scores percentiles, and standard scores are covered.

As a contribution to test theory, students of testing should find *Psychological Tests and Personal Decisions* (12) a valuable resource. It, along with Goldman's text, (20) focuses attention on the relationship between tests and decision making.

> An almost universal characteristic of counseling ... is that it deals with decisions and plans ... Counseling is usually able to give help in making decisions and plans for the future and in choosing among alternating courses of action in the world of reality. (20, p. 25)

"A decision can be defined as the process of selecting one action from a number of alternative courses of action." (7, p. 1) In this connection, it is wise to remember that the results of tests are not decisions but merely leads or clues to be investigated. One makes a decision after sufficient data are obtained to provide an adequate basis for the judgment.

A guiding principle long advocated by investment companies is most pertinent here: "Before you invest, investigate." Before a client makes a decision concerning data derived from testing, he should investigate.

Ahmann and Glock provide updated discussions of tests and specific examples of measuring educational and behavioral objectives. (2)

Measurement in Education, Psychology, and Guidance (1) is concerned with individual testing, vocational interests and aptitudes testing, various approaches to personality assessment, group testing, and educational diagnosis.

A good treatise on principles and concepts, the reasons why psychological measurement proceeds as it does, and the why to the how of psychological measurement are offered in *Tests and Measurements*. (8)

While there are many tests and instruments available for use by counselors, the authors believe it would be helpful to both the student and the practitioner to have a list of recommended tools for various situations. The following tools are recommended for consideration; their choice is, of course, influenced by their use by the authors, each of whom has been and still is a practicing counselor.

☞ *Scholastic Aptitude*

1. Otis Quick-Scoring Mental Ability Tests

2. Wechsler Adult Intelligence Scale (R)

3. Wechsler Intelligence Scale for Children (R)

4. American College Testing Program Examination

5. College Entrance Examination Scholastic Aptitude Test

6. Graduate Record Examinations

7. Miller Analogies Test

☞ Aptitudes (other than scholastic)

Art

1. Meier Art Tests (33)

2. Knauber Art Ability Test (28)

Manual

1. O'Connor Finger Dexterity (36)

2. O'Connor Tweezer Dexterity (37)

3. Crawford Small Parts Dexterity Test (11)

4. Stromberg Dexterity Test (43)

5. Purdue Pegboard (39)

6. Minnesota Rate of Manipulation Test (6)

Mechanical

1. Minnesota Spatial Relations Test (46)

2. Revised Minnesota Paper Form Board Test (31)

3. MacQuarrie Test for Mechanical Ability (includes Manual Dexterity) (32)

Clerical

Minnesota Clerical Test (5)

Quantitative

Quantitative Evaluative Device (42)

English

Cooperative English Tests (17)

Multiple Aptitudes

1. Flanagan Aptitude Classification Tests (9)

2. Employee Aptitude Survey (40)

3. Guilford-Zimmerman Aptitude Survey (25)

4. Rating Scale of Vocational Aptitudes (14)

Vocational Interests

1. Kuder Preference Record – Vocational (29)

2. Strong-Campbell Vocational Interest Test

3. California Occupational Preference Survey (27)

4. Rating Scale of Vocational Interests (15)

Needs

1. Edwards Personal Preference Schedule (18)

2. Self-Rating Scale of Psychological Needs (24)

Personality Traits

1. Guilford-Zimmerman Temperament Survey (26)

2. California Psychological Inventory (21)

3. Self-Rating Scale of Personality Traits (23)

Problem Check List

Mooney Problem Check List (35)

Vocational Values

Rating Scale of Vocational Values (16)

Case History

The California Pre-Counseling Self-Analysis Protocol Booklet (13)

Records (see Chapter 7)

1. Counseling Record

2. Personal Data Form

3. Cumulative Record

Instruments (see p. 98)

1. California Career Study Guide

2. Designing Your Career

☞ *References*

1. *American College Testing Program Examination.* Iowa City, Iowa: American College Testing Program, 1970.

2. Anastasi, Anne. *Psychological Testing.* New York: The Macmillan Company, 1968.

3. Andrew, Dorothy M., and Donald G. Paterson. *Minnesota Clerical Test.* New York: The Psychological Corporation, 1946.

4. Betts, Gilbert L., and W. A. Ziegler. *Minnesota Rate of Manipulation Test.* Minneapolis, Minnesota: Educational Test Bureau, 1946.

5. *College Entrance Examination Scholastic Aptitude Test.* Princeton, New Jersey: College Entrance Examination Board by Educational Testing Service, 1970.

6. Crawford, John E., and Dorothea M. Crawford. *Crawford Small Parts Dexterity Test.* New York: The Psychological Corporation, 1956.

7. Cronbach, Lee J., and Goldine C. Gleser. *Psychological Tests and Personnel Decisions.* Urbana, Illinois: University of Illinois Press, 1965.

8. Demos, George D., and Bruce Grant. *The California Pre-Counseling Self-Analysis Protocol Booklet.* Los Angeles, California: Western Psychological Services, 1965.

9. Demos, George D., and Bruce Grant. *Rating Scale of Vocational Aptitudes.* San Diego, California: Educational and Industrial Testing Service, 1966.

10. Demos, George D., and Bruce Grant. *Rating Scale of Vocational Interests*. San Diego, California: Educational and Industrial Testing Service, 1966.

11. Demos, George D., and Bruce Grant. *Rating Scale of Vocational Values*. San Diego, California: Educational and Industrial Testing Service, 1966.

12. Derrick, Clarence, David P. Harris, and Biron Walker. *Cooperative English Tests*. Princeton, New Jersey: Cooperative Test Division, Educational Testing Service, 1960.

13. Edwards, Allen L. *Edwards Personal Preference Schedule*. New York: The Psychological Corporation, 1959.

14. Flanagan, John C. *Flanagan Aptitude Classification Tests*. Chicago: Science Research Associates, Inc., 1953.

15. Gough, Harrison G. *California Psychological Inventory*. Palo Alto, California: Consulting Psychologists Press, 1960.

16. *Graduate Record Examinations*. Princeton, New Jersey: Educational Testing Service, 1963.

17. Grant, Bruce, and George D. Demos. *Self-Rating Scale of Personality Traits*. (From *California Career Study Guide: Self-Evaluation in Career Planning*) Los Angeles, California: Western Psychological Services, 1964.

18. Grant, Bruce, and George D. Demos. *Self-Rating Scale of Psychological Needs*. (From *California Career Study Guide: Self-Evaluation in Career Planning*) Los Angeles, California: Western Psychological Services, 1964.

19. Guilford, J. P., and Wayne S. Zimmerman. *Guilford-Zimmerman Aptitude Survey*. Beverly Hills, California: Sheridan Supply Company, 1956.

20. Guilford, J. P., and Wayne S. Zimmerman. *Guilford-Zimmerman Temperament Survey*. Beverly Hills, California: Sheridan Supply Company, 1949.

21. Knapp, Robert R., Bruce Grant, and George D. Demos. *California Occupational Preference Survey*. San Diego, California: Educational and Industrial Testing Service, 1966.

22. Knauber, Alma Jordan. *Knauber Art Ability Test*. Cincinnati, Ohio: Alma Jordan Knauber, 1935.

23. Kuder, G. Frederic, *Kuder Preference Record – Vocational.* Chicago: Science Research Associates, Inc., 1960.

24. Lennon, Roger T. *A Glossary of 100 Measurement Terms.* Yonkers-on-Hudson, New York: World Book Company, (no date).

25. Linkert, Rensis, and William H. Quasha. *Revised Minnesota Paper Form Board Test.* New York: Psychological Corporation, 1948.

26. MacQuarrie, T. W. *MacQuarrie Test for Mechanical Ability.* Monterey, California: The California Test Bureau, 1943.

27. Meier, Norman Charles. *Meier Art Tests.* Iowa City, Iowa: Bureau of Educational Research and Service, 1940.

28. Miller, W. S. *Miller Analogies Test.* New York: Psychological Corporation, 1960.

29. Mooney, Ross L., and Leonard V. Gordon. *Mooney Problem Check List, 1950 Revision.* New York: The Psychological Corporation, 1950.

30. O'Connor, Johnson. *O'Connor Finger Dexterity Test.* Chicago: C. H. Stoelting Company, 1926.

31. O'Connor, Johnson. *O'Connor Tweezer Dexterity Test.* Chicago: C. H. Stoelting Company, 1928.

32. Otis, Arthur S. *Otis Quick-Scoring Mental Ability Tests.* New York: Harcourt, Brace & World, 1954.

33. *Purdue Pegboard.* Chicago: Science Research Associates, Inc., 1948.

34. Ruch, Floyd L., and William W. Ruch. *Employee Aptitude Survey.* Los Angeles: Psychological Services, Inc., 1963.

35. Seashore, Carl E., Don Lewis, and Joseph G. Saetveit. *Seashore Measure of Musical Talents, Revised Edition.* New York: Psychological Corporation, 1960.

36. Stake, R. E. *Quantitative Evaluative Devise.* Adams, Nebraska: Lincoln Test Service, 1962.

37. Stromberg, Eleroy L. *Stromberg Dexterity Test.* New York: The Psychological Corporation, 1951.

38. Strong, Edward K. *Strong Vocational Interest Blank for Men.* Palo Alto, California: Consulting Psychologists Press, 1938.

39. Strong, Edward K. *Strong Vocational Interest Blank for Women.* Palo Alto, California: Consulting Psychologists Press, 1948.

40. Trabue, M. R., Donald G. Paterson, Richard M. Eliott, L. Dewey Anderson, Herbert A. Toops, and E. Heidbreder. *Minnesota Spatial*

Relations Test. Minneapolis, Minnesota: Educational Test Bureau, 1930.

41. Wechsler, David. *Wechsler Adult Intelligence Scale*. New York: The Psychological Corporation, 1955.

42. Wechsler, David. *Wechsler Intelligence Scale for Children*. New York: The Psychological Corporation, 1949.

☞ *Suggested Additional Readings*

Blanck, Rubin, and Gertrude Blanck. *Marriage and Personal Development*. New York: Columbia University Press, 1968.

Bolton, Brian, and Marceline E. Jacques, eds. *Rehabilitation Counseling*. Baltimore: University Park Press, 1978.

Burgum, Thomas, and Scott Anderson. *The Counselor and the Law*. Washington, D.C.: American Personnel and Guidance Association, 1975.

Callis, Robert. *Ethical Standards Casebook*. Washington, D.C.: American Personnel and Guidance Association, 1976.

Canon, Harry J. "Developing Staff Potential." In *Student Services,* edited by Ursula Delworth and Gary R. Hanson, pp. 439–455. San Francisco: Jossey-Bass, 1980.

Dameron, Joseph D., ed. *The Professional Counselor: Competencies, Performance Guidelines, and Assessment*. Falls Church, Virginia: American Personnel and Guidance Association, 1980.

Danish, Steven J., and Michael A. Smyer. "Unintended Consequences of Requiring a License to Help." *American Psychologist* 36, no. 1 (1981), pp. 13–21.

Delworth, Ursula, and Gary R. Hanson. "Conclusion: Structure of the Profession and Recommended Curriculum." In *Student Services,* edited by Ursula Delworth and Gary R. Hanson, pp. 473–485. San Francisco: Jossey-Bass, 1980.

Drapela, Victor J., ed. *Guidance and Counseling Around the World*. Washington, D.C.: University Press of America, 1979.

Fretz, Bruce R., and David H. Mills. "Professional Certification in Counseling Psychology." *Counseling Psychologist* 9, no. 1 (1980), pp. 2–17.

Giroux, Roy F., Donald A. Biggs, Alan M. Hoffman, and John J. Pietrofesa, eds. *College Student Development Revisited: Programs, Issues, and Practices.* Rev. ed. Falls Church, Virginia: American Personnel and Guidance Association, 1979.

Herr, Edwin L. *Guidance and Counseling in the Schools: The Past, Present, and Future.* Falls Church, Virginia: American Personnel and Guidance Association, 1979.

Lewis, Judith A., and Michael D. Lewis. *Community Counseling: A Human Services Approach.* New York: John Wiley and Sons, 1977.

Miller, Theodore K., and D. Stanley Carpenter. "Professional Preparation for Today and Tomorrow." In *Student Development in Higher Education,* edited by Don C. Creamer, pp. 181–204. Cincinnati: American College Personnel Association, 1980.

Shertzer, Bruce, and Shelley C. Stone. *Fundamentals of Guidance.* 4th ed. Boston: Houghton Mifflin Co., 1981.

Stude, E. W., and Don L. Goodyear. *Ethics and the Counselor.* Fullerton, California: Personnel and Guidance Association, 1975.

Part V

THE PREPARATION OF THE COUNSELOR

Chapter 20

UNDERGRADUATE EDUCATION

A mong the several problems involved in the education of the counselor is the fact that few undergraduate students have chosen the career of counseling, and an even smaller number have received any professional help in seeking the undergraduate education they should obtain.

In the sense that there are premedical or predental courses of study, there simply isn't any precounseling curriculum.

Public school counselors usually are developed after a few years of teaching, from which for one reason or another they decide to move to counseling. Agency counselors often spring from a background of social work or sociology.

The authors have had as colleagues in college counseling centers individuals with doctorates in counseling, educational psychology, clinical psychology, counseling psychology, sociology, philosophy, and English.

Counselors, teachers, social workers, etc., are unfortunately permitted to practice with an extreme variance in education that ranges from less than a bachelor's degree to the doctorate. The legal profession also has the situation in which most lawyers acquire the L.L.B. while some, without any additional years of education, are granted an L.L.D. or J.D., depending entirely upon the policy of the particular law school from which the legal student is graduated.

Contrast the above with the precise and uncompromising position of the education of the physician and dentist. While there may be some variation in premedical or predental requirements for admission to medical or dental schools, once the candidate is accepted in either institution, he/she faces a four-year curriculum leading to the M.D. and D.D.S. degree. There is no such thing as a partially or incompletely trained physician or dentist. Of course, for the physician who wishes to specialize, there is the necessity of completing three or more years of residency (following the standard one year of internship).

We are dealing with the undergraduate education only in this chapter (saving the rest for the next one, Chapter 21, on graduate education), because it is the view of the authors that there should be a precounseling program (as there is premed, prelegal, etc.) at the undergraduate level and also because of the fact that some professional courses must be taken prior to graduate school.

Because of the massive numbers of teachers and counselors required to operate the public schools of this nation, the ideal of a uniformity of preparation probably must remain only a dream of wishful thinking into which sorely harassed educational administrators may retreat, faced as they are with professional staffs that too often range from the incompetent to the master teacher and master counselor.

The salary schedule usually provides for yearly increments on a seniority basis up to a point, then demands further education (usually under the label "professional growth"). An additional degree or a specified number of graduate units beyond the bachelor's or master's degree is required before the annual seniority increase is resumed.

There is little doubt that years of experience usually make a lawyer a better lawyer, a physician a better physician, a teacher a better teacher, and a counselor a better counselor, and there is a rational justification for rewarding years of experience with salary increments.

The authors' hope in making a proposal for undergraduate education for counselors in this chapter is that colleges will continue to sharpen their liberal education requirements and expand their preprofessional curriculums to include precounseling.

It has been said that the lawyer is the last of the intellectual generalists. Certainly, the counselor must be included in this category, for in dealing with the diversity of human problems, plans, decisions, and adjustments, the counselor has occasion to draw upon a wide reservoir of knowledge. Much of this knowledge, particularly in the sense of knowing enough about so many things that appropriate referrals may be made, must come from the undergraduate years before the specialization of graduate studies.

The counselor desperately needs an adequate liberal education with an emphasis in the social sciences, i.e., psychology and sociology.

The courses in the four-year program outlined above are categorized below in terms of departments and the number of units included per each department. Electives (15 units) are provided for adding to a department if a particular college insists on a subject major.

The counselor who is training to counsel in a college, agency or in a private practice may eliminate enough units in education to produce sufficient units which may be distributed among the recommended electives or used to complete a major in a particular subject.

The student may wonder at the freedom exercised by the authors in labeling this undergraduate program as "liberal education," particularly when there are several courses that appear to be strictly vocational, especially when these vocational courses are included as preparation for teachers.

Departments	Units	Departments	Units
English	9	Industrial Technology	3
Social Science	3	Criminology	1
Biology	3	Preprofessional:	
Health	3	Medical, Dental, Veterinarian,	
Art	1	Medical Legal, and	
Music	1	Theological	
Physical Education	4	Curriculums	
Physiology	3	(Interdisciplinary)	2
Philosophy	6	Journalism	1
Business	7	Sociology	3
Engineering	1	Anthropology	3
Nursing	1	Theater Arts	1
Recreation	1	Home Economics	1
Psychology	9	Mathematics	3
Education	21	Economics	3
Industrial Arts	1	Electives	<u>15</u>
			120

The authors believe that the inclusion of such courses as "Introduction to Engineering," "Introduction to Law Enforcement," etc., serves the purpose of enriching the counselor trainee's background by giving him/her an academic glimpse into several careers or career areas. And since he/she obviously is not taking any of these courses as preparation for engineering or law, etc., they serve well the function of contributing to his/her general education, while at the same time introducing him/her to the world of work with which he/she will relate so closely in his/her practice of counseling – even as a generalist.

The insight into home economics afforded by that course has contributions for men as well as women, and home economists usually are delighted to have the opportunity of exposing men to the complexities and ramifications of their field.

☞ References

1. Blocker, Donald H. "Wanted: A Science of Human Effectiveness." **Personnel and Guidance Journal,** March 1966, pp. 729–733.

2. Demos, George D., and Bruce Grant. "College and University Counseling." From **Guidelines for Guidance: Readings in the Philosophy of Guidance,** edited by Carlton E. Beck. Dubuque, Iowa: W. C. Brown and Company, 1966.

3. Isaacson, Lee E. "Standards for the Preparation of Guidance and Personnel Workers – In Colleges and Universities." **Counselor Education and Supervision,** Spring 1968, pp. 187–192.

4. Richardson, H. D. "Preparation for Counseling as a Profession." *Counselor Education and Supervision,* Winter 1963, pp. 124–128.

5. Ryan, Charles W. "Preparation of Counselors in Ohio Catholic Schools." *Counselor Education and Supervision,* Winter 1968, pp. 119–123.

6. Shertzer, Bruce, and Joan England. "Follow-up Data on Counselor Education Graduates – Relevant, Self-Revealing, or What?" *Counselor Education and Supervision,* Summer 1968, pp. 363–370.

☞ Suggested Additional Reading

Smith, C. E., and Oscar G. Mink. *Foundations of Guidance and Counseling*. Philadelphia: J. B. Lippincott Company, 1969.

Chapter 21

GRADUATE EDUCATION

While there has never been any question about the need for graduate education in the preparation of counselors, there certainly has been considerable disagreement on what kind and how much graduate study there should be.

The roots of the difficulty are found in the long-standing and still-running disagreements between the education and psychology departments in many colleges. Empire building and/or seekers of supposed prestige by alignment with one department or the other have done little to foster cooperative interdisciplinary education of counselors.

It is time to end the battle for supremacy over which department wins the upper hand in counselor education. As a solution to the dilemma of choosing between the two, the authors propose the formation of a department of counseling as an entity separate from both the education and psychology departments, yet as closely related to each as brothers.

As with any new discipline, it will take considerable time for counseling as a science to gain academic acceptance. How soon this date arrives will depend upon the efforts of the faculty who become members of the new department. Since most of them will come from the departments of education and psychology, the critical factor in making counseling a reality as an academic department will rest in the hands of these pioneering education and psychology professors. It will depend on whether or not they can think of themselves and function as professors of counseling. If they can't, then the battle will continue between education and psychology, with the friction even more evident and devastating, since the different factions will have been thrown even closer together. It remains to be seen if this proposal of a counseling department is accepted and put into practice, and whether highly intelligent academicians can overcome past differences, jealousies, prestige seeking, and empire building in order to join together with their professional colleagues in the exciting adventure of integrating knowledge from their own and other disciplines to create a science of counseling.

If this proposal cannot be realized, then each college must resolve its own dilemma of whether to assign counselor training to the education department or to the psychology department.

There used to be an argument over how much education – one or two graduate years? This difference of opinion has practically disappeared on the grounds that one year simply does not permit the inclusion of all that must go into the adequate preparation of the counselor who is a generalist, let alone the individual who elects to qualify himself/herself for a specialization.

Prior to studying the authors' recommendations of specific subjects in the graduate program, the reader should familiarize himself/herself with the proposals made by several authorities in counselor education.

Ohlsen (8) reports on standards for the preparation of elementary school counselors. Professional studies include:

1. Counseling theories and techniques

2. Group procedures in guidance and counseling

3. Professional identification, the profession, and its ethics

4. Role definition, program development, and coordination of elementary school guidance services

5. The consultation process

6. Individual appraisal

7. Vocational development theory, including the use of appropriate materials for elementary school children

8. Research skills to enable the elementary school counselor to understand the relevant research and to appraise the outcomes of his services

"Standards for Counselor Education in the Preparation of Secondary School Counselors" (11) includes the following sections:

1. Philosophy and Objectives

2. Curriculum: Program of Studies and Supervised Experiences

3. Selection, Retention, Endorsement, and Placement

4. Support for the Counselors Education Program, Administrative Relationships, and Institutional Resources

Isaacson's report on "Standards for the Preparation of Guidance and Personnel Workers – In Colleges and Universities" (7) offers needed information regarding the higher education level. It is proposed that "understanding and competency in the following areas should be included in the didactic portion of preparation":

1. Student Personnel Work in Higher Education

2. Higher Education as a Social Institution

3. Human Growth and Development

4. Social and Cultural Foundations

5. Methods, Techniques, and Concepts Used by Student Personnel Workers

6. Research and Evaluation

7. Preparation in Specialized Fields

Blocker presents an interesting viewpoint in his proposal that

> ... the general concept of human effectiveness can be used to organize a body of knowledge that can extend the boundaries of the underlying discipline in ways helpful to counselors of all value orientations. The counselor is uniquely interested in the etiology of human effectiveness, in the study of those causes that underlie effective living.
>
> What is needed for counselor education is an organized body of knowledge about the development of human effectiveness. (3)

In Richardson's proposal for preparation for counseling as a profession, he suggests the following:

> The basic and advanced graduate course areas required in the core or trunk of the program model include:

1. **Social Sciences:** Sociology, Anthropology, Political Science, Economics

2. **Education:** Principles or Philosophy

3. **Psychology:** Psychological Tests, Educational Psychology or Learning Theories, Descriptive Statistics and Statistical Analysis, Developmental Psychology or Personality Development, Individual Testing

4. **Counselor Education:** Principles of Counseling and Guidance; Analysis of the Individual; Career Development: Educational and Vocational Group Procedures; Information Materials: Educational, Vocational, and Personal-Social; Counseling Practicum; Group Counseling; Research Methods: Data Processing and Programming; Advanced Counseling and

Supervised Practice; Philosophies and Theories of Counseling; Dissertation and Research Seminar in Experimental Design. (10)

Viewing counselor preparation from the eyes of school superintendents is possible in examining Peters' and Thompson's article. They report the responses of school superintendents who were requested to rank counselor duties in order of their perceived importance. Five points were given to a first choice, four to a second choice, etc.

		Points
1.	Individual counseling	75
2.	Test administration and interpretation	47
3.	Group counseling	24
4.	Informational services	23
5.	Working with staff and administration	23
6.	Utilization of effective communication in school-community and parent-child relationships	21
7.	Utilization of emphatic insight in understanding student behavior, homes and background	17
8.	Research, evaluation, and student follow-up	11 (9)

From this it is easy to realize the kinds of subjects these superintendents would prefer their counselors to have taken in the counselor education programs from which they emerged.

The late Clarence W. Failor pioneered several excellent proposals for counselor education.

Essential as related courses in child growth and development, psychology, sociology, and other social studies are, they are foundation stones, and not substitutes for, special training in guidance. The customary courses in the guidance sequence which are called for by all the 42 states that certify counselors and which are common in most counselor education institutions are:

1. Foundations of Guidance and Pupil Personnel Services which stresses the philosophy and principles of guidance services

2. Individual Inventory Service which provides competencies in all types of observations and reports in helping the individual better understand himself and his potentialities

3. Socio-Economic Information Services embracing knowledges about sources and use of educational, occupational and social information in which areas pupils must make choices

4. Group Techniques in Guidance which stresses method as well as content

5. Counseling Techniques which provides competencies in the most unique but not exclusive phase of guidance services in schools

6. Organization and Administration of Guidance Services

7. Some practical experiences in applying the knowledge and skills obtained in the preceding sequence (6)

The authors recommend the following programs:

1. Two-year graduate program for generalists, leading to a master's degree

2. Three-year graduate program for career counseling specialization, leading to a doctoral degree

3. Three-year graduate program for personal-social specialization, leading to a doctoral degree

4. Three-year graduate program for marriage and family counseling specialization, leading to a doctoral degree

The breakdown of each of the foregoing programs into subjects is given below. Adjustments will, of course, have to be made by each individual college to conform to prevailing staff philosophy and in accordance with any credential or licensing requirements in the particular state involved.

The authors recommend that colleges have a Department of Counseling. The courses which should be offered by this department are identified as "C"; courses which should be offered by the psychology department are labeled "P"; by the education department, "E"; by the sociology department, "S".

If the college is unable to have a Department of Counseling, the subjects (assigned below to the counseling department) should be distributed among the education and psychology departments according to whatever philosophy or policies prevail in a given institution.

☞ California Requirements for Marriage/Family, Child Counselor License Eligibility

Content Areas

I. Human Biological, Psychological, and Social Development
II. Human Sexuality
III. Psychopathology
IV. Cross Cultural Mores and Values
V. Theories of Marriage, Family, and Child Counseling
VI. Professional Ethics and Law
VII. Human Communication
VIII. Applied Psychotherapeutic Techniques of Marriage, Family, and Child Counseling
IX. Research Methodology

X. Survey Course in Psychological Testing

☞ *References*

1. "ACES Corner" (Comments by Dr. Robert Hoppock). *Counselor Education and Supervision,* Summer, 1968, pp. 396–397.

2. "Association Activities: Guidelines for Graduate Programs in the Preparation of Student Personnel Workers in Higher Education." *Personnel and Guidance Journal,* January, 1969, pp. 493–498.

3. Blocker, Donald H. "Wanted: A Science of Human Effectiveness." *Personnel and Guidance Journal,* March, 1966, pp. 729–733.

4. Collins, Charles C. "Junior College Counseling: A Critical View." *Personnel and Guidance Journal,* February, 1965, pp. 546–550.

5. Demos, George D., and Bruce Grant. "College and University Counseling." From *Guidelines for Guidance: Readings in the Philosophy of Guidance,* edited by Carlton E. Beck. Dubuque, Iowa: W. C. Brown and Company, 1966.

6. Failor, Clarence W. "Who Should Counsel in the Schools?" *News and Views,* School of Education, University of Colorado, January, 1960, pp. 4–5.

7. Isaacson, Lee E. "Standards for the Preparation of Guidance and Personnel Workers – In Colleges and Universities." *Counselor Education and Supervision,* Spring, 1968, pp. 187–192.

8. Ohlsen, Merle M. "Standards for the Preparation of Elementary School Counselors." *Counselor Education and Supervision,* Spring, 1968, pp. 172–178.

9. Peters, Herman J., and Charles L. Thompson. "School Superintendents View Counselor Preparation." *Counselor Education and Supervision,* Summer, 1968, pp. 379–386.

10. Richardson, H. D. "Preparation for Counseling as a Profession." *Counselor Education and Supervision,* Winter, 1968, pp. 124–128.

11. "Standards for Counselor Education in the Preparation of Secondary School Counselors." *Personnel and Guidance Journal,* June, 1964, pp. 1061–1072.

☞ *Suggested Additional Readings*

Gallagher, Phillip J., and George D. Demos. *The Counseling Center in Higher Education.* Springfield, Illinois: Charles C. Thomas, 1970.

Hill, George. "Standards for the Preparation of Secondary School Counselors." *Counselor Education and Supervision,* Spring, 1968, pp. 179–186.

Miller, Lyle L., Editor. *Challenge for Change in Counselor Education* (A collection of the writings of C. Harold McGully). Minneapolis, Minnesota: Burgess Publishing Company, 1969.

Parker, Clyde A. *Counseling Theories and Counselor Education.* Boston: Houghton Mifflin Co., 1968.

Ryan, Charles W. "Preparation of Counselors in Ohio Catholic Schools." *Counselor Education and Supervision,* Winter, 1968, pp. 119–123.

Shertzer, Bruce, and Joan England. "Follow-up Data on Counselor Education Graduates – Relevant, Self-Revealing, or What?" *Counselor Education and Supervision,* Summer, 1968, pp. 363–370.

Wrenn, C. Gilbert. "The Selection and Education of Student Personnel Workers." *Personnel and Guidance Journal,* 31, 1952, pp. 9–14.

Chapter 22

WORK EXPERIENCE

F or many years, counselor educators have been talking about the
virtues of having counselors, especially those in public schools, get
experience in work outside the schools before beginning their careers as
counselors. Recommendations about the length of time the counselor
should be engaged in nonteaching and noncounseling work experience
range from a few months to a year or two.

The advantages of such an approach are obvious. It would give
the counselor an enriched background for vocational and educational
counseling in particular, and indirectly it could contribute to his/her
effectiveness in personal-social counseling. Furthermore, the extension
of time should contribute significantly to his maturation development.

Assuming the adoption of one year of work experience, the counselor
trainee would then become involved in a program such as the following:

1. Four-year curriculum in liberal education, leading to a bachelor's
   degree

2. Year of work experience

3. First year of graduate education

4. Second year of graduate education

5. (For specialists) Third year of graduate education

This program would represent a minimal time investment of
seven years for generalists and eight years for specialists. While this
might be an excellent arrangement, it is not feasible from the following
standpoint: requiring another year to be added to a six-year program
for public school counselors could mean that the seven years plus, say,

three to five years of teaching would find the individual involved in ten to twelve years of preparation for counseling.

If this ten-to-twelve-year program were made mandatory, from a practical standpoint educators probably would thereby legislate public school counselors out of existence, for even the most dedicated would hesitate to embark on a ten-to-twelve-year voyage of preparation leading to a long, overworked series of years, with salaries far below education, experience, and professional contributions.

While the authors firmly believe in the value of the workexperience concept in counselor education, they propose to achieve it in another way.

The counselor trainee, whenever he/she selects a counseling career, should be initiated into a planned summer-work program. If started at the end of the freshman academic year, this would mean the student would work for approximately three months each summer during the four undergraduate years, a total of 12 months divided into four three-month segments. Each summer the work should be in different industries, companies, and occupations.

On an optional basis, those students who wish to work part-time throughout all or part of the academic year should combine this with the summer program.

Wages would be earned in all of the work experience, with the student functioning as an employee, who would have to produce to his employer's satisfaction.

During the summer between the first and second graduate years (and when applicable – between the second and third years) the student would devote the time to research in the industries in which he/she did not have time to work during the previous years. Several companies and occupations existing within these industries should also be studied, and, if time permits, research into the industries, companies, and occupations in which the student already has worked should be done.

In this plan, the student may begin his/her work experience at whatever point in his/her educational program he decides to become a counselor.

Several colleges have for years offered excellent work experience programs for their undergraduates, not as preparation for counseling, but as part of the overall educational development of the students.

Antioch College, Yellow Springs, Ohio, was a pioneer in this type of program in which students attend school for a semester or two, then leave to work for a period of time. This is done on an alternate basis. "At the Yellow Springs campus, students take classroom studies alternately with three-month stretches of full-time work. To graduate they must accumulate 90 credits for full-time work in addition to 160 for classroom instruction." (1)

For potential counselors to follow such a program as Antioch's would be fine except for the added years required to qualify as a counselor.

Many high schools and junior colleges offer work experience programs, which in most instances originated in the need to help integrate nonacademic students into the world of work. A work experience program for the academically talented high school students would be a tremendous asset to them, and especially valuable to future teachers and counselors.

Norris, Zeran, and Hatch (4) offer information regarding work experience programs in high schools and junior colleges. Further helpful information regarding these programs in public schools is given by Tyler in his **Report of the Study of Work Experience Programs in California High Schools and Junior Colleges.** (5) He identifies the work experience program as work experience education and defines what this encompasses.

What one massive urban school district, Los Angeles, did in work experience is reported in **Work Experience Jobs.** (6)

Concerning work experience throughout the country, Armsby's **Cooperative Education in the United States** (2) is an informative source.

In **Chapter 21, Graduate Education,** the authors cited five factors which should be pursued in depth in counselor education. Numbers two and three of these points must be included here as particularly apropos to the theme of this chapter.

2. Present and possible future environments of individuals – with strong emphasis on the world of work (supported by enriched background in economics and sociology)

3. A variety of work experiences outside the college or public school communities

If the counselor trainee is to derive maximal educational benefits from participating in work experiences, he/she must do the work expected of him/her by the employers while at the same time obtaining as much knowledge as possible about his/her work environment.

Some of the important aspects to be learned are the advantages and disadvantages of whatever work in which he/she is engaged; relating the current experience with previous ones; getting the feel of what it is like to be in such work; and identifying the factors of significance in the performance of the work.

The student, though performing as a worker, should keep continuously in mind that the main reason for his/her being in the work experience program is to learn, not just his/her particular job, but as many related aspects as time and energy permit about the total industry and company in which he/she is working.

For the student who would like to have a frame of reference for his/ her investigation of the industries, companies, and occupations included in his/her work experience, **Designing Your Career** (3) offers lists of "Topics to Investigate in Studying Industries" (p. 6) and "Topics to Investigate in Studying Occupations." (p. 13)

There should be no question in the public mind about counselors being realists and educators who have lived enough to know what life is in a variety of environments. Let not the situation arise in which a parent would say to a too-young counselor, "No damn young whippersnapper is going to practice on my boy while he/she learns his/her profession."

If counselors are to get experience while still in their twenties or thirties, the work experience program offers perhaps the most encouragement for properly "aging" the counselor-to-be, so that he/she will acquire a sufficient degree of sophistication to warrant his/her being permitted to help others make wise choices and adjustments.

☞ *References*

1. "Antioch's Alternative: Students Required to Hold Off-Campus Jobs." *Los Angeles Times,* Part 1A, September 10, 1969, p. 4.
2. Demos, George D., and Bruce Grant. *Designing Your Career.* Columbia, Missouri: Lucas Brothers, 1965.

COAST to COAST PROFESSIONAL SERVICES, INC.
THE PTSD CLINICS PROJECT/EXECUTIVE SUMMARY

EXECUTIVE SUMMARY

PROJECT OVERVIEW: PTSD CLINICS is the establishment of clinics for the treatment of PTSD (Post Traumatic Stress Disorder). The initial focus is the returning military personnel from war zones because they suffer severely from PTSD and the military hospital is not equipped to handle this problem. These clinics are designed as mostly out-patient but we determined a need for residence facilities for the more acute cases. The clinics sites are located across the country starting at location close to military facilities where personnel returning from war zones would be stationed. Other locations in major cities where abuse to women and children is high would be the next focus area. The initial budget is the procurement of facilities and equipment, as well as, the recruitment of qualified personnel and training of personnel.

THE PROBLEM: It has been estimated that one family out of five in this country has a member who suffers from mental illness. This affects not only the patient, but the other family members also. The problem is more frequent and severe among the members of our military forces than among the general population. Estimates run as high as two out of five returning home from the war suffer from PTSD. It is a form of mental illness of more serious nature than what you could call average (if there is such a thing as "average"). Mental illness to any degree is debilitating to the individual who suffers from it.

An unpleasant (even scandalous) series of events began to happen within the families of servicemen returning from Iraq. The military hierarchy began to look for solutions. First they turned to their medical personnel. The response was, "we are equipped to deal with physical problems. This is mental. It's beyond the scope of our practice." They next turned to the Chaplains' Corps. The response was, "we deal with spiritual matters, not mental illness." It became apparent that no one branch of the service was designed to deal with this type of problem. A combination of skills is needed. When you look at the total population, then add drug and alcohol addiction, dishonesty and moral decay in general, America is being overwhelmed. We needn't repeat stories here to make the point. Everyone is aware of how large the problem has become.

Proposed Approach: Therapy always is individualized to meet the specific concerns and needs of each unique trauma survivor, based upon careful interview and questionnaire assessments at the beginning of (and during) treatment. Trauma therapy is done only when the patient is not currently in crisis. If a patient is severely depressed or suicidal, experiencing extreme panic or disorganized thinking, in need of drug or alcohol detoxification, or currently exposed to trauma (such as by ongoing domestic or community violence, abuse, or homelessness), these crisis problems must be handled first. When a shared plan of therapy has been developed within an atmosphere of trust and open discussion by the patient and therapist, a detailed exploration of trauma memories is done to enable the survivor to cope with post-traumatic memories, reminders, and feelings without feeling overwhelmed or emotionally numb. The goal of "trauma focused" exploration is to enable the survivor to gain a realistic sense of self-esteem and self-confidence in dealing with bad memories and upsetting feelings caused by trauma; trauma memories usually do not go away entirely as a result of therapy, but become manageable with new coping skills. Trauma exploration can be done in several ways, depending upon the type of post-traumatic problems a survivor is experiencing. These types of problems are not limited to PTSD, but include at least five different post-traumatic conditions.

Usually within several months after starting treatment, the patient will report feeling better and will probably seem more cheerful and optimistic. The patient's performance at school or work (for example increased attendance, better grades, or improved performance evaluation at work), Home or family (for example improved ability get along with family members, or increased participation in family chores), Friends or community (for example, frequent socializing with friends).

The number of people that would benefit is exponential because it is not only the individual that benefits but everyone (Family, friends, co-workers, employers, students, etc.) The individual has personal contact. Left untreated the PTSD victim exhibit behavioral difficulties (such as impulsivity, aggression, sexual acting out, eating disorders, alcohol/drug abuse, and self-destructive actions), extreme emotional difficulties (such as intense rage, depression, or panic) and mental difficulties (such as fragmented thoughts, dissociation, and amnesia). This would cause an economic drain on police and medical resources, for the individual as well as the family and others they would associate or contact. The amount that could be saved as well as the lives saved is impossible to calculate, but it is a significant number

THE APPLICANT

PTSD Clinics
16641 Edgewater Lane
Huntington Beach, CA 92649
Ph: 714-846-1572
hhyc97@aol.com
California corporation No. 2718479 dated January 29, 2005 EIN 56-2499974
BANK
California Bank & Trust, Huntington Beach, CA Branch –
ABA/122003396   Acct # 3120171646

Board of Directors
Dr. George Demos, Chairman and President/CEO
    16641 Edgewater Lane   (714) 846-1572
    Huntington Beach, CA 92649

Dr Earl Beecher, Vice president
    16222 Monterey Lane #328 (714) 377-7447
    Huntington Beach, CA 92649
Anthony Merson, MBA, CFO
    15952 Plumwood Street   (714) 893-6716

Westminster, CA 92683

Dr. Lonnie Hammargren, Director
   4318 Ridgecrest Drive   (702) 596-6669
   Las Vegas, NV 89115

Rev. Joseph P. Howe, Director
   1118 Sheridan Road   (847) 431-3074
   North Chicago, IL 60064

Carl W. Kirnbauer J.D

Dr. Richard (Burk) Marrs   (714) 392-2441
   19325 Brooktrail Lane,
   Huntington Beach, CA. 92648

Program Team:

Dr. George Demos is a retired Clinical Psychologist, and Professor of Psychology at several universities in Southern California.

Dr. Lonnie Hammargren is a former Lieutenant Governor for the State of Nevada (1995-1999) member of the UNLV Board of Regents and state Board of Education. He is an accomplished neurosurgeon and spent several years as a NASA flight surgeon. In Vietnam he was the Commander of the 25th Medical Detachment of the 173rd Airborne Brigade.

Dr. Earl Beecher was a Professor of Business Administration (full time 33 years at CSULB, and part time at seven others (UCLA, UCI, CSULA, Pepperdine, etc.).

Anthony Merson has a MBA from Pepperdine University and worked as the CFO for various companies over the last 20 years. He is a retired Army Captain with 27 years in the California Army National Guard.

Rev. Joseph P. Howe is pastor of the North Shore Baptist Church and Director of World Ministries to the Armed Forces co-located in North Chicago, IL. He has been a chaplain, Lieutenant Colonel, in the U.S. Air Force and has lectured for many foreign militaries and universities throughout the world.

Carl W. Kirnbauer J.D. California Real Estate Broker, License #00370404. Specializing in large scale residential income and commercial properties, tenants-in-common residential income property acquisitions and management, reverse mortgages. Provided FHA Certifications for various large scale condominium projects.

Dr. Richard (Burk) Marrs, Doctorate Degree from UCLA in 1970 in philosophy-critical analysis and in applied psychology, and taught applied psychology in the classroom to teachers for over 30-years. I was and still am an expert in treating PTSD veterans and their families with problems from the Vietnam war.

PROJECT NAME: **PTSD CLINICS**

DESCRIPTION: The PTSD Clinics are to be established clinics located across the country and available to those individuals who have been diagnosed with PTSD or think that they may have PTSD. Most of the clinics are store front facilities that can be built up to create the setting needed to make the patients feel at-ease and provide offices for one-on-one therapy. Estimates run as high as two out of five returning home from the war suffer from PTSD. It is a form of mental illness of more serious nature than what you could call average (if there is such a thing as "average"). Mental illness to any degree is debilitating to the individual who suffers from it. With these numbers demonstrate the need for an extensive number of clinics to treat even a small percentage of those afflicted. We also plan for an in-patient type facility to treat the acute cases that arise. One or two acquisitions are a small hotel or motel could be converted into the proper in-patient clinic. The staff size would vary depending on the size and demand of the clinic, but any where from 10 to 40 professionally train people per clinic. This would include: Psychiatrist, Psychologist, Therapist, Nurses, and clinical assistants as well as administrative personnel. We estimate over 3000 direct jobs and over 6000 indirect jobs created.

The most effective kind of treatment for PTSD is cognitive-behavioral psychotherapy. Medication is sometimes used in conjunction with cognitive-behavioral therapy for patients who are at risk to hurt themselves or others, have symptoms that are extremely debilitating, or who do not respond to psychotherapy. Cognitive-behavioral therapy involves working with the individual's thoughts to change the way he or she thinks, feels, and acts. *Exposure therapy,* a form of cognitive-behavioral therapy that is especially effective for PTSD, requires the patient to imagine the trauma in a safe, controlled environment. The therapist helps the patient confront and gain control of the fear and distress that is associated with the trauma. While the patient recalls the traumatic memories, he or she uses relaxation skills to cope with the distress brought about by recalling the trauma. Relaxation skills are taught early in the treatment and may include meditation, progressive muscle relaxation, and breathing retraining. Cognitive-behavioral therapy may also include cognitive restructuring, in which the patient learns new ways of thinking about the trauma that minimize anxiety, guilt, or depression. Patients also learn to recognize "triggers" for the symptoms and use coping skills such as relaxation and cognitive restructuring to minimize the likelihood of experiencing a complete relapse of symptoms. Usually the mental health specialist will gauge the success of intervention services by observing changes in your patient's behavior and functioning, and by administering standardized rating scales for PTSD when appropriate. Because of our extensive knowledge of the patient's behavior, we will observe our patient's ability to get along with peers or other family members.

We plan on using professional organizations to recruit our staff and we have developed a training program to standardize the treatment at each of the clinics. The key members of our organization have extensive contacts with military, veterans, and medical organizations to identify those people that we want to help. We plan on developing educational programs on PTSD that can be given to the military and other organizations that will help them in identifying those that might be afflicted with PTSD.

Our business plan uses medical insurance billings to insure that the program will continue after the humanitarian funds are depleted.

PROJECT SCHEDULE & ESTIMATES

Schedule: Depends on indentifying the clinic sites and feasibility study. Interim operations include hiring and training of staff in a temporary location until build-out and occupancy qualifications are accomplished.

Development Costs: The initial cost of procuring the proper facilities to use as clinics is estimated in Annex -1

Operation & Maintenance: O&M Costs are summarized in Annex-1

Revenues: Billing those patients's who have medical insurance. We plan negotiating a contract with the military and/or VA. Also affiliate with or get approval from HMO.

FINANCIAL REQUIREMENTS

See ANNEX-1

Appendix 1

DEPTH INTERVIEWING

D epth interviewing is more art than science and more hunch and intuition than objective interpretation. It is as much a matter of heart as of mind, and skill comes only from extensive practice. This booklet is offered as a compilation of clues and reminders to help those who interview refine and expand their interviewing skills.

Our thoughts about the depth interview represent a condensation of reactions that represent a total of 59 years of interviewing experiences. We have tried to avoid the "cook-book" aspects of interviewing that can be found in any standard text. Instead, we sat down and discussed what we do when we interview. Our findings are our own. We hope our comments are informative, pertinent, and helpful.

☞ What Is a Depth Interview?

As the phrase suggests, the depth interview goes beneath the surface of objective data. It seeks to get underneath the social mask which makes a person appear normal and typical and uncover those "psychological" aspects that make him/her more or less unique. In a broad sense it is an attempt to find out what makes this human being tick. It is to discover the basic choice points in his/her system of values and attitudes which predict future behavior and to expose potential for developing additional competence.

The depth interview, as we analyze it, seeks to assess the individual's:

1. **Mental Characteristics**–his/her intelligence and how he/she uses it.

2. **Emotional Make-Up**–his/her stability, control, temperament, and general mood tone.

3. **People Skills**–his/her sociability, aggressiveness, and characteristic ways of dealing with others.

4. **Motives**–his/her ambitions, drives, needs, and values.

5. **Insights**–his/her degree of understanding of himself/herself and others.

6. **Maturity**–his/her degree of social, emotional, and mental maturity.

7. **Personal Organization**–his/her reliability, dependability, personal integration, and environmental compatability.

8. **Leadership**–his/her ability to organize and direct the efforts of others and the style(s) he/she uses.

9. **Potential**–his/her ability to grow and develop as a person.

10. **Hang-Ups**–those things that hinder his/her personal adjustment and development.

All of the above and more are the ingredients of a depth interview.[1] However, in practice, it is often slanted for a specific purpose. Perhaps the most frequent is determining whether this person has what it takes for a certain job. More uniquely the therapist uses it to get an understanding of the starting point and causes of personal problems.

---

[1] While we talk of mental, emotional, social, motivational, and other attributes, we must also be aware of how one may blend into another and how often one has a distinct effect on others. For example, emotional depression will reduce mental speed and efficiency. It will change attitudes, and it will drastically reduce social mobility and skills. In short it will seriously (and usually adversely) influence all other aspects of the individual's psychological make-up.

☞ *Getting Started*

While the past is the best predictor of the future, it does not necessarily describe the potential for change. This will be a function of the person's reaction to his/her current needs; and the interview should reveal them. Further, there should be a relationship between life experiences and the present psychological make-up. Therefore, the source of data in the depth interview is the person himself/herself. He/she and he/she alone provides the clues. The interviewer speaks only to encourage the interviewee to tell about himself/herself.

One way to get started is to say something like this: "We are here to take a look at you. The only way I can tune in on you and understand you is for you to tell me about yourself. So tell me about yourself, your earliest memories, your childhood, your family, your schooling, your work experiences, your marriage, your hobbies, and interests (past and present), how you use your spare time, and anything else that is important to you." If this is too much for him/her to grasp at once you know you have a person who needs things simplified for him/her and may have trouble choosing and making decisions.

☞ *Beware of the Halo*

Interviewers are people and people have biases. Our research has shown that an interviewer easily becomes a victim of an intellectual halo. Our predictive misses have most often centered around overestimating the abilities and behavior of people who score high on intelligence tests or have much education or both. It is quite common for interviewers to have ethnic, religious, and vocational biases. Too often, we are inclined to see what we want to see in terms of what we wish to happen or believe should happen.

Hence we suggest that your attitude as an interviewer should be, "You never know: let's see what turns up."

☞ *Listening with the Third Ear*

The depth interview demands sensitive and intense listening; this is what Theodor Reik implied in his book, **Listening With The Third Ear** (Grove Press, New York, 1948). The interviewer makes his/her ears the basic tool; his/her mouth is complementary and used primarily to elicit more listening data.

Sensitive listening is a simultaneous process wherein the content of what is said is enriched through trying to understand such questions as:

1. How did he/she feel when he/she said that?

2. What made him/her bring this subject up?

3. Is he/she revealing all that he/she feels?

4. Is this statement in harmony with and does it enrich what he/she has said before?

In a good interview both the interviewee and interviewer feel they have given a good account of their feelings, ideas, and behaviors and that each has understood the other.

As you listen, you will often be unsure of what a statement means. The simplest approach is to ask. You might say something like this:

1. I'm not sure I understand, can you tell me more?

2. What does this mean to you?

3. How did you feel about that, and how do you feel about it now?

4. Do you mind explaining this more fully?

Sensitive listening is the basic tool for demonstrating empathy (sensitivity to and understanding of the needs and feelings of the other person). The more fully you communicate that you are really trying to understand, the more likely the interviewee is to open up. Thus, it is axiomatic that depth interviewing encourages a wide range of emotional responses, and the interviewer needs to be able to cope with these.

☞ *Develop Your Own Format (Stay Flexible)*

The ideal depth interview would be done without recording apparatus or written notes. Most of us, however, cannot do this and still produce an accurate and useful interview report.

Our suggestion is that you take the notes that are vital to you in understanding this person. At times you may need to take down in your own note-hand exactly what he/she says. Also, you may have a need for certain vital statistics such as birthday, job, length of marriage, and so on.

Many interviewers fill out a more or less complete personal history form containing space for data on:

1. **Growing up history**–parents, siblings, home, relatives, etc.

2. **School history**–extent, grades, subjects, extracurriculars.

3. **Marital history**–marital adjustment, children, problems.

4. **Work history**–in more or less detail.

5. **Reading**–preferences, variety, extent.

6. **Hobbies**–duration, kinds, intensity.

7. **Significant experiences**–those that influenced his/her life.

8. **Philosophy**–what are his/her guiding principles?

Other questions that can be used to verify or deny conclusions drawn are:

1. How would your wife/husband (or other significant person) describe you?

2. Describe your best friend (boss, associate, etc.).

3. What more do you want to learn?

4. What new experiences would you like to have?

5. What would you do if you had a million dollars?

6. What kind of an animal would you like to be?

7. What would you do differently?

8. What characteristics would you like to improve in yourself?

9. If you had a magic wand, what would you do?

10. If you could live in any period of history which would you choose?

One of the ever present problems during the depth interview is whether or not to do any descriptive and interpretative writing. Our suggestion is that you should try to do as much as possible. Then much of your write-up time can be devoted to refinement. A simple way to do this is to list numbers representing the assessment categories on your data form or on a separate sheet and get as much down as possible. A simplified example follows:

1. **Mental**–Very bright, not always careful, inclined to disregard some facts, bends data for his/her own purposes, more of a thinker than a doer, likes theory, may ignore specifics, creative in an undisciplined manner.

2. **Emotional**–Repressed much of time with flat effect, overplays calm and objective approach, seeks "safe" environment, calmness shattered by censure or blame, somewhat afraid of failure, stable when he/she can call his shots.

3. **People**–High need for approval, fairly sociable, careful, non-aggressive and non-dominant, contentious when threatened, otherwise easy-going, not a sales-type, not outgoing.

4. **Motives and Insights**–Strong drive for conformity, average drive for personal achievement, needs well regulated environment, basically conventional, sees himself/herself as more adventurous than he/she is and is inclined to ignore his/her faults, his/her perceptions of others are largely colored by his/her own needs, finds difficulty understanding human motives.

5. **Leadership**–Average desire to lead, tends to be a benevolent autocrat, leans heavily on policy, rules and regulations, some tendency to withhold delegation, fair knowledge of management principles, run of mill management potential because of average initiating habits.

Given as much data as the above example contains, the final write-up becomes primarily a matter of checking, revising, and expanding your observations into a meaningful document.

When you are conducting a depth interview you are following a path through a person's mind. By following the twists and turns you encounter as his/her story unfolds, you can understand him/her and insert your interpretations of his/her meaning into the appropriate chapters of his/her story.

☞ *Nonverbal Clues*

While the bulk of the findings in a depth interview comes from what is said, there is a considerable amount of nonverbal communication. Initially, and as the task progresses, there are many signs to be noted.
Some of them are:

1. Does he/she come on like gangbusters, frankly, carefully, suspiciously, with humor, etc?

2. What does his/her handshake indicate?

3. What are the signs of nervousness and when?

4. Is he/she tense when he/she says he/she is relaxed or vice versa?

5. Does he/she try to do his/her share, or less or more?

6. What changes occur as the interview progresses?

7. Is this a fun experience, a task to be completed or an ordeal for him/her?

☞ *Play It Loose*

The trouble with any format is that it tends to box in the interviewer. Our preference, therefore, is to play it loose! If he/she digresses or explains too fully, follow him/her and see what it means. Keep yourself as flexible, as unstructured, and as observant as possible. If you do your job right, you will find it hard, exhausting work but very satisfying. You really do not need to know his/her reading habits, his/her hobbies as such; what you are trying to do is to understand him/her and this understanding may unfold from any area of his/her life. When he/she opens a door, enter and explore. Help him/her to open these doors. Watch for sudden changes in his/her behavior. These mean that something is going through his/her mind that you should investigate.

☞ *Digging Deeper*

Only long and laborious practice in the depth interview yields results that are satisfying. When you are not sure how deep to dig, the best advice is to follow the Golden Rule. Each new interview is a fresh experience from which, hopefully, we learn something and get closer to the true essence of the person interviewed. A clear objective for the interview is also essential.

In the pages that follow we have made some statements that can serve as reminders as you labor at the ever challenging task of entering the bewildering world of the other person.

☞ *Should You Use Tests?*

When test results are available by all means use them. In many cases test results will confirm interview findings. In some cases you will find that there is disagreement. This may cause you some difficulty, but your only task is to get the truth. When what you get from the interview is different from a personality test score, look harder and then play your own hunch; make your own decision. We are convinced that a skillful depth interview can yield findings that are generally more accurate than test results. This is especially true in the personality and motivational areas, while it is not quite so valid in the mental realm.

Our position is that a sensitive depth interview can yield an accurate picture of a person without test results. A description of a person based solely on test scores loses much in the translation and is likely to be both sterile and inaccurate.

☞ *Mental Behavior*

It is quite simple to get an estimation of the intelligence quotient, and we have frequently found a high correlation between test scores and interview estimates. In addition the interview can give us information about mental qualities and dynamics that no test score will reveal. As you interview you can note:

1. How does he/she plot the course of his/her interview behavior? Is he/she careful, deliberate, impulsive, methodical, etc.?

2. How do his/her answers flow? Are his/her thoughts free-flowing, sporadic, or highly organized?

3. How detailed is he/she? Is he/she conventional or stereotyped?

4. When he/she squirms, is he/she holding things in?

5. Does he/she choke on the abstract concept? Does he/she have a need to file, catalog, put concepts into neat compartments?

6. Is he/she sure? Does he/she have confidence in his/her own answers? Is he/she dogmatic? Opinionated?

7. Is his/her mind open or closed? Will he/she examine facts and accept those he/she does not like?

8. Get him/her to repeat an incident. Does he/she improve, change, clarify, mix facts up, forget essentials, etc.?

9. How does he/she react to problems? With zest, diligence, joy, apprehension, doubt, effort, etc.?

10. Does he/she stretch his/her data, garble them, expand them, document them, take chances with them?

11. When does he/she hesitate? Is he/she deliberate when not sure? When does he/she take calculated risks?

12. How creative is he/she, resourceful, ingenious, imitative, or innovative?

13. Is he/she analytical, broad, comprehensive, natural, compulsive, perfectionist, or careless?

☞ *Emotional Make-up*

Since people vary in mood from time to time, it is essential to determine whether or not your subject's present feeling tone is characteristic of him/her, is a function of a current mood, or an emotional reaction to the contemporary situation. The interview itself can be a stressful experience that is more threatening for some than for others. When a man/woman has just lost a job, he/she is likely to be much less sure of himself/herself; the recently bereaved tend to be more despondent; the recently promoted happier, and so on. The following questions are designed to help you peer into his/her emotional past and present.

1. When you shook his/her hand was his/her palm wet or dry?

2. Does he/she show stress or strain?

3. Ask him/her to tell you about his/her troubles, his/her worries, his/her fears, and his/her anxieties.

4. Is he/she placid, hostile, apprehensive, poised, or unhinged?

5. Is he/she totally defensive, confident, tense, or relaxed?

6. If you note a sign of disturbance, you might want to ask him/her about it later.

7. How does he/she react to threat, to challenge, to stress, or to danger?

8. Is he/she intense, tight, distressed inside, or disturbed?

9. Does his/her tone, expression, and language change – and when?

10. What is his/her emotional attitude toward life?

11. Can he/she compete without becoming irritated?

12. What are his/her anxieties, what do they mean, and when does he/she get too much stimulation for his/her resources to handle?

13. Does he/she have wide or narrow swings in mood?

14. When does he/she usually show anger, sadness, joy, or any other feeling?

15. What does his/her ulcer, heart trouble, migraine, or any other symptoms signify to him/her?

16. What triggers his/her emotions?

17. What is his/her emotional control?

18. What evidence does he/she give of emotional dependence?

19. What is his/her emotional security blanket?

20. What will he/she do under pressure?

☞ *Human Relation Skills*

Nearly everyone has a self-image of a rather personable, cooperative, and friendly person. Few label themselves as contentious, anti-people, and suspicious. Therefore, the interviewer must interpret on the basis of faint evidence. Everyone says he/she is interested in people, so it is a matter of degree. The following suggestions are designed to help you place this person on a realistic scale:

1. Is he/she more interested in things or people? How does he/she spend his/her spare time? Does he/she seek out others?

2. What are his/her general attitudes toward people?

3. Is he/she likely to speak first or second?

4. Does he/she like people, is he/she afraid, suspicious, or uneasy? How did he/she react to the interview?

5. What is his/her general openness?

6. Does he/she take the interpersonal initiative?

7. Where does he/she go by preference?

8. Does he/she reject you, pull or push you, embrace you, avoid you?

9. Ask him/her what he/she would do at a cocktail party.

10. Is he/she competitive, contentious, or cooperative?

11. Ask him/her what he/she would do in a strange town.

12. Ask him/her how important people are to him/her.

13. Does he/she use or exploit others?

14. Can he/she play alone as well as with others?

15. How much does he/she give or take from people?

16. How openly does he/she disclose himself/herself?

17. Does he/she dominate, persuade, move in, or sit by?

18. Does he/she come through as authentic or phony?

19. Does he/she tend to play games and if so, what ones?

☞ *Motives and Insights*

These areas are most difficult to uncover. In most men/women motives are multiple and subject to change. Genuine understanding of people is often very difficult. Further, there are those who have a rather accurate feel for themselves and others, but who have difficulty in putting their understanding into words.

Perhaps the most direct road to the revelation of a person's motivations is to find out what his/her self-image is. Since he/she wants to project this self-image to the world, it provides a key to his/her motivational structure. For instance, the man/woman whose self-image revolves around the idea that he/she is tough-minded, hard, efficient, and driving is likely to behave in a ruthless and heavy-handed manner.

It is possible to divide insight into two separate categories: self-understanding and understanding of others. Thus, one person can understand himself/herself rather well and be essentially inept when it comes to understanding the other person. A highly outgoing person on the other hand may be quite sensitive to others and blind to his/her own needs, faults, strong points, etc. The following points should give you assistance in moving into this difficult area:

1. What turns him/her on?

2. How does he/she respond to praise?

3. What would he/she do if he/she could not talk, and had to start a new business?

4. What are his/her goals and expectations?

5. What satisfies him/her?

6. Is he/she very sensitive or a "bull in the china shop"?

7. Does he/she question his/her motives and study them?

8. Does he/she question the motives of others?

9. What does he/she do for fun – and why?

10. Can he/she communicate understanding?

11. Ask him/her to describe his/her best friend – and what makes him/her that way?

12. How does he/she react to the very aggressive individual?

13. How does he/she motivate others?

14. How does he/she turn people on?

15. How does he/she get people to laugh, to work, to think, etc.?

16. How sensitive is he/she to others?

17. Does he/she question his/her own actions, motives, feelings, etc.?

18. Can he/she articulate insight in a total sense?

19. Is he/she sensitive to mood changes in others?

20. Can he/she detach – can he/she leave his/her own frame of reference?

21. Is he/she realistic in his/her self-appraisal?

22. Will he/she do the right thing at the right time?

23. Does he/she take constructive action on his/her weaknesses?

24. How does he/she react to criticism?

25. Does he/she sincerely want to learn and improve?

☞ *Leadership*

Not all people are destined to be leaders and many do not want to be. We frequently find ourselves pointing this out in specific cases. At times we may describe the interviewee's ability to be a teamworker and a responsible citizen.

A person may not be in a leadership position but may still possess some of the requirements for effective supervision. Among these, personal organization, personal discipline, and personal responsibility are paramount.

The ability to organize and direct the efforts of others is of great value to any man or woman. When demonstrated, it opens up all sorts of opportunities. For young people especially it is the swiftest and surest road to job success. To get at his/her leadership ability and style we should try to find out:

1. How interested is he/she in leadership – has he/she read anything in this area?

2. Does he/she think in terms of pushing or pulling others?

3. Does he/she know when to push and when to pull?

4. Does he/she have a range of options and the flexibility to use them?

5. Does he/she supervise fluidly or in a mechanical manner?

6. Does he/she push hard toward results?

7. When and how does he/she praise?

8. How and when would he/she fire?

9. How does he/she demonstrate that he/she is fair?

10. How well do subordinates like him/her?

11. Will people really follow him/her?

12. Is he/she willing to listen to subordinates, peers, superiors?

13. Can he/she sell his/her point of view to others?

14. Can he/she tolerate inconsequential conversation, is he/she patient, will he/she wait?

15. Is he/she receptive to ideas and suggestions of subordinates?

16. How does he/she get along with his/her peers?

17. Does he/she listen to and evaluate feed-back?

18. Does he/she use participative procedures?

19. Is he/she results minded?

20. Does he/she have supervisory objectives?

21. Can he/she discipline?

22. Can he/she put a person back together and give him/her hope?

23. Does he/she show compassion and consideration?

24. Will he/she and can he/she teach others?

25. Does he/she evidence responsibility, sincerity, determination, and hope?

☞ *Summarizing and Reporting*

The test of effectiveness of any depth interview is the ability of the interviewer to write a report which will communicate the essence of the interview to himself/herself and others. One of the most common feelings interviewers have after an interview is that they wish they had had more time to probe more deeply and ask more questions. Frequently, these questions occur only after the interview is over and the interviewer feels that he/she must make some of his/her statements by inference. The more skilled the interviewer becomes the less frequently he/she is troubled with this nagging doubt. Obviously, all human beings are too complex to be totally captured in a single interview just as a snapshot does not tell completely how a person looks. Thus, when it comes to writing a report the interviewer finds himself/herself caught in the dilemma of uncertainty of the completeness of his/her data and his/her desire to fairly report his/her understanding of another human being. We have found it helpful for the interviewer to ask himself/herself certain kinds of questions about the interview material and the report. Perhaps the best way to make a judgment of the adequacy of the personal data in a report is to compare the history of the individual and his/her current behavior. With this in mind ask the following questions:

1. Adequacy of data. Does the history of the individual explain his/her current behavior?

2. Consistency of mental effort. Is his/her history of change and growth in keeping with the interviewer's current estimates of his/her mental ability in dealing with his/her opportunities?

3. Emotional consistency. Is he/she able to maintain his/her course of action and adjust to the circumstances without experiencing undue stress, anger, or bitterness?

4. Adequacy of social skills. Is he/she able to maintain his/her friendships and satisfactory relationships with others in spite of the changes in his/her or their circumstances?

5. Understanding of motivations for change. What produces change? Does his/her explanation of the influences of change in his/her life correspond to the significant events he/she describes?

6. Leadership qualities. Does he/she try to change or maintain status quo? Does he/she change before or after the significant event described? Do others respond appropriately to the changes in his/her life? Does he/she respond appropriately to changes which occur in the lives of others?

7. Test of mutuality of the report. Can the interviewee agree that the interviewer's report clearly and fairly portrays his/her presentation in the interview?

Remember that the interview, as we present it, is designed to be a relationship, an expression of mutual trust between you as interviewer and the other person as interviewee. The interview is a helping function. Your task, therefore, becomes one of learning how to make the interview a helping relationship. The purpose of the ways to establish communication that we have discussed is to enable you as interviewer to zero in upon a growth process in the interviewee. This, you will discover, involves a change in you as well as in your client. In fact, you should emerge from each interview experience a slightly different (indeed better) person for having gone through the mutual disclosure process that the effective interview must involve. Just as you seek to learn as much about the person across the table as you can, so too should he/she come to know you much better. Only through the establishment of such mutuality can the interview be the helping relationship for which it is designed.

Readings in this area that will be of assistance to you follow:

Benjamin, A. **The Helping Interview,** Houghton-Mifflin, 1969. A beautifully done description of the interview.

Garrett, A. **Interviewing: Principles and Methods,** Service Association of America, 1958. A must for the beginner.

Jourard, S. **Disclosing Man to Himself,** Van Nostrand, 1968. The role and importance of disclosure in the interview.

Maslow, A. **Toward a Psychology of Being,** Harper and Row, 1968. A sensitive description of man as he could be.

Shertzer, B. & Stone, S. **Fundamentals of Counseling,** Houghton-Mifflin, 1968. A thorough coverage of counseling topics – well organized and documented.

☞ *Illustrative Report Number One*

Note: The following write-up is a non-technical but skillful description of a young business person. Paragraph one describes his/her social impact and skills, paragraph two is an accurate description of his/her problem-solving ability, while paragraphs three, four, and five are generally addressed to his/her emotional make-up, his/her motives and insights, and his/her leadership ability respectively. The only test used was a brief fifteen-minute test of mental ability. These statements, therefore, resulted mainly from a depth interview which was less than two hours long.

1. He/she wants to have the rules of the game described before he/she enters a contest. He/she believes that he/she has the right to know what he/she is getting into before he/she commits himself/herself. He/she supports this conviction in both word and deed. He/she prefers to speak directly to the point and to have others speak with equal openness. He/she is suspicious of the fast talking person who speaks without seeming to say very much. He/she prefers action to words. He/she makes a desirable impression upon others and maintains this. By and large, he/she takes people as they come while reserving the right to become close to those only of his/her choosing. He/she is more reserved than outgoing, yet he/she can participate because he/she enjoys people and the variety of guises they present. He/she is shrewd and he/she is unlikely to be taken by the personal entrepreneur. He/she insists upon his/her right to examination. He/she can carry conviction to the other fellow.

2. He/she prefers to find a point at which a problem originated so that he/she can begin his attack upon it at this juncture. As he/she progresses toward his/her solution, he/she exercises a reasonable care to keep pertinent data bearing its appropriate load. He/she rather enjoys the analytical process. His/her practice is to isolate a bench mark or two and then to fit details about them. It is important to him/her that he/she reach a solution that works out in practice. He/she is oriented toward the pragmatic operation. Problems challenge him/her. He/she likes to involve himself/herself with data that are amenable to quantification. He/she likes to see a solution stand on its own factual merit. The intangible and the amorphous have small appeal to him/her. He/she is more interested in getting his/her hand and his/her mind actively involved than in manipulating ideas at the sheerly theoretical level. In general, he/she is capable of thinking on a high superior plane. He/she reserves the privilege of making up his/her own mind about things.

3. His/her needs for activity argue against the sedentary task. While he/she has a normal tolerance for frustration, his/her patience grows thin when things seem to be getting nowhere. He/she has drives to achieve and to be profitably engaged. Once he/she has begun upon a course of action, he/she wants to follow through to its completion. Obstacles in his/her path will increase his/her determination to make out. He/she can overwhelm such by the sheer intensity of his/her attack. He/she has a streak of stubbornness. He/she supports himself/herself and his/her programs. He/she can be a formidable opponent when he/she is convinced that right is on his/her side. Generally, he/she keeps his/her cool and tries to think his/her way through the difficult period. He/she does a rather slow burn and, when the irritation continues, is likely to attack the source. This will be a planned procedure and not a bull-like rush.

4. He/she is an autonomous person with underlying needs for independence. He/she perceives himself/herself as competent to make his/her own life decisions. It is important to him/her that he/she receive value for the effort he/she expends. Life experience has taught him/her that he/she must put out if he/she wishes to gain. He/she does not easily tolerate failing himself/herself. There is too much pride in him/her to permit him/her to accept something for nothing. He/she has gained in personal insight as a result of some things that have happened to him/her. He/she has demonstrated that he/she can learn from the experience. He/she sees himself/herself as a responsible individual and he/she is one. He/she is hardheaded and tough. He/she can live through the traumatic event without despair.

5. He/she needs to be doing. He/she prefers to work within a structured environment where the lines and levels are known. Within such a system, however, he/she wants a free hand to cope with the duties that are his/hers. When he/she feels that he/she is capable of carrying the load, he/she does not want gratuitous assistance nor to have noses poked over his/her shoulder. He/

she accepts responsibility well. In fact, he/she wants to be accountable for something. He/she thrills to achievement and to the evidence of success that it presents. He/she can function on his/her own and initiate his/her own behavior. He/she likes to tie things together and to bring a congeries of parts into a unitary whole. When he/she has resolved one task, he/she wants to move on to another one.

☞ *Illustrative Report Number Two*

Paragraphs one and two of the following report describe mental functions, paragraphs three and four give the emotional make-up, paragraphs five and six report test results, paragraphs seven and eight give social skills and impact, paragraph nine describes insights, and paragraph ten gives his/her leadership style. The Conclusion and Summary indicates best area of job placement, and it makes definite suggestions of his/her own personal improvement and development.

1. He/she is superior in mental ability, ranking in the upper 2% of the general population and in the upper 17% when compared with supervision. Mentally, he/she is alert, quick, and broad. He/she is direct in his/her thinking, but he/she is also creative and ingenious so he/she frequently puts an unexpected twist into his/her ideas. He/she is imaginative and rather liberal in his/her thinking and will take to new ideas faster than most.

2. While he/she can be factual, logical, and analytical, his/her inclination is to take a look at several details and reach a conclusion. Thus, he/she uses induction frequently rather than the more common deduction, and he/she is quick to reach decisions. He/she has good verbal and mathematical ability, and he/she is more articulate than most engineers. He/she has a lot of intellectual curiosity and ranges widely in his/her thinking. His/her practical judgments are usually good.

3. His/her emotions are fluid and spontaneous. Thus, he/she is arriving at good control through maturity and experience, but they are too strong and too flexible to be under complete control. He/she is an exceedingly active and direct person who wants to move fast and cover a lot of territory. He/she rarely disseminates, and his/her feelings are expressed quickly and definitely. Likewise, they are dissipated quickly and leave little residual tension.

4. He/she is an intense person who goes at things at full tilt. He/she continually strives to prove himself/herself. He/she is a fierce competitor. He/she is frequently happy and exuberant; on occasion he/she gets down. Overall, he/she is optimistic and is learning to keep his/her swings in mood within normal limits. He/she is frequently impatient and inclined to be somewhat impulsive. He/she is rather tough-minded and has a quick, rough-and-ready sense of humor.

5. On the personal attitude test, he/she scored average in all traits except aggressiveness, on which he/she was moderately high, and in independence and flexibility, on which he/she was very high. While he/she admits to some feelings of inferiority and to sensitivity, he/she is fundamentally a well-adjusted person who rises to challenge and who can stand considerable job pressure.

6. His/her measured interests are: Writing 70%, Management 60%, Sales 60%, Accounting 50%, Service 50%, Engineering 30%, Teaching 20%, and Mechanical 10%. This is a broad interest pattern, and it emphasizes activity in spite of the high Writing score.

7. His/her human relation skills are fundamentally good and natural. Because of his/her energy and his/her positiveness, he/she has definite likes and dislikes and is quick to express them. He/she is spontaneous and open with others and has considerable persuasive skill.

8. His/her sociability and friendliness is of a very personal sort. In fact, he/she is probably more competent and content in new or unusual situations than he/she is in more formal or better structured ones. In face-to-face conversation he/she is stimulating and purposeful. He/she likes a rapid-paced operation and will become bored by routine. By nature, he/she is rather outgoing and extroversive.

9. His/her understanding of human behavior is objective and based on personal experience. He/she is not highly introspective and does not live within himself/herself extensively, since he/she likes to transfer his/her thoughts into action as soon as possible. He/she is ambitious. He/she has a rather natural and somewhat rough-and-ready feel for others.

10. He/she is a good leader with rather natural talents to organize, stimulate and direct. He/she is inclined to supervise with many innovations and in a very personal and direct manner. There is some evidence that he/she prefers to work things out on the run over planning them in detail in advance. He/she is an active leader and at this stage in his/her development he/she fits the concept of a line supervisor better than that of a staff officer. He/she is inclined to supervise somewhat too closely and too specifically. His/her drive, force, and enthusiasm are superior.

☞ Conclusions and Prognosis:

Insofar as his/her psychological characteristics are concerned, Mr./Ms. Jones has high qualifications for the more active phases of business management. He/she likes variety and challenge and will do his/her best work under such conditions. We feel that his/her drive and quick mental ability are outstanding. For his/her maximum personal development he/she should consider:

1. Being somewhat more methodical and analytical in his/her thinking. This would force him/her to be a little more conservative and would keep him/her from getting too far ahead of his/her associates.

2. Making sure that in his/her haste to get things done that he/she does not leave too many loose ends.

3. Testing his/her feelings, his/her thoughts, and his/her reactions to people against the criterion of maturity. He/she should not diminish his/her drive, but he/she could make it a little less tinged with impatience and a little more adapted to method and routine.

4. Retaining his/her aggressiveness but making it a little more subtle and indirect.

5. Making sure that he/she delegates as much as possible, that he/she plans for the long haul as well as the present, and that he/she learns as much as he/she can about the motivational and developmental aspects of management.

Appendix 2

PERSONALITY THEORY GUIDE

☞ *Personality Theory Guide**

	Freud, Sigmund	Jung, Carl	Adler, Alfred	Horney, Karen
Name or View of Theory Practitioner or Scientist	Psychoanalysis A Practitioner	A Psychology of the ID A Practitioner	Individual Psychology A Practitioner	The Cultural Basis of Neurosis: Intrapsychic Processes and a Practitioner Human Relations
Dynamism of Operation	Libido (generalized sex drive) and Thanatos (Death Instinct)	Tensions created between opposites in personality. Self preservation – basic motive Libido generalized drive not especially sex	Power Social Interest (Self Assertion)	Basic Anxiety produced by anything which disturbs child's security. Feelings of isolation and helplessness. Child's desire for safety and satisfaction.
Principles of Operation	ID – seeks pleasure satisfaction (primary process) EGO – reality principle SUPEREGO Conscience guilt Ego ideal pride	Equivalence between opposites Entropy (balance sought) Theory of opposites Symbolization Conscious and unconscious reciprocal reality Libido moves between progression and regression Constellation of a complex	Inferiority Striving for Superiority Fictional Finalism (ex: belief in a hereafter) Compensation and Overcompensation	
Acceptance of Unconscious	Yes	Yes	No. Person is goal directed	Yes

---

* By George D. Demos, California State University, Long Beach

Mechanism or Constructs	ID – Cathexis (Primary Process) Repetition compulsion EGO – Reality principle Secondary process	EGO (Self) Personal unconscious complexes Collective Unconscious Anima (soul) Shadow (evil or animal) Attitudes (intraversion or extraversion) Functions-sensations (Feelings through intuition) Other archetypes	Originally believed in Organ Inferiority Later – Inferiority Overcompensating "Style of Life" Creative Self Self Ideal Character Traits Complexes Inferiority– Superiority Redeemer Proof (fear of failure) Predestination Masculine protest	Self Actualization (Attempt of Actual Self to match Idealized Image, created by person to protect himself from feeling of helplessness – becomes a force in itself.) Creative or Real Self

Sullivan, Harry S.	Murray H.	Lewin, Kurt	Rogers, Carl	Miller & Dollard
Interpersonal Psychology A Practitioner	Personology Scientist	Field Theory Scientist	"Self" Therapy A Practitioner	Stimulus-Response Scientist
Tension need or anxiety (absence of euphoria which individual seeks) Anxiety arises out of parataxic distortions emphatized from Mother et al.	Motivation is release of tension satisfaction All starts with need. A cycle operates to build up tension for satisfaction	Behavior is a function of the psychological field Need - tension - vector valence	Self strives for consistency, maintain itself and actualize itself.	Wish - Cue - Response Reward - Habit, Conditioned Response Primary and secondary drives Seeks reduction of tension
By using "good me", "bad me" etc, guards person from anxiety. Anxiety arises from tension resulting from threats, real or imagined. Attitudes transferred to child by empathy of mother, including parataxic anxiety.	"Need-Press" Thema Unity, themes Regnant processes in configurations in brain Primary Needs Secondary Needs Proactive and reactive Overt and covert Subsidiation Proceedings Durance Serial programs Needs 1. Process activity 2. Modal 3. Effect	Principles deriving an event Boundary connections 1. Relatedness 2. Concreteness 3. Contemporaneity Person and environment Life space Fact integration of psychological facts Person is goal directed Interdependence of behavior	1. Need for positive regard by others 2. Need for positive self regard 3. Need for conditions of worth Symbolization or nonsymbolization Organism acts as a whole in the phenomenological field. Person is goal directed Introjections of self Values from others	Reinforcement – gradient of reinforcement Extinction – gradient of extinction Discrimination – gradient of discrimination Generalization and gradient of reinforcement leads to anticipatory responses reasoning (by tying words to ideas) Anticipatory response of not thinking that which is fearful, uncomfortable, gradient of avoidance, gradient of approach Displacement (redirect response after denial to new object
Doubtful (Goal directed)	No (Goal directed)	Not determined	Yes	Yes (explained by stimulus generalization)

A Single Ego System includes Self System "Good me", "Bad me", etc. Arises out of anxiety Dynamisms, Personification. *Cognitive Processes* Protaxis, Parataxis, Syntaxis *Defense Mechanisms* Selective inattention Consensual validation Dissociation Sublimation Consensual Validation (Similar to Rogers Reality Check)	Ordination Press alpha and beta Needs integrate Value-Vector Scheme Complementary and Supplementary projection. *Id* same as U.C. of Freud's impulses to self and society *Ego* – Still central organizer of personality Not solely inhibitor or repressor. A promotor *Super-Ego* – like Freud's but Ego Ideal is person at his future best acceptable to the U.C. Person learns from interpersonal contacts and experiences.	Inner process Central layer Peripheral layer Motorium Permeal Boundaries Life Space Regions Psychological Field Locomoton Need – Tension and vector valence Boundaries, Energy Process Dynamic Restructuring Equalization – proceeds Integration Repression Retrogression 2 Dimensional Topology + time-Horology + reality-unreality dimensions	The Self (nuclear) In the Organism (whole) In the Phenomenal Field Seeks Actualization Values attached to experiences Checking of experiences against reality Similar to Sullivan Consensual validation	Reflexes Innate Hierarchy of Responses Primary and Secondary Drives Habit Resultant Responses Secondary Generalization Allowance of Cultural experience

	Freud, Sigmund	Jung, Carl	Adler, Alfred	Horney, Karen
Developmental Phases	Oral Anal Urethral Phallic Oedipus Latent stages Homosexual Genital	Early Years Energy invested in survival Later – Sexual values appear As man grows Introversion and self-deployment	No developmental plan Oedipus important only with pamperd child	No universal phases

Typology	Based on development phases	Eight types of Intraversion and Extraversion, subdivided into thinking, feeling, sensation and intuition	Hippocratic Types
			1.Sabguine – little inferiority
			2. Coleric – tense aggressive
			3. Melancholic – Overwhelmedbyinferiority
			4. Phlegmatic – lost contact with life
			
			Later View
			1. Socially useful
			2. Goal active but socially interested type
			3. Avoiding one
			4. "Getting type
			
			(Numbers of Hippocratic types correspond to Later types)
				1. Moving toward people
				2. Moving away from people
				3. Moving against people with need of
				  a. power
				  b. exploitation
				  c. prestige
				  d. personal achievement
				  e. self sufficiency and independence
				  f. perfection and unassailability

Therapy and Relationships	Back of couch to Analyst Transference Relationship	Face to face Directive approach by Analyst	Face to face Social relationship and directive approach by analyst	No fixed positions between therapist and patient. A directive relationship
Goal	Free patient from "knots" (conflicts)	Self actualization Individuation Sublimation	Socialization	Growth of Real Self
Method of Therapy	Free Association Dream Analysis Treat every "knot" as it appears Unstructured process Explore the past Help Ego handle repressed materials and change feelings about them. Achieve sublimations	Explore present and future	Attempts to redirect patient from striving for power to socialized goals. Start with complexes. Diagnosis based on style of life established in youth. Treats every difficulty in style of life. Starts from present.	Attempts to treat patient from present, treats whole pattern of distortion. Attempt to deal with consequences of uniqueness Directive attack on distortions

Causes of Neurosis	Repressed anxiety usually involving involving unresolved or badly resolved oedipus	Energy discharge is blocked and can't be released through sublimated or instinctual channels. This causes repression into the unconscious where it becomes heavily charged and may explode into ego in irrational fashion	Neurotic person strives for own power and self-aggrandizement due to feeling of inferiority. Selfish goals. Has style of life that is self-defeating. All that is not "fitting" in neurotic person is excluded	Lost flexibility in relation to choice of behavior. Distortions between actual self and idealized image. Narcissism is not self love but self inflation based on inferiority feelings.

Sullivan, Harry S.	Murray, H.	Lewin, Kurt	Rogers, Carl	Miller & Dollard
Infancy Childhood Juvenile Preadolescence Early Adolescence Late Adolescence Adulthood	No universal developmental phases.	Differentiation of personal processes Area of Environment in life space. Integration a continuous process. No discrete changes in development.	None Posed	None Posed

Fixation at a level of
  Infancy
  Childhood
  Juvenile
  Preadolescence
  Early Adolescence
  Late Adolescence
  Adulthood
	No Development Phases	None Post	None Posed	None Posed

No fixed positions between patient and therapist. Therapist is a participant observer with empathic understanding.	No therapy system in this schema	None (not a therapy) None (not a therapy)	Face to face Directive	Mixed – no firm prescribed manner Directive
Eliminate Parataxic Disturbances	None Posed	None Posed	Integration of organismic reality and self picture. Revise value system.	Release patient from defensive anticipatory response
Structured Interview Works from Present to the future	None	None (not a therapy)	Minimum of interpolation Minimum of transference	Promote adjustive behavior Extinguished anticipatory responses by reducing anxiety A relearning process Teach a hopeful but realistic outlook
Parataxic distortions Character syndromes Which lead to mass dissociation. The more anxiety, the more inflated the self system and the more dissociated it is. This interferes with constructive social living	An Idiopathic explanation Each is a person unto himself Usually when needs and pressure patterns are in conflict.	Not described but environmental pressure without ability to locomote Conflict of opposing vectors A barrier which cannot be passed or circumvented may cause regressive behavior or rationalization	Tension and maladjustment between self and organism. Psychological maladjustment exists where organism denies to awareness significant experiences; not symbolized into self-structure Gestalt – Tension. Incorrect value system	Child not equipped for complex learning Learning dilemmas where responses a person can make are not drive reducing. Defense mechanism of anticipatory neurotic responses attached to cues and stimuli which are not fear producing for others. Mixed pleasurable and unpleasurable activities. Disorientation, delusion, confusion, hallucination. Infancy transitory psychosis

	Freud, Sigmund	Jung, Carl	Adler, Alfred	Horney, Karen
Adjustment	When individual is free to use his energies for purposes he wishes without having them bound up in a shaky defense structure.	When energy flows freely throughout psyche without being bottled up in any of the opposites.	When individual has faced his inferiority and overcome it, when he has adopted a "style of life" which is not self defeating.	Actual and real image almost identical Where energies not bound up in a neurotic mechanism to bolster up distorted idealized image.
Prevention of Neurosis	Based on wholesome resolution of oedipus. Requires adequately masculine father and feminine mother.	Not determined	Parents will neither 1. Overprotect child 2. Nor neglect him nor 3. Allow inferiorities so that he will not be a. deprived of social feeling b. revengeful or c. compensative or overcompensative	Informed and wholesome parents will be cautious of creating unnecessary anxiety in child to unnecessarily threaten his safety and satisfaction.
Terminology Creative Self	Character	Self	Creative self (style of life crative)	Real Self
Sublimation	Sublimation		Social rather than personal goals	
Cathexis	Cathexis			
Repression	Repression		All that dares not fit into style of life is repressed.	
Neurotic				
Distortion				Neurotic Distortion
Reliance on Heredity	Yes	Yes	Yes	No
Reliance on early development as a formative factor	Yes	No	Yes	Yes
Self concept included in theory	No	No	Yes	Yes
Reliance on biological or social science	Biological	Biological	Social	Social

Sullivan Harry S.	Murray, H.	Lewin, Kurt	Rogers, Carl	Miller & Dollar
When individual behavior not controlled by parataxic distortions but is able to make rational syntaxic decisions	A Benign Super Ego and an Ingenious Ego combine to permit adequate expression of Id impulses in an acceptable social setting. (culturally approved)	When individual is free to locomote to chosen goals without excess energy bottled up in inner processes.	When the concept of self is such that all of the sensory and visceral experiences of the organism are, or may be, assimilated on a symbolic level into a consistent relationship with the concept of self	When individual is free of anticipatory neurotic responses and thus is enabled to thin, act and live more rationally.
Informed and wholesome parents will be "real people" and thus not infect child with parataxic anxieties.	None Posed	Healthy child "knows the ground on which he stands" child must know his security and be absorbed by its warmth and strength.	Where there is a complete absence of threat to self-structure experiences which are inconsistent with self may be perceived and examined and the structure of the self revised to assimilate and include it.	Parents primary role is to maintain drive stimuli at a low level. Permissive gratifying and make few learning demands before child is adequately equipped.
Self System	Regnant Process Patterns	Non Posed	Self	None Posed
Sublimation	Subsidation	Substitute locomotion		Displacement (generalize to a more acceptable stimulus)
Dissociation and Selective Inattention	Needs integrate	Need and force	None posed	None posed
			Symbolization or distorted Symbolization	Anticipatory response of "Not thinking"
				Gradient of Reinforcement temporarily contiguous Reward or punishment will be associated with stimulus
No	No	No	Yes – Organism actualizes itself along lines of heredity.	No
Yes	Yes	Not determined	Not determined	Yes
Yes	Not determined	Not determined	Yes	Not determined
Social	Social	Social	Both Biological and Social	Social

	Freud, Sigmund	Jung, Carl	Adler, Alfred	Horney, Karen
Acceptance of unconscious determinants in theory	Yes Built into the Id	Yes Built into the Id	No	Yes (Items too threatening to Idealized Image)
Assumptions of theory	Behavior is a product of interaction between three systems (Super-ego, Id and Ego) Anxiety, Pleasure Principle. A closed thermodynamic system	There is more than sex in man's motivation – including aims. Racial origins of personality rather than infantile origins.	Man's behavior motivated by social urges (self assertion)	Aggression is not inborn Oedipus not a sexual conflict between child and parents, but an anxiety growing out of care of child by parents. Security "Hunger" Emphasis on culture
Criticisms of theory	1. Too much weight on heredity and to little on social factors. 2. Uncontrolled, unrecorded, probably biased observations. 3. Theory based on "special" cases. 4. Unquantified, unobservable observations. 5. Difficulty in testing hypotheses. 6. Did not allow for other cultures.	1. Created a perception of personality seemingly rigid and obsessional. 2. Often inconsistent and circular decisions. 3. Theory exceedingly involved.	1. Scheme is superficial. 2. Scheme not systematic or consistent (aggression became creative power of ego-example). 3. Doesn't explain what shapes man's mind and goal. 4. Inferiority probably not universal.	1. Personality model is inferior to Freud's in clarity, consistency and elaboration. 2. Rejection of Libido leaves many factors unexplained (the unconscious, resistance, repression, dreams, etc.).
Contributions	Gave man his first usable Personality Theory on which to build a treatment program, further research and further theory.	1. The Dream Series Method. 2. Active Imagination Method. 3. Theory valuable for study of history of mysticism and an understanding of irrational thinking.	1. Emphasis on environment and goal. 2. Recognized striving for power in western society. 3. Introduced style of life concept. 4. Led us away from biological elements of Freudian psychology.	Emphasis on acquired factors, especially based on helplessness of child.

Sullivan, Harry S.	Murray H.	Lewin, Kurt	Rogers, Carl	Miller & Dollard
Yes	Yes	Not determined	Yes – The unconscious is made up of unsymbolized items.	Yes – Items never conscious. Items learned before words. Items repressed.
Social Interaction (Interpersonal contact makes personality) Accepts Teleology as behavior mechanism. Accepts Field Theory Training can't be effective until structure is established	Seeks compromise between clinical complexity and investigative economy. Brain is locus of personality. Needs and pressures as determinants of behavior. Accepts Field Theory. Does not seek Diagnosis but Formulation.	Importance of environment. Psychological Life Space is a closed system. Importance of need and goal. Interdependence of behavior.	Organism reacts as a whole to phenomenal field and seeks to maintain, enhance and actualize itself. Strives for consistency. Behavior is goal directed.	There is a continuum between animal and human behavior. Nothing occurs with the personality other than stimulus and response
1. Not original in his "effect of society on person." Not much added and too much subtracted by reducing the personality to a single system of the ego. 2. Doesn't explain how society molds its members. 3. Its interpersonal relations difficulty a neurosis, a neurotic symptom or a cause of neurosis?	1. So broad a theory that it loses its vigor. 2. Suffers from inability to explain transformed motives and development of motives. 3. Too complex a taxonomy. 4. Too much poetry and too little positivism	1. Topology and vectoral representations really add nothing new. 2. Life Space is not a closed system. The objective environment must be considered. 3. Doesn't consider past history. 4. Misused Mathematical and Physical concepts.	1. Theory not completely formulated. 2. Depends more on self-respect than others. Rogers believes that a person is pretty much what he says he is. 3. Much unconscious behavior is unexplained.	1. Concern is with simple behavior, but this may not explain much of complicated activity. 2. Tenuous assumption of phylogenetic continuity of psychology. 3. When it moves to men, it adopts and hoc definitions. 4. No prior definition for S & R. 5. Very little known about S & R. The hyphen theory.

1. Great stimulus to research probably due to more objective language spanning gap between theory and observation. 2. New insights on group relations.	1. Seeks formulation rather than diagnosis. 2. Careful treatment of motivational process. 3. System provided to "unsnarl" complex information and multitude of needs and pressures. 4. Merger of internal and external motivation theory.	1. Research contributions great. 2. Some psychological concepts made more explicit. 3. Field Theory is more psychological than behaviorism. 4. Brought in consideration. 5. Man no longer hollow. Has needs, intentions, hopes.	Adds concept of Self to Theory.	1. Very explicit and efficient as a theory. 2. Adds learning process explanation. 3. Social Anthropology and Clinical Psychoanalysis added to Experimentalist Focus. 4. Ready to submit to experiment. 5. Less reification. 6. Looks the way a theory should look.

Why Do So Many People Act CRAZY ?????????
And What Solutions Can Be Used To Stop This Craziness

By Dr. Buck Marrs

*GET SANE BY OWNING ALL OF YOUR PERCEPTIONS

First of all, turn-on your Crap-Detectors!!! Separate any of the following ideas/solutions as being useful or just plane CRAP!! Like all estimated 7-billion people on this planet, we all make day-to-day, moment-to-moment, 24-hours a day decisions according to our own perceptions. A study in 2015 suggests that all humans have 2500-3000 perceptions a day.

> TAKE PERSONAL RESPONSIBILITY FOR ALL OF YOUR MOMENT- TO-MOMENT, DAY-TO- DAY PERCEPTIONS FROM BIRTH TO DEATH AND PERHAPS BEYOND!!

> STOP BLAMING ANYONE ELSE FOR YOUR PERCEPTIONS!!

> STOP PLAYING THE VICTIM GAME!!

> IF WE ALL ARE RESPONSIBLE FOR ALL OF OUR PERCEPTIONS, THERE ARE NO VICTIMS, EVEN WITH BAD ENCOUNTERS WITH OTHER HUMANS AND OBJECTS … to be explained in more detail later.

> ALL OF OUR PERCEPTIONS COME FROM MULTIPLE PARTS OF OUR BODIES AND BRAINS––MEMORY, ANALYSIS INTUITION, INSTINCTS, OUT GUT FEELINGS, OUR HEARTS, AND ETC.

> *HOW WE TREAT ALL OTHER PERSONS IS EXACTLY HOW WE FEEL ABOUT OURSELVES AT THAT MOMENT. IF WE ARE LOVING TOWARD ANOTHER PERSON, THIS SHOWS EXACTLY HOW WE FEEL ABOUT OURSELVES AT THAT*

MOMENT, IF WE ARE UPSET OR ANGRY WITH ANOTHER PERSON, THIS IS EXACTLY HOW WE FEEL ABOUT OURSELVES AT THAT MOMENT. A great "Saturday Night Live" Skit I saw years ago had a female psychotherapist doing therapy telling a couple to "look at each other" and then "look at yourself", repeating the line of "look at yourself" many times. SO … …
LOOK AT YOURSELF--LOOK AT YOURSELF---
LOOK AT YOURSELF!!!!

I have had the privilege of teaching primarily university graduate students for 42-years at California State University, Long Beach and had a clinical psychotherapist practice for over 35-years as a second profession and have tested all of my theories and procedures on tens of thousands of people of ages 5-90 with very little disagreement.

And I still hold that I have learned more from them than they have learned from me. I have never met another human being that I did not learn something from through talking and listening, and from their body language, while connecting to my own unique perceptions. Even though all humans on this planet are more alike than different, each human experiences his/her unique perceptions separately and grows differently.

WE ARE ALL DIFFERENT!!!!!!!

My perceptions about myself are that I love all of my family--wife, two daughters and one son and their families, my sister, … (I can't stop hugging my 6 grandchildren) … all of my beloved friends, and etc. . I don't like most female makeup--red lipstick … major YUK, dark eye shadow (I could puke!),, botoxed puffy faces, butt cracks … (real ugly), child molesters, pickles, some raisons, … … .. I can go on for days …

My major points with these small examples are that no one forced me to like/love or dislike/hate anyone or anything. I DID ALL OF THIS BY MYSELF. I AM NOT A VICTIM.. THESE ARE ALL MY PERCEPTIONS … ALWAYS HAVE BEEN, AND ALWAYS WILL BE!!!!

I AM TOTALLY RESPONSIBLE FOR HOW I HAVE CHANGED AND GROWN FROM BIRTH TO NOW AND SO ARE YOU!!!!!!!

* CHANGE ... ADAPTATION ... PROBLEMS ... NEUROSIS ... SELF CONTROL

Change------and-------ADAPTATION TO CHANGE (or PROBLEMS) are normal, natural, constant, seemingly random and spontaneous, and are necessary and seem to be out of our control. We are in the constant process of adapting to changes within our bodies and to changes outside of us in the environment and in our relationships with others. And, changes/problems seem to be indifferent to how we feel about them.

This is called PERSONAL GROWTH. We need to adapt to changes every day during sleep and awake times to learn. This is the basic process we all start at birth which continues until death (and/or after death according to your perceptions).

NEUROSIS (a form of mental illness) occurs when an individual misunderstands and mishandles a problem by TRANSFERRING THE OWNERSHIP AND RESPONSIBILITY FOR NORMAL TENSION (INCUBATION) ONTO SOMEONE ELSE OR SOME ENTITY OR INSTITUTION. The individual then works mistakenly on the other party as an illusionary means of resolving the self-inflicted tension connected to his/her own adaptation.

In fact, ALL TENSION IS SELF-INFLICTED AS EXPERIENCED BY THE INDIVIDUAL'S PERCEPTIONS. AND EXPERIENCES!! NEUROSIS occurs when an individual does not trust his/her own perceptions and feelings connected to adapting to a problem and experiences INDIRECT SELF-ACCEPTANCE by transferring control of his feelings and himself with any of the following acts: blaming. ... defending. ... arguing ... making excuses ... giving reasons for his/ her feelings. ... attacking- verbal or physical ... name- calling. ... compromising (giving in and being angry) ... playing the right/ wrong game ... proving to others ... judging ... guilt ... jealousy ... obsessiveness ... attempting to control others ... ... threatening ... accusing ... power struggles ... tantrums or hysterical outburst ... playing the victim ... and etc.

When any of the above occurs, the misdirected neurotic person usually attempts to control the other person under the illusion that he/ she will gain his/her self-control. A healthy person will usually resist someone trying to control him/her by resisting and then leaving. In fact, the neurotic person is in process of going out-of-self-control and usually feels even more tension, while attempting even harder to control the other party. The neurotic person fails as the healthy person repels naturally. Depression may occur as the neurotic person tries in-vain to control him/herself with the illusion that this can happen if only the other person would be in his/her control. Relief of tension or satisfaction rarely to never occurs WHEN A PERSON ATTEMPTS TO CONTROL HIMSELF/HERSELF BY ILLUSIONARILY CONTROLLING ANOTHER.

*THE PROCESS OF
CHANGE--PROBLEMS---ADAPTATION--NEUROSIS--SANITY

CHANGE (normal, natural, constant,
random, spontaneous, indifferent)

1. INCUBATION--(always a tension state)--based in FEAR as the primary feeling with secondary feelings of anxiety, upset, anger, frustration sadness, hurt, etc.

2. Our brains search for alternative forms of solutions leading to ACTION.

3. Release of tension which is SATISFACTION AND RESOLUTION.

4. We are now ready for new problems to be re-cycled which is GROWTH.

ADAPTATION (normal, natural, constant, random, spontaneous, indifferent) (Going from 'change' to 'adaptation' represents the experiencing or processing of normal problems.)

UNHEALTHY ADAPTATION--THE "VICTIM"--(OR, INDIRECT SELF-ACCEPTANCE AS AN ACT OF NEUROSIS)

* going-out-of-control by dissociating from yourself by focusing on others to resolve the tension instead of focusing on yourself.
* transfers responsibility for feelings (incubation-problems) to others
* is unable to problem-solve because of too much tension
* is incapable of being content, satisfied, happy or problem solving
* increases stress by not staying with yourself by not keeping the mind in the current time-frame of here-and-now with too much thinking about controlling others
* performs act of disassociation: arguing, blaming attacking, name calling, accusing, threatening, jealousy, power struggles, suffering, whining, defending, making excuses, judging, prejudice, racism, playing the right/wrong game, arrogance, bragging, vanity, acts of 'machismo., tantrums, and ETC.

HEALTHY/SANE ADAPTATION
* stays in self-control by keeping associated with self
* no transference of responsibility for feelings to others
* accepts own fear with the incubation
* adapts to the problem in a responsible time and moves-on to GROWTH
* is available to be content, peaceful, happy and more loving
* stays in or regains self-control by keeping one's mind in the "here and now" and is more relaxed by controlling and/or shutting-down all thinking (the more we think, the more we give ourselves stress and tension)

THE FOLLOWING PROCEDURESM WORK IN COMBINATION AND/OR INDIVIDUALLY FOR MOST HUMANS

* talking to others without attacking using "I" Messages (explained later)
* meditation
* exercise
* connecting to your tears, BOTH MALES AND FEMALES
* jogging
* walking
* self-hypnosis
* yoga
* deep breathing
* tai-chi
* repetitive prayer
* playing a musical instrument or doing art work
* repetitive knitting
* talk therapy
* group therapy
* listening to acceptable music
* reconnecting with nature--the beach, mountains, surfing, etc.
* being totally honest with yourself and others
* AA/DA meetings
* medication
* accupressure
* ETC.

USE "I" MESSAGES (no "YOU" messages). Negotiate problems as a family with everyone putting everything on the table and finding solutions that everyone can live with. Renew the Method 3 Negotiation Process at a later time and re-negotiate.

** Either manic or depressive episodes can be triggered by (1) a situational conflict or episode, or without a situational conflict or (2) by a biochemical imbalance which might need to be controlled with mood balancing medication: Prozac, Paxil, Zoloft, etc.

CONTROL THEORY AND PRACTICE

DEFINITION: "Control" is the power to guide or manage.

FALLACY: One person has the power to control another person or group.
(The position held here is that there is no such process as one person controlling another person's mind or heart!)

THE NEED TO CONTROL: One person needs to control another when he/she is afraid that he/she cannot handle his/her own feelings in relationship to the behavior of the other person. The controller TRANSFERS his/her self-fear onto the other person by putting-out verbal and/or physical messages in an attempt to coerce the other person to change.

SELF CONTROL: All there is, is **self-control!** People choose to control themselves, or they choose not to control themselves as they attempt to adapt to whatever environment they are in, regardless of how someone is attempting to control them.

RESISTANCE: When one person attempts to physically or verbally control another person perhaps even with force, a NORMAL reaction is to resist physically and/or mentally being controlled. When a person resists mentally, he/she DOES NOT FEEL SAFE and is usually angry or afraid. When an angry or afraid person LOSES INTERNAL CONTROL, he/she may act-out his/her fear/anger with some outburst verbally or physically.
(Or, when people feel safe, they normally have stronger internal or self control!)

It follows, therefore, that one person should not attempt to control another person with verbal or physical force or coercion (which is impossible) unless he/she wants to deal with normal resistance!!

(And of course, we need to control our children to keep them safe!)

*WE TEND TO GET BACK FROM OTHERS WHAT WE PUT OUT TO THEM! (Modeling-----Copying, Modeling---Copying ... ETC)

*PUTTING OUT SAFETY AND RESPECT TO OTHERS WILL CUE THE OTHER PERSON TO RESPOND TO YOU WITH SAFETY AND RESPECT! (Modeling---Copying)

*IMAGE OF YOURSELF---HOW YOU AND I FEEL ABOUT OURSELVES AT ANY GIVEN TIME IS EXACTLY HOW WE TREAT OTHERS!!!!

IF WE ARE FEELING SAFE AND LOVING WITH OURSELVES, THIS IS TYPICALLY HOW WE WILL TREAT OTHERS AT THAT MOMENT!!! IF WE ARE PERSONALLY GOING THROUGH SOME FEAR/ ANGER/MANIC/DEPRESSION ABOUT OURSELVES, THIS MAY BE HOW WE MIGHT TREAT ANOTHER PERSON IF WE ARE GOING THROUGH A "NEUROTIC", OUT-OF-SELF CONTROL EPISODE!!!

TO DESCRIBE THIS ANOTHER WAY, HOW OTHER PEOPLE TREAT US AT ANY MOMENT DESCRIBES EXACTLY HOW THEY FEEL ABOUT THEMSELVES AT THAT MOMENT!!! IF ANOTHER PERSON TREATS YOU OR ME WITH RESPECT AND/OR LOVINGNESS, THEY ARE SHOWING US EXACTLY HOW THEY FEEL ABOUT THEMSELVES AT THAT MOMENT!!!

WHEN ANOTHER PERSON TREATS YOU OR ME WITH ANGER AND/OR DISTRUST, THEY ARE SHOWING US

EXACTLY HOW THEY FEEL ABOUT THEMSELVES AT THAT MOMENT!!!

TYPICAL MESSAGES TO OTHERS THAT ARE CONTROLLING AND MAY START ARGUMENTS

1. ORDERING, DIRECTING, COMMANDING
   (Telling the other person to do something, or giving them an order or command)

2. WARNING, ADMONISHING, THREATENING
   (Telling the other person what consequences will occur if he/she acts out.)

3. MORALIZING, PREACHING, OBLIGING
   (Telling someone what he/she should or should not do)

4. PERSUADING WITH LOGIC, ARGUING, INSTRUCTING, LECTURING
   ((Trying to influence a person with fact, logic, counter-arguments, information)

5. JUDGING, CRITICIZING, DISAGREEING, BLAMING
   (Making negative comments or evaluations)

6. INTERPRETING, ANALYZING, DIAGNOSING
   (Telling the other person what are his/her motives and/or analyzing why he/she is doing or saying something, communicating that you have him/her figured out)

7. NAME-CALLING, RIDICULING, SHAMING
   (Making judgment statements, stereotyping or categorizing him/her)

8. ADVISING, GIVING SOLUTIONS OR SUGGESTIONS
   (Telling someone how to solve his/her own problems)

9. REASSURING, SYMPATHIZING, CONSOLING
   (These acts "may" act as a form of 'babying' the other person which may reinforce the person acting as a baby)

10. PROBING, QUESTIONING, INTERROGATING
    (Trying to find reasons, motives, causes while searching for more information to help YOU solve his/her problems---again, a form of babying)

11. WITHDRAWING, DISTRACTING, HUMORING
    (Trying to get the person away from their problems by withdrawing yourself from their problems using distractions by kidding and pushing their problems aside)

BIBLIOGRAPHY

Axline, Virginia M., Dibs: In Search of Self. New York; Ballantine Books, 1969.

Baker, Eva and Popham, W. James, Systematic Instruction. Englewood Cliffs, New Jersey: Prentice-Hall, Inc., 1970.

Bloom, B. (Ed.). Taxonomy of Educational Objectives; Handbook I: Cognitive Domain. New York: Longman Green, 1956.

Bruner, Jerome S., The Process of Education. Cambridge, Mass: Harvard University Press, 1960.

Department of Home Economics, Techniques for Effective Teaching, National Education Association, 1966.

Dewey, John, Experience and Education. New York: Macmillan Co., 1955.

Ginott, Haim G., Between Parent and Child. New York: Macmillan Co, 1965.

Gordon, Thomas, Parent Effectiveness Training. Peter H. Wyden, Inc./ Publisher, New York, 1972.

Harty, L. and B. Monroe, Objectives for Instructional Objectives. Active Response Manual, Insgroup, Inc., Long Beach, California, 1970.

Jourard, Sydney M., The Transparent Self. New York: D. Van Nostrand, 1964.

Mager, Robert F., Preparing Instructional Objectives. Palo Alto, California: Fearon Publishers, 1962.

Neill, A.S. Summerhill. New York: Hart Publishing Co., 1960.

Postman, Neil and Weingartner, Charles, Teaching as a Subversive Activity. Delacorte Press/New York, 1969.

Putney, Shell, and Putney, Gail, The Adjusted American. New York: Harper, 1964.

Rogers, Carl R., On Becoming a Person. Boston: Houghton Mifflin, 1963.

Rogers, Carl R., Freedom To Learn. Columbus, Ohio: Charles E. Merrill, 1969.

Tyler, Ralph W., Basic Principles of Curriculum and Instruction. Chicago, Illinois: University of Chicago Press, 1950.

THREE STYLES OF CONFLICT RESOLUTION

* **From birth, no one wants to be controlled by another.**

** **When someone attempts to control us, it is natural to resist.**

*** **Or, control solicits resistance!!**

**** **When some one attempts to control another, he/she is frightened and is coming from a place of no personal power. (And, at the same time, he/she is giving their power over to the other person they are attempting to control.)**

Method I--The Use of Authority/Coercion

> * I win (with the use of coercion or threat of taking away some kind of freedom of the person to be controlled)
>
> * You lose (giving-in out of fear of loss of freedom which solicits resistance)
>
> * A reward/punishment system (The person using coercion must have something the other person wants to allow himself to be controlled)

> This method of control is the most commonly used by teachers (and parents), and is expected by both students (and children). Teachers must control the curriculum and instructional processes by definition giving directions most of the time that cannot be negotiated. This method of control is necessary because it is efficient and expected.
>
> *** Method I should be used until students start to resist this kind of control, and then Method II or III should be used.

Method III--- Permissiveness

> * I (the teacher) intentionally loses or give-in for now dealing with the conflict at a more convenient time.
>
> *The student wins for now with the conflict being dealt with at a more convenient time for the teacher possibly keeping classroom instruction more in tact.

The position held here is that all misbehavior by students should be dealt with in a proficient manner allowing no misbehavior to be ignored with the teacher keeping his/her personal power by choosing when, where and how conflicts are to be dealt with.

Method III----Negotiation for Alternatives Where Everyone Wins
The position held here is that all conflicts of needs (timely, tangible) are negotiable, while all conflicts of values (not timely nor tangibly-religion, politics, etc.) are not negotiable.

1. Make an appointment to meet and confer. Use class time, or make an appointment with an individual or group that is agreeable to all.
2. Identify the problem. Use "I" messages to explain your conflict talking about yourself (avoiding the word "you") while referring to the 'acts' or 'behaviors' about the other person that are not acceptable. Then, shift to 'active listening' where you are primarily silent giving acknowledgement (not agreement) that you are respectfully listening to the other side(s) of the conflict.
3. Brainstorming for alternative ways of behaving that are agreeable to most parties will happen naturally as all parties are listening to each other.
4. Pick one set of change of behaviors that are agreeable to all persons with normal consequences that will occur if the new agreements are not kept.
5. Decide WHO, does WHAT, WHEN, WHERE, and HOW. This is the end of this meeting at this time. (Perhaps these new agreements/behaviors with consequences should be put into a written contract signed by all parties including students, teacher, parents, and/or an administrator??)
6. Act-out the new agreements/behaviors for a reasonable time.
7. Meet again within a reasonable time re-cycling steps 1-5 evaluating how the new agreements/behaviors are working revising anything that has not worked.

Brain Compatible Instruction and Management

by Buck Marrs

All teachers are entertainers ... or, they should be. A definition of "entertaining" is when a teacher holds the attention of the class pleasantly. To understand how this is done, a description of how the human brain operates is in order. The human brain is an incredibly complex organ that needs much stimulation from as many different medias as possible.

The brain will stay focused only on that which it finds interesting, and will search for patterns of understanding that make sense. The primary job of the brain seems to be to figure out how to adapt to any new problem or environment encountered. The brain must participate actively with any new problem, while processing data randomly and spontaneously. Also, students need to feel safe by understanding what is expected of them. Students who do not feel safe usually act inappropriately. Teachers need to make class rules clear and enforce them with consistency. Over ninety percent of classroom control problems can be prevented with:

- brain-compatible instructional sequencing,
- "Withitness" and body language, and
- positive reinforcement.

Instructional sequencing for all age levels should include as much student participation as possible to be brain compatible and to hold a student's attention. Cooperative grouping with much student talking is vital. Talking is one of the most natural methods in which humans actively participate and problem solve. Indeed, to tell a student to stop talking is to require his brain to act in a most unnatural way –– to stop problem solving and learning.

This is why teachers receive resistance from students when told to stop talking. The more students are allowed to talk about ideas and concepts, the more these ideas and concepts are stored into short-term memory.

Information not actively processed or not found interesting will not be stored into short-term memory.

In addition, inquiry instruction, where the teacher offers students problems to solve by answering open-ended questions seems more brain compatible. "Why", "how", and "what" type questions seem to offer more challenging inquires than "who", "when", or "where" questions. Again, cooperative groups with about three students offers each student the opportunity to talk and share with others while getting valuable feedback from peers, using a conversational style of talking without being controlled by an adult teacher.

Indeed, the more actively involved students are in the instructional process, the more the brain participates, and the more information is stored into short-term memory. The theories offered here suggest that we learn and retain approximately 90% of what we teach to others. This is why teachers may be the best and most active learners in their classrooms. Also, students learn and retain over 80% of what is experienced directly or practiced, over 40% of what is discussed with others, 20% of what they see and hear, 15% of what they see, and 10% of what they hear.

The strong message for teachers here is that the worst information delivery and teaching method is when the teacher stands and delivers information, using lecture as the primary tool for instruction. Just listening to someone talking is the least brain active method of learning. Most college students listening to a 20-minute lecture will recall less than 25% of what was said, losing over 75% of the information presented. Elementary, middle, and high school students will learn less from the lecture method of instruction than will college students because older students have longer attention spans than do younger students. Clearly, we humans at all age levels have shorter attention spans and lower retention when our brains are not actively involved. Students who are not actively involved in a lesson will tend to exhibit less self control, as well.

Normal instructional sequencing and lesson planning should include as much brain compatible activity as possible:

1. A brief preview of the lesson should be given first. Here, the teacher gives students the objectives and purposes for the lesson while reviewing the previous lesson. The teacher should always write the instructional agenda on the board for the visual learner and talk about the agenda for the auditory learner. This can be done with teacher-talk, question and answer discussion, or cooperative grouping in two's or three's. Students reviewing materials in cooperative groups will participate more actively and can help each other with homework. When students are actively involved talking, the teacher can take care of clerical duties or monitor groups with appropriate coaching.

2. Data and examples should be given, and a demonstration can be offered when possible. The teacher can present data with examples and demonstrate using audio-visual displays of concepts being presented. Usually, examples from students are more brain compatible using a question and answer inquiry format.

3. Questions are asked about materials just presented in steps 1 and 2. Here students are invited to actively participate giving the teacher necessary feedback about students' understanding. If students do not understand, the teacher repeats either steps 1 or 2, or both. Students gain from this inquiry discussion by hearing other students' answers along with the teacher's coaching. A question and answer session leads to inquiry instruction when the following is used: questions are asked by both teacher and students, answers hopefully are given, the teacher repeats the answers for all to hear, and acknowledgment is given about the accuracy of the answer. Positive reinforcement should be given. The teacher must never give a student a negative comment about a response. This sequence is repeated until the teacher feels

satisfied that students understand the materials before going on to step 4.

4. Appropriate practice is given where students have the opportunity to do something with the concepts or skills presented in the previous steps. Again, cooperative grouping allows students the chance to teach each other by actively participating using talking and listening as they randomly search for their own unique patterns of understanding with which they can associate to concepts being presented. Students can use manipulatives and visuals while actually making or doing something that helps them further learn by more actively processing data from a teacher's objectives. Here, the experiential learner is best served by actively participating with the concepts or skills.

5. Closure on a lesson can be accomplished by the teacher reviewing the lesson with a question and answer session, cooperative grouping while students review, or with a brief teacher lecture. Each lesson can be concluded with a preview of how the day's data will be used in future lessons or with a homework assignment whereby students get important reinforcing practice with the new data. This provides a transition to the next day's lesson which can start with step one, repeating the instructional cycle.

This style of instructional sequencing covers all bases for thorough brain compatibility, and the sequencing can change order. Lessons can be started with step three-inquiry (questions and answers), and then practice followed with necessary data or demonstration, and again followed with more practice. Or, a sequence can be started with reasonable practice as a form of problem solving followed by questions and then data concluding with more practice. Lesson plans and sequencing should be created to meet the needs of each class. Teachers are encouraged to be creative.

When a student or much of the class starts to go off-task by talking out of turn or with physical movement, this signals the teacher that his instruction may not be brain-compatible, and that he needs to change instructional gears to another step of sequencing that is more interesting. Kounin (Charles, 1996, p.45) used the term "satiation" when students have processed the same data too long, and they need to move on to the next related concept or the next more active instructional step. It is the teacher's job to read the faces and body language of his students and to change instructional gears to keep a class on task.

Even when a teacher's instruction is brain-compatible, some students may still go off-task by acting out with over talking and/or with too much physical movement. These behaviors can easily be controlled with "Withitness" and "Body Language". Teachers display "Withitness" when they give total attention to their class and when they can be seen at all times by their students. Teachers who keep strong eye-contact by casually skimming and scanning their class rarely have students who go off-task. Students of all ages (K through graduate school) usually keep their eyes on how observant their teacher is, and will stay on-task if they feel their teacher is observing them. Teachers that keep a superior standing position while skimming and scanning most of the time can be seen by students, and are using body language that is most attentive.

When a student still goes off-task, a teacher can effortlessly walk closer to the student and use strong eye-contact. Students will normally bring themselves back on-task when this kind of intervention is used. Also, teachers who normally walk around all parts of their rooms casually keeping strong "Withitness" prevent off-task behavior with their movement and their eye-contact. Indeed, teachers who appear on-task themselves will cue their students to stay on-task. Interventions using body language are usually effortless and non-assertive.

Skinner (Charles, 1996, p. 24) postulates the notion that positive reinforcement stimulates the repetition of positive behavior by reinforcing the kind of desired behavior with positive physical signals or with positive verbal cues (thank you, please, great idea, strong comment, etc.) while ignoring behavior that is not desired. Using respectful comments will tend to bring respectful comments in return from students. Negative and controlling comments from teachers are not respectful (e.g., judgments, sarcasm, name-calling, ridiculing, etc.). We all tend to copy respectful models, and we tend to get back from other people what we put out to them. And, 'catching-them-being-good' and positive reinforcement seems to work with most students most of the time.

Indeed, all students at all ages want to get along by cooperating to avoid pain. We teachers are functioning in the place of their parents. We may be the best models of respectfulness for our students to follow. Brain compatible instruction is respectful as are withitness, body language and positive reinforcement. All of these management procedures will create a safe and productive learning environment which will usually prevent control problems, and which will help students be happier and hence, learn more.

☞ Extension Activities/Questions

1. What must a teacher do to make his/her teaching "brain compatible"?

2. What can a teacher do to bring his/her class back on-task during an instructional lesson?

3. Why should all teachers be "entertainers"?

☞ References

Charles, C.M. (1996) *Building Classroom Discipline.* Longman Publishers, New York.

Richard (Buck) Marrs has been a full time professor in the Department of Teacher Education at California State University, Long Beach since 1968, and has supervised over four hundred students in grades K-12. Also, he has been a practicing psychotherapist since 1972 specializing in treating families and their dysfunctional children and adolescents.

Staying Sane While Working with the "Out of Control" Student

by Buck Marrs

Losing control physically and/or mentally is one of each humans' most primal fears. Undoubtedly, all teachers fear that if a student goes out of control, they too will go out of control. As a consequence, teachers are under the impression that it is their primary job to keep their students in control. Nothing could be farther from the truth! Two unhealthy myths seem to be the basis for these misconceptions.

Myth number one is that one person has the power to control another person. Strong teachers have the strength or power to control their students. Parents have the wisdom and power to control their children. Husbands and wives have the power to control their spouses. Nothing could be further from the truth. Ask any wise, experienced teacher, parent, or spouse, and he/she will tell you that their students have never been in their control, that their children were out of their control from birth, and that their spouses have always been out of their control.

The position held here is that no one person has the power or wisdom to control another persons' mind or heart. One person may have the power to control another person physically, but will never have the power to control his/her mind. The person being controlled physically always has the ability to resist mentally. As a matter of fact, when someone attempts to control another, the natural and normal reaction is to resist. So, when a teacher attempts to control a student, they should expect the student to resist. And, the teacher in this case started the problem in the first place by attempting to control the student. This process of resisting when someone attempts to control another is normal for all animals of lower and higher orders. Therefore, it is a waste of time for a teacher to attempt to control students, unless the teacher is intending to start the resistance process. In cases like this, controlling teachers (parents and spouses, as well) are their own worst enemies because they are the ones who start the fights by soliciting resistance. Over controlling teachers do not handle their own fear healthily.

All there is, then, is self-control and self-responsibility. People choose to control themselves, or they choose not to control themselves, as they attempt to adapt to whatever environment they are in, regardless of how someone else is attempting to control them. This is how we all stay in control ourselves. Students may resist a teacher's attempt to control them as a natural means of maintaining their own self-control. And, a teacher may resist a student's attempt to control him as a natural means of staying in control of himself. To put this another way, when a teacher attempts to control a student, the student may resist because he doesn't feel safe changing his behavior, and may act out with anger and frustration. Fear, anger and frustration are normal reactions of resistance! The primary drive within all humans is to stay safe by maintaining ones' own self-control and self-dignity. It is natural to respond with fear and resistance when someone else attempts to control us.

It follows, therefore, that one person should not attempt to control another with verbal or physical coercion (which is impossible, anyway) unless he wants to deal with normal resistance. Control solicits resistance!

Following are typical teacher (and parent) messages that may be controlling and which tend to start resistance and arguments. Even though many of these messages are normal during instruction, they should be avoided during a conflict.

1. Ordering, Directing, Commanding –– telling the student to do something, or giving him an order or command;

2. Warning, Admonishing, Threatening –– telling the student what consequences will occur if he does something, alluding to the use of power;

3. Moralizing, Preaching, Obliging –– telling the student what he should or should not do;

4. Persuading With Logic, Arguing, Lecturing –– trying to influence with facts, counter-arguments, or your own opinion;

5. Judging, Criticizing, Disagreeing, Blaming –– making negative judgments or evaluations of a student;

6. Interpreting, Analyzing, Diagnosing –– telling the student what are his motives, communicating that you have him figured out;

7. Name-Calling, Ridiculing, Shaming –– making a student feel foolish, stereotyping or categorizing him;

8. Advising, Giving Solutions, Or Suggestions –– telling the student how to solve his own problems;

9. Reassuring, Sympathizing, Consoling, Supporting –– trying to make the student feel better, talking him out of his feelings, denying the strength of his feelings, trying to make his feelings go away;

10. Probing, Questioning, Interrogating –– trying to find reasons, motives, causes, searching for more information; or

11. Withdrawing, Humoring, Distracting –– trying to get the student away from his conflict, withdrawing from the problem yourself, distracting the student, kidding him out of his feelings, pushing the problem aside.

Myth number two is that one person has the power to inflict hurt, pain, or anger onto another person. This mild to moderate psychological disorder is called *neurosis*. Neurosis occurs when a person misunderstands and mishandles a problem by transferring the ownership and responsibility for normal tension (fear, anger, anxiety, frustration, etc.) onto someone else or some entity or institution. An example could be that during a classroom meeting, a student tells the teacher that he thinks the class stinks and is boring. The facts are that when a student verbally attacks a teacher in front of the class, the student is responsible for the attack, and the teacher is responsible for his/her response to the attack with fear, anger, or calmness. A student (or anyone else for that matter) does not have the power to make a teacher afraid or angry. Fear and/or anger is what the teacher does to himself/herself in response to the student's attack. A student (or anyone else for that matter) does not have the power to inflict tension on any of us at any time. When a person acts neurotically by transferring responsibility for his/her feelings to someone else, he/she is in the process of taking himself out of control.

Another definition of a neurotic episode is when a person experiences *indirect-self acceptance*. This occurs when a neurotic person thinks someone else is responsible for their emotional discomfort and transfers blame to the other person. At this time, the person is mistakenly giving the attacker the power to inflict fear or anger, hence the indirect self-acceptance. *(In fact, all tension is self-inflicted as experienced by the individual!)*

Typical episodes of neurotic transference are as follows: *blaming, arguing, making excuses, defending, attacking (physical or verbal), name-calling, giving reasons for feelings, jealousy, guilt, compromising (giving in and being angry), accusing, threatening, attempting to control another, power struggles, tantrums or hysterical outbursts, playing the victim, and etc.* All of these behaviors are examples of going out of control.

When any of the above occur, the misdirected student may attempt to control another under the illusion that he will regain his own self-control. In fact, the neurotic student is in the process of going more out-of-control himself, and usually feels more self-inflicted tension which may lead to depression. This neurotic cycle of self-inflicted discomfort and pain ends when the student stops transferring responsibility to others and stops being a victim. At this moment, the person starts to take responsibility for what he is doing to himself.

A teacher can stay in control of himself when encountering a neurotic student by avoiding all of the controlling messages mentioned above, and by not acting neurotic himself. The skill of *"active listening"* usually works effectively here. Active listening is an intentional intervention whereby the teacher simply remains *silent* when a student is arguing and going out of control, keeps eye contact, and mirrors back what is being said while giving respectful verbal acknowledgment. When responding back, the teacher uses *"I-messages"* by simply talking about himself (I'm feeling.. and my needs are …) and about what he will do and what he will not do, and by avoiding arguing by not defending or giving reasons for his feelings. A small number of students may be habitually neurotic and may act out consistently with disrespect. These behaviors should never be tolerated.

Some understanding about what happens to a person who goes out of control seems in order. All people have mood swings which can be charted. Picture a horizontal line moving up and down with some consistency. Normal mood swings do not go up or down to any extreme unless a person is adapting to some immediate crisis. During a crisis, a person's mood may go to a very high or manic state where the individual experiences too much excitement and may go out of control with intense fear, anxiety, or anger. Or, the mood may swing to an extreme low of depression with intense sadness, fear, hurt, or hopelessness. With extremely high or low mood swings, the person is going out of control and may act out in extreme ways: panic, tantrums, yelling, or screaming, or become physically violent or suicidal. At this time, the out of control person is usually experiencing extreme bio-chemical changes which will affect his neurological patterns and behavior. Some people behave out of balance with extreme mood swings without having a crisis and may suffer from psychological disorders. Clearly, their brain chemistry may not be normal, and they may be candidates for medical intervention. Thankfully, most people who have extreme neurological imbalances can be helped with prescribed medication from a well-trained medical doctor. In these cases, a teacher must refer these problem students to a school counselor or psychologist for a more accurate diagnosis and further referral. Some imbalances are due to diet and can be easily controlled.

Students who are going out of control on a regular basis may act out with hyper-activity, attention deficit, obsessive/compulsiveness, extreme argumentativeness, defiance, too much physical movement, lethargy or sleeping in class, insecurity, feelings of inadequacy, verbal abusiveness, extreme disrespect, suicidal or perhaps violent tendencies.

Surely, the teacher needs to intervene as soon as possible with out of control behavior in the classroom. Most importantly, the teacher needs to stay in control of himself. Active listening and "I" messages are great skills to help the teacher stay in control. Avoiding controlling messages are key in preventing an out of control student from going further out of control. Teachers must not feed a student's neurosis by attempting to control him. Do not start with or participate in the control/resistance cycle. Soft interventions should be used first. A soft intervention is more passive and non-assertive for the teacher and is non-controlling, and tends to prevent misbehavior. Soft interventions also take less energy for the teacher.

Allow no inappropriate behavior to go unnoticed. Always intervene as soon as possible. Use positive re-enforcement as your primary tool of management.

Examples of soft interventions are: a teacher needs to keep strong eye-contact with the class and with some students in particular, use body movement around the room, use body movement towards a student who is going out of control, stay visible at all times, visually skim and scan the room regularly, use a physical cue (finger to lips) and stare (looking "bad"), flick the lights to get attention or ring a bell and then wait and stare, tap a student's desk and stare, use a gentle touch on an arm with some brief verbal cue "Please join us", etc.

Interventions within the whole class should last no more than 2 to 3 seconds. A teacher should intervene quickly and then change the subject by continuing instruction while walking away. Do not allow an intervention to disrupt the whole class unless there is an emergency. Never present verbal data while any student is talking out of turn. Make a verbal intervention to a student ("I'll wait until I have everyone's attention before I continue") and then wait with silence until all eyes are on the teacher. Presenting verbal data to a class that is not paying attention and/or talking trains students not to pay attention and not to listen.

Hard interventions are more active, intrusive, and assertive to aggressive being more personal. Hard interventions take more energy for the teacher and the student. Examples of hard to harder interventions are: verbally mention the student's name and look "bad", address the entire class with an 'I' message describing the behavior not accepted and how the teacher feels, describe how the teacher is unable to function when this behavior occurs, verbally describe to the class the behavior that is acceptable and thank individuals with positive verbal cues for acting appropriately, give rewards (tokens) to students or the entire class for good behavior, negotiate when possible with students the consequences that restrict freedom for inappropriate behavior that the teacher can live with and enforce *(all consequences must be enforced with consistency)*. Hold a conference with a student or a group of students or the entire class to discuss the behavior that is not liked and the consequences that will result *with no threats--just consequences on a business-like basis*, hold a conference with an administrator or a counselor with the student to discuss a behavior contract with consequences, solicit help from parents on the phone and/or with a conference about the behavioral contract, restrict the student with some detention that can be enforced, restrict the student from the class for a brief period, expel the student from school as the last resort. Any rumor of a potentially suicidal and/ or violent student should be reported to an administrator immediately. *Always* take such rumors seriously!

Sadly, violence in schools seems to be on the increase. Potentially violent students can be spotted in the primary grades. Children in need should be diagnosed, monitored, and taught more constructive conflict resolution skills through role-playing, anger-controlling techniques, and behavior modification. Adult mentoring programs can link a responsible adult with a child or adolescent in need. In the schools, group therapy models can be used where students learn from each other reducing fear, alienation, and anger. Indeed, teachers often take the place of the parents when the student is in school, and teachers have the responsibility for each student, as does the parent. Oftentimes, teachers are the healthiest model for students to copy.

☞ Extension Activities/Questions

1. How can a teacher stay in-control during a classroom conflict?

2. Why does "control solicit resistance"?

3. Why are all arguments neurotic?

☞ References

Charles, C.M. (1996.) *Building Classroom Discipline.* Longman Publishers, New York.

Printed in the United States
By Bookmasters